Managing the Library Automation Project

John Corbin

ORYX PRESS
1985

The rare Arabian Oryx is believed to have inspired the myth of the unicorn. This desert antelope became virtually extinct in the early 1960s. At that time several groups of international conservationists arranged to have 9 animals sent to the Phoenix Zoo to be the nucleus of a captive breeding herd. Today the Oryx population is over 400, and herds have been returned to reserves in Israel, Jordan, and Oman.

♾ The paper used in this publication meets the minimum requirements of American National Standard for Information Science—Permanence of Paper for Printed Library Materials, ANSI Z39.48, 1984.

Library of Congress Cataloging-in-Publication Data

Corbin, John Boyd.
    Managing the library automation project.

    Bibliography: p.
    Includes index.
    1.Libraries—Automation.   I. Title.
Z678.9.C635   1985   025'.0028'5   85-15461
ISBN 0-89774-151-X

Contents

Preface

The purpose of this book is to provide a practical handbook and guide for the librarian untrained in systems development, and perhaps even unfamiliar with computers, who is nonetheless responsible for developing an automated library system. An automated library system is developed and integrated into the library organization in an effort referred to as a library automation project, and skill and time is required to plan and implement the system successfully. In most small or not-so-wealthy libraries, no one has the training and experience required to perform the exacting, time-consuming, yet absolutely vital job of laying an adequate groundwork for these radically new and complex systems.

The emphasis of this book is upon the planning, organization, management, and step-by-step process of a library automation project; it is a completely revised edition of *Developing Computer-Based Library Systems,* published in 1981 by The Oryx Press.

The text of the book is organized into four parts coinciding with major phases of an automation project. Part I presents, in two chapters of introductory concepts, overviews of an automated library system, computers, and related technology. Part II includes two chapters on project organization and management. The first describes project organization and staffing and the second, project planning and control. Part III has three chapters on system procurement, including a chapter on requirements for an automated library system; the request for proposal; and bid solicitation, evaluation, and award. Part IV covers system installation and operation. It has four chapters: the first discusses site preparation; the second, database conversion; the third, staff and user education and training; and the fourth, system installation, acceptance, and operation.

The Appendices include a sample list of the phases, activities, and steps of a library automation project; sample job descriptions for staff who will be involved with a project; lists of typical hardware, equipment, and supplies for automated library systems; and a complete sample Request for Proposal for an integrated library system. A Glossary contains definitions of terms included in the book, and a Selected Bibliography of allied readings which might be helpful to the beginning project manager is provided.

The author wishes to acknowledge his gratitude to Dana Rooks, who read the manuscript and made many useful suggestions for its improvement. Appreciation must also be expressed to my staff and colleagues at the University of Houston—University Park who have been patient with me during the preparation of this book.

Part I
Introductory
Concepts

Chapter 1
The Automated Library
System

It is an amazing fact that computers were first manufactured commercially in 1954, a mere 30-odd years ago. Since then, this ubiquitous machine, of initial interest only to a handful of scientists, has become society's workhorse, whose impact as a catalyst for change rivals that of the industrial revolution of the nineteenth century and the mass production, marketing, and communications industries of the twentieth. Libraries were early users of computers, and today automated systems in libraries are no longer the unusual. Indeed, the unautomated library is moving farther and farther from the mainstream of our profession.

A library automation project is concerned with the successful acquisition and integration of an automated system into the library organization. This requires the planning and coordination of many activities and events involving a variety of people within and outside the library. It is important that each of these individuals has a basic understanding of the concept of an automated library system. The purpose of this chapter is to provide a general overview of an automated library system. It includes the following topics:

- Definition of an automated library system
- Elements of an automated library system
- Methods of developing an automated library system
- Effects of using an automated library system

DEFINITION OF AN AUTOMATED LIBRARY SYSTEM

A library comprises a number of separate but interrelated and interacting parts called systems, which are organized sets of activities, tasks, or operations performed on information, library materials, or other items to achieve a specified end result or purpose. Examples of large systems in the library include acquisitions, cataloging, circulation, and reference (see Figure 1-1).

Figure 1-1. Systems and Subsystems of a Library.

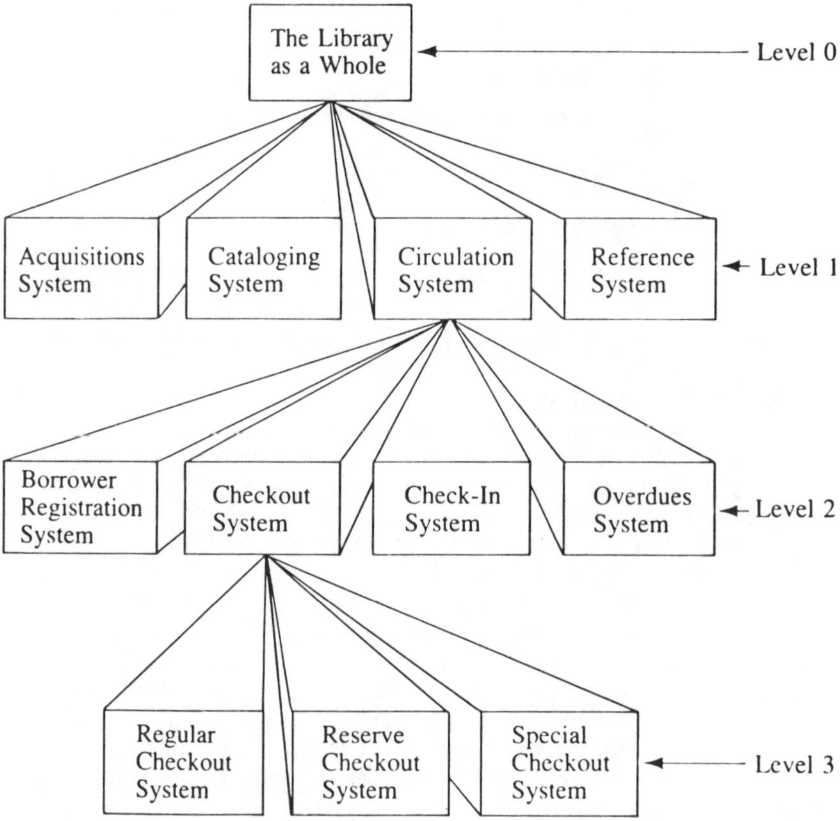

In the traditional manual library system, staff perform the various tasks required to complete each operation, but if a computer is used to perform some processing operations, an automated library system results. In such a system, humans and the computer usually share responsibility for performing the work. For example, a staff member might perform the first five operations; a computer, the next 100 operations; a staff member, the next 10 operations; and so on. Due to this sharing of responsibilities, today's automated library systems actually should be referred to as "human-machine systems," or, literally, "systems in which humans are assisted by a computer." Completely automated library systems, in which no human intervention and control are necessary, do not exist and are not likely to until the end of the century or beyond.

ELEMENTS OF AN AUTOMATED LIBRARY SYSTEM

An automated library system, regardless of its nature, size, or whether in an academic, public, special, or school library, will consist of a number of interrelated and interacting elements, including system purpose, processing and workflow, resources, management and leadership, and environment. A block diagram depicting these elements is shown in Figure 1-2.

Figure 1-2. A Block Diagram Depicting the Elements of an Automated Library System.

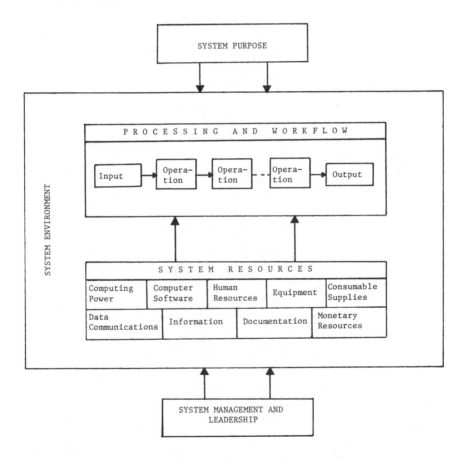

System Purpose

A primary element of an automated library system is its purpose. An automated library system must have a goal, mission, reason for being, or purpose, which provides a focal point for developing the system and for operating and managing the system, once it is implemented.

Example: The purpose of the cataloging system is to process materials to be added to the library's collections in an efficient and timely manner and to provide access to these materials through effective bibliographic control mechanisms.

Example: The purpose of the online catalog is to decentralize access to bibliographic and availability information for materials in the library's collections.

Thus, the purpose of an automated library system is the same as that of its parallel manual library system. The computer is merely a tool (albeit a marvelous one) enabling the library staff to do specific tasks faster, less expensively, or more accurately than a staff using manual methods.

System Processing and Workflow

Each automated library system requires the processing of information or physical objects. This processing and workflow in a system consists of input, processing operations, and output.

System Input. Each automated library system requires an input of information, library materials, or other items as "raw material" to be converted or processed into a desired end product. An acquisitions system, for example, might require an input of bibliographic, fund accounting, and location or inventory information about items to be acquired. A material labelling system might require an input of both materials to be processed and locational, bibliographic, and inventory information which will be placed on the identifying labels. Although selection slips, order cards, and other processing forms may be required to record and transport information, a system usually is concerned only with the information contained in or represented by these media, rather than with the forms themselves; the forms are merely containers of information to be processed.

The computer itself accepts information as input, and that information must be in a form acceptable to it; that is, in a machine-readable form.

System Processing Operations. Each automated library system has a set or group of processing operations, which are performed in an orderly and predetermined sequence, on the input of information or physical items. The information or items input into the system are converted to the desired end product as the step-by-step tasks are completed. The movement of information, materials, and other items through the processing steps within a system is referred to as workflow.

Common processing operations that the computer can perform include information verification, sorting, merging, calculation, comparison, storage, retrieval, reproduction, and dissemination. The computer cannot perform direct physical acts, although it can be used to control other machines which might perform physical operations. Physical operations such as moving, inserting, pasting, opening, closing, gathering, cutting, lifting, removing, turning, etc., must be performed by humans or machines other than the computer.

System Output. An automated library system produces a defined end result called output; output equals processed input. Examples of system output include materials acquired and physically processed; books cataloged and classified; records and reports prepared; lists and bibliographies produced; interlibrary loan transactions completed; reference questions answered; and other products or results achieved by performing prescribed information processing and physical operations on input. The output of a system also can be defined as a conditional change in information or materials. For example, output can be verified information (unverified information is processed into verified information) or labelled materials (unlabelled materials are processed into labelled materials).

While the computer can accept and process information in a machine-readable form only, its output can be in human-readable form or in a form which is both human-readable and machine-readable. Common human-readable output of the computer are a visual display on a cathode ray tube (CRT) screen and printed or typed documents. Common machine-readable but not human-readable output are magnetic tape, magnetic disk, punched cards, and punched paper tape.

System Resources

A number of resources are essential to support an automated library system. These include computing power, computer software, data communications, information, human resources, documentation, equipment, consumable supplies, and monetary resources.

Computing Power. Each automated library system requires access to computing power, either from an in-house machine or from a machine located elsewhere in a computing center serving the library. The computer is discussed in depth in Chapter 2.

Computer Software. A computer cannot operate without software, which are sets of step-by-step instructions that command the machine to perform processing operations on information. Computer software is discussed in Chapter 2. A list of typical hardware for an automated library system is shown in Appendix C.

Data Communications. For terminals and other devices connected to a remote computer, a data communications system may be needed. Through data communications, computing power can be brought into the library at any point where it is needed, even though the computer itself might be located blocks or miles away. Data communications are discussed in Chapter 2. A list of typical data communications equipment for automated library systems is shown in Appendix C.

Information. Information, which also is discussed in Chapter 2, is a very important resource in an automated library system. Information is generated, acquired, organized, stored, retrieved, and disseminated in a library system for use by patrons and staff.

Human Resources. Human resources are required by an automated library system to develop, operate, manage, and maintain the system. Some of this work may be performed by the same people, or different staff may be required for each, depending upon the size and nature of the automated system. The staff who will develop the automated system are discussed in Chapter 3, and the staff who will operate, manage, and maintain the system after it is installed are discussed in Chapters 10 and 11.

Documentation. Several types of documentation are essential to an automated library system. Documentation refers to the written descriptions of various aspects of the system, to be used by library staff and others for instructional and reference purposes while installing, operating, managing, and maintaining the system. Documentation for an automated library system is discussed in Chapters 5 and 10.

Equipment. An automated library system requires peripheral equipment such as desks, chairs, cabinets, tables, and other machines and equipment in order to operate the library properly. A list of typical equipment which might be needed by an automated library system is included in Appendix C.

Consumable Supplies. Supplies such as paper, custom forms, labels, printer ribbons, magnetic tape, cleaning materials, and energy are consumed by a system as it is operated. A list of common supplies which might be needed by an automated library system is also included in Appendix C.

Monetary Resources. Money is required to acquire, install, operate, and maintain an automated library system. Since any system must be purchased within the limits of a budget imposed upon it, the availability of monetary resources dictates the size and capabilities of the system acquired. Also, available monetary resources will dictate the amount of other resources such as staff, equipment, and supplies available to operate the system. These restrictions, in turn, limit the type, quality, and quantity of the system output. A financial and cost plan for an automated system is discussed in Chapter 4.

System Management and Leadership

An automated library system, like a manual system, requires effective management and leadership if it is to be successful. A well-trained and motivated staff is needed to plan, organize, coordinate, and supervise the activities of the system on both a day-to-day and a long-range basis. There are many approaches to, or styles of, management that may be used in administering an automated system. Basically, the approach or style used in an automated system will be the same used to manage a manual system.

System Environment

An automated system must exist and operate in an environment designed for the needs of the system. The system must be housed and operated in a finite amount of physical space, with proper levels of lighting, temperature, humidity, noise control, and cleanliness. It should be noted that several parts of a system which use some or all of the same resources can occupy the same physical space. For example, the charge, renewal, and discharge functions of an automated circulation system can all operate in the same physical space, using some of the same resources.

Some computers require special levels of cleanliness, air conditioning, and humidity controls in order to function properly. The design and construction of special facilities for a computer housed in the library are described in Chapter 8. Other aspects of system environment are discussed in Chapter 11.

METHODS OF DEVELOPING AN AUTOMATED LIBRARY SYSTEM

Automated library systems can be characterized by their method of acquisition or development. This section discusses turnkey, adapted, locally developed, and shared systems.

Turnkey Systems

The most prevalent method today of developing an automated library system is to purchase and install a turnkey system. A turnkey system is one which has been designed, programmed, and tested by an organization or company, then offered for sale or lease to libraries, ready to be installed and operated.

These packaged or off-the-shelf systems typically include a computer and all other essential hardware, software, and documentation such as descriptive, training, and reference manuals. Some turnkey system vendors will provide and install both the hardware and software, train the library staff to operate and manage the system, and then provide ongoing maintenance and support of the hardware and software. Other vendors will provide only the software, documentation, and training and require the library to be responsible for acquiring and maintaining the necessary hardware.

Developing an automated library system by purchasing and installing a turnkey system has both advantages and disadvantages.

Advantages of Turnkey Systems. A great advantage to acquiring and installing a turnkey system is that the library can examine the systems of several vendors operating in other libraries before a commitment is made to purchase a specific system. Both good and bad features of each system can be evaluated to obtain a more balanced comparison between the various systems being considered. Some other advantages include the following:

1. A turnkey system frequently can be acquired and installed in the library within a few months or under a year.
2. The costly and time-consuming design, programming, and testing of the system by the library can be eliminated because the vendor will already have spent the months or possibly years that must be devoted to these important activities.
3. The library need not have access to computer and systems specialists because this expertise is provided by the turnkey system vendor.
4. Most of the newer and more popular turnkey systems can be readily tailored to satisfy most library requirements.
5. The vendor will be responsible for making the system work in the library.
6. While the library staff must learn to operate and manage the turnkey system, it is not necessary that the staff have a special computer background as a prerequisite.
7. No recurring transaction or service fees, other than hardware and software maintenance, will have to be paid.
8. Although it might at first glance appear expensive, the turnkey system could cost less than other locally adapted or locally developed systems, if all developmental and operating costs are considered in the comparison.

Disadvantages of Turnkey Systems. There are some disadvantages to a library acquiring and installing a turnkey system:

1. A turnkey system will be designed for average or typical libraries and therefore might have undesirable features which must be accepted by the library. The system also might lack desirable features, thus forcing the library to compromise its individual needs to a packaged system.
2. Some turnkey systems are inflexible and cannot be altered, once installed, to meet changing needs and conditions within the library without extensive and costly overhauls or complete replacement.
3. Space in the library or in a computing center serving the library must be provided for the computer system supporting the turnkey system.

4. The computer must be housed in a nonpublic area where electrical power, heating and air conditioning, security, noise, and dust can be controlled.
5. While the general library staff need not have previous data processing or computer knowledge and experience, the library will require someone with sufficient expertise to manage the project, install the system, and operate and manage the system after its installation.

Adapted Systems

Another method of developing an automated library system is to locate a suitable system, then duplicate and adapt the software for local installation and operation. The system could be installed to operate on an in-house computer or on a computer located in a computing center serving the library. This method has some advantages and disadvantages.

Advantages of Adapted Systems. The primary advantage of adapting the system of another library could be that the borrowing library can eliminate the costly and time-consuming design, programming, and testing of the system, because the originating library already will have performed these activities. Another advantage is that, as with turnkey systems, the library can examine the operational system before it decides to acquire and adapt the software for local use.

Disadvantages of Adapted Systems. There are also some disadvantages to adapting the system of another library:

1. The borrowed system might reflect all the policies and idiosyncrasies of the original library, which may be different from those of the library wishing to use the system.
2. The borrowing library must have access to computer and systems specialists to adapt, install, maintain, and enhance the application software for local use.
3. While previous data processing or computer knowledge and experience might not be required of the library staff, someone will have to manage the project to adapt and install the system and to operate and manage it after implementation.
4. Space in the library or in a computing center serving the library must be provided for the computer and auxiliary equipment needed to support the system.
5. More time and money might be spent in adapting another library's system compared to purchasing a turnkey system, with the possibility that the end result is a less effective system.

Locally Developed Systems

A third method of developing an automated system is to design, program, document, install, and test a system locally, from scratch. The software may be maintained and operated on an in-house computer or on a computer located in a computing center serving the library. As with each of the previous options, there are both advantages and disadvantages to locally developed systems.

Advantages of Locally Developed Systems. There are some advantages to developing an automated system locally from scratch:

1. The system can be designed to meet the exact needs and requirements of the library.
2. The library can maintain control over all aspects of the system's development, installation, and operation.
3. No recurring transaction fees will be involved.

Disadvantages of Locally Developed Systems. There are likewise some distinct disadvantages to developing a system locally from scratch:

1. Local development is the most difficult and time-consuming method of acquiring an automated library system.
2. The library must have access to highly specialized computer and systems specialists to design, program, test, install, and maintain the system.
3. Several years might pass before the library would have a smoothly running operational system.
4. The library itself must acquire, house, and maintain a computer system and other essential hardware to support the automated system, or, use equipment in a computing center serving the library.
5. If all expenses are considered, the costs of developing, operating, and maintaining a locally developed system probably will be as great as, if not more than, a turnkey, adapted, or shared system, with the potential for poorer results.

There is a general consensus today that a library should not design again a system that many others have developed and that could be obtained through other methods.

Shared Systems

A last method of developing an automated library system is to share a system with other libraries through networking. A shared system is one that has been developed or acquired by a library, consortium, company, or other organization, then offered for use by selected or many libraries through a data communications network.

The system to be shared may be a turnkey or adapted system or may have been developed from scratch by the organization.

Typically, the library involved in sharing the automated system will have one or more computer terminals connected via communication links to the system computer, which may be located in the same city, the next state, or even thousands of miles from the library. A library can contract with the organization or firm for services such as cataloging, file conversion, bibliographic verification, acquisitions, interlibrary loans, serials control, online reference services, and even circulation. Payment for use of the systems may be through membership dues and/or access and transaction fees.

Sharing an automated library system with others has some advantages, as well as disadvantages.

Advantages of Shared Systems. Using a system shared with other libraries through networking provides the following advantages:

1. As with a turnkey system, a great advantage to sharing an automated system is that the library can examine the system actually operating in other libraries and see the system's good and bad features before it decides to use the system.
2. The library need not have a computer available locally in order to gain the benefits of an automated library system.
3. Usually, the equipment needed to access a shared system can be installed in the library within a few months.
4. The library is not required to invest time or money in designing, programming, and testing the system.
5. The organization or firm offering the system will be responsible for making the system work in the library.
6. The library need not have access to computer and systems specialists because this expertise will be provided by the organization or firm vending the system.
7. If it is unhappy with the services provided, the library can withdraw from participation with little loss of capital investment.
8. The vending organization or firm usually assists in installing and maintaining essential hardware in the library and in training the library staff to use the system.
9. While the library staff must learn to operate the in-house equipment and use the system, they will not be required to have any specialized computer background as a prerequisite.

Disadvantages of Shared Systems. There could be some disadvantages to using a shared system:

1. The library generally will have little if anything to say about the services received; it usually must use the available services on a take-it-or-leave-it basis.

2. Because many basic decisions are made by a network operations office or commercial firm, the library might feel a loss of control over important events that affect it.
3. The shared system might have undesirable features which must be accepted by the library or might lack desirable features which will force the library to compromise its needs to those of the shared system.
4. While the library can avoid the costs of acquiring and maintaining a computer system and software by sharing a system with others, its membership dues or transaction and access fees are recurring expenses which will have to be paid each year.

EFFECTS OF USING AN AUTOMATED LIBRARY SYSTEM

When properly designed, installed, operated, and managed, an automated library system can offer many benefits to a library, but any system will have some limitations. Some observable effects of using an automated library system can be noted, particularly in regard to operations, staffing, services, accountability, and costs.

Operations

Operations in an automated library system usually are more complex and require more precision in their execution than in a manual system. Automated operations are, in most cases, detailed and require smooth interaction to avoid errors and delays in service. The automated system is more sensitive to dysfunction than the traditional manual system. Errors made in the workflow, or steps omitted, create a ripple effect in an automated system. Many operations are interactive and interrelated throughout the system, and the output of many parts of an operation then become input to others. Usually, operations cannot be omitted or rearranged without serious repercussions in an automated system, and when one operation fails, the work flow could stop or the system could fail completely. This is not always the case in a manual system.

Staffing

The use of an automated library system could result in a reduction of staff necessary for the functioning of the system. Some staff who are eliminated from the automated system could be retained and shifted to other programs. More often, the computer serves to relieve staff from performing undesirable or repetitive tasks, leaving them free to perform more rewarding and stimulating duties in the same system. Some staff may be given different responsibilities in the automated system and will have to be retrained for their new duties.

Services

An important and beneficial effect of library automation can be seen in improved services to users because the computer is capable of performing repetitive and routine work faster and more accurately than humans.

In addition, since an increased amount of work can be performed in the automated library system, the computer could enable the library to offer new services never before possible with a manual system.

Example: Terminals can be made available to the public for a fee to enable online search of commercial databases.

Example: Terminals can be made available to the public for a fee to provide word processing capabilities.

Accountability

The use of a computer to support a library system should result in better control over materials and services through the availability of more current and comprehensive files and faster and more accurate notices and reports than in a manual system. The result could be better accountability to users, management, and taxpayers.

Costs

Aside from the problem of job displacement, the cost of installing and operating an automated library system is its most controversial aspect.

A prevalent argument has been that an automated system should not be considered unless it can be proven to be less expensive than the manual system it replaces. But it must be remembered that an automated system often is radically different from a manual system, so it is difficult to obtain accurate cost figures for a comparison between the two, particularly in advance of the installation of the machine system. Installation of an automated library system is expensive, and the costs of maintaining the system could be more expensive than the manual system it replaces. If the computer can support more than one system, then costs could be spread over each system served, thus reducing operating costs for each. For example, the cost of maintaining a computer system for a circulation system might be $30,000 a year. But if that same computer is used also to support an acquisitions system and an online catalog, the costs could be divided three ways, or $10,000 per system. The more systems a computer supports, the less the cost per system being supported. Of course, the library still must pay the total cost of maintaining the system.

Another argument is that the use of a computer could stabilize the operating costs of a system. The costs of human labor are increasing steadily, while the costs of acquiring, installing, and maintaining a computer system are dropping, or at least not rising as rapidly as labor costs. A stabilization of operating costs for a system could take place, but every effort to streamline procedures and workflow must be made before this can be accomplished. Sharing the computer supporting the system, as discussed above, can reduce the direct cost of operating that system but not the overall costs to the library.

Chapter 2
The Computer and Related Technology

Relatively few libraries had hope of or interest in using computers prior to the 1970s. During the past few years, however, growing demands for new and sophisticated approaches to information access and dissemination, an inability to cope with an expanding and increasingly complex information base, rising operating costs, and insufficient funding have forced librarians to seek better and more cost-efficient systems for providing services. The use of well-designed automated systems potentially could alleviate some of these pressures. Computers now are commonplace in most institutions and organizations where libraries exist or in networks serving libraries; hence, most libraries have ready access to computing power. Indeed, technological advances and competition within the computer industry have reduced the size and cost of hardware to the point that many libraries can afford to have their own in-house computers dedicated to their sole use.

This chapter reviews some fundamentals of computers and related technology. Specifically, it includes:

- Definition and characteristics of a computer
- Capabilities and limitations of the computer
- Computer sizes
- Location of the computer
- Components of the computer system
- Computer processing modes
- Computer software
- Machine-readable information
- Data communications

DEFINITION AND CHARACTERISTICS OF A COMPUTER

A computer is an electronic device or machine which accepts and automatically performs prescribed sequences of processing operations on information to achieve a desired end result. The type of computer of interest to librarians is the general purpose digital computer, which operates on information expressed as digits of the binary or other number system. This machine processes information by counting and comparing digits; that is, by adding, subtracting, multiplying, and dividing symbols or digits expressing information and comparing them to determine if they are the same or different.

The general purpose computer has an internal storage unit or memory where information to be processed and interchangeable sets of processing instructions called programs are stored. This capability enables the machine to perform long sequences of repetitive and time-consuming operations accurately and automatically over a long period of time without human direction and interference. The set of instructions on which the computer operates can be easily removed, erased, and replaced when required.

CAPABILITIES AND LIMITATIONS OF THE COMPUTER

A computer has many capabilities which make it a desirable library tool, but it also has its limitations because most systems represent a compromise between availabile technology, cost, and size considerations.

Capabilities of the Computer

A digital computer basically can be used to control processes, store and retrieve information, maintain files of information, perform computations on information, and arrange and rearrange information. In addition, it can:

1. Perform large volumes of repetitive, time-consuming operations automatically and accurately over a long period of time.
2. Operate at high speeds, measured in one one-millionth of a second or less.
3. Direct itself in a predetermined manner once it is provided with information and a set of instructions.
4. Process one job at a time or several jobs almost simultaneously.
5. Receive an input of information and instructions from remote locations, process the input, and transmit the results back to a remote user.
6. Choose among alternatives in processing information in a way that is equivalent to making decisions.

Limitations of the Computer

The computer does have limitations, and libraries must be aware of these in considering an automated system.

1. The computer cannot perform without sets of instructions; it must have a set of instructions for every application or job it is to perform. Every operation and decision to be made by the computer must be foreseen in advance by humans and the alternatives specified in the programs.
2. While it can perform at incredible speeds, a computer can do nothing that it is not programmed to do. Computers cannot perform any operation that cannot be performed by humans.
3. The computer can operate only on information, and that information must be in a form that it can recognize and then convert to a machine-readable form.
4. It can detect, but generally cannot correct, inaccurate information fed into it; the results of computer processing are only as accurate as the input placed into the system.
5. The computer is not capable of performing all necessary operations in a library system; in all cases, humans must specify which information is to be collected and how it is to be organized, stored, retrieved, arranged and rearranged, and disseminated.

COMPUTER SIZES

Many sizes of computers, with varying capabilities and levels of sophistication, are available to support an automated library system. The size categories are not precisely defined in the industry and can be misleading. While modern computers are arbitrarily classed as micro-, mini-, or mainframe computers, it is important to remember that size bears little relationship to a computer's ability to perform well. Some small computers are capable of performing as well as, and sometimes better than, other larger machines. For example, by adding available options to a microcomputer, its storage capacity, processing power, versatility, and cost can equal or exceed that of a larger minicomputer.

Microcomputers

The microcomputer is the smallest class or size of computer today. It is a programmable machine, as small as a postage stamp or as large as a portable typewriter, useful in a wide range of home, business, industrial, and library applications. Usually, the microcomputer is restricted to handling only one application and user at a time. It often is used as an integral part of a larger computer system. For example, a microcomputer might control communications from a number of visual display terminals connected to a larger computer, or the microcomputer might be a part of the terminal itself, performing such preprocessing functions as information editing and error detection before transmitting data to the larger machine. This size of machine can be operated anywhere in the library, without requiring special air conditioning. However, excessive heat and humidity can nonetheless cause damage to the machine.

Minicomputers

The minicomputer also is a small, programmable machine which is fast and reliable and useful in a wide range of business, industrial, and library applications. The machine might be the size of an office typewriter and fit on a desk, although most are housed in floor-standing cabinets along with other essential equipment. Some minicomputers can handle only one application at a time, but most can handle several sets of instructions and users simultaneously. Most are used independently of other computer systems, while others are connected to larger systems and dependent upon them for mass storage and some processing. Some of the smaller minicomputers do not require special air conditioning and humidity controls, but most do, particularly if large disk drives are used. The very large minicomputers are sometimes referred to as superminicomputers.

Mainframe Computers

Any size of computer larger than the minicomputer is usually referred to as a mainframe computer. This type of computer is fast and versatile, with the capabilities of handling large amounts of mass storage, a wide range of auxiliary equipment, and many applications and users at the same time. The mainframe computer is most often found in a computing center serving a number of different users, but some large libraries have this size of machine in-house, dedicated to their sole use. A small mainframe computer without auxiliary equipment might be the size of an office copier, requiring as little as 400 or more than 1,000 square feet of physical space, depending upon its peripheral equipment. A large mainframe computer might require thousands of square feet of floor space for the system, its peripheral equipment, and the staff for its operation and maintenance. Special air conditioning and humidity controls are required for mainframe computers.

LOCATION OF THE COMPUTER

The computer supporting an automated library system can be located either in the library or in a computing center serving the library. There are advantages and disadvantages to either location.

The Computer Located in the Library

The primary advantage to locating the computer supporting an automated system in the library is that the library can retain complete control over the system. The library would not be dependent upon another department or agency to operate and maintain its system or supply it with computing power. The library probably would be the sole user of the machine. The disadvantage to having the computer in the library is that special air conditioned and humidity-controlled quarters might have to be provided for the system as well as high capacity power circuits that have to be protected from transient power surges. In addition, the library will have to train its staff to operate and manage the system.

The Computer Located Outside the Library

The advantages to having the computer supporting its automated system outside the library in another department or agency is that the library would not have to provide space and a controlled environment for housing the system and the staff required for its operation and management. The major disadvantage is that the library might feel a loss of autonomy when it must depend upon another unit for its computing power. The library might not be able to control the hours the computer is available for use; staff in the computing center may not be available at the right times to operate the machine or prepare reports; and the library may be required to pay what it considers an inordinate sum of money for computing services.

If the computer supporting an automated library system is shared with other departments or agencies, the library may have problems gaining sufficient auxiliary storage, assistance in enhancing its software, and priority on the machines. In some cases, staff who understand the library's software and how to troubleshoot and solve problems may not be readily available. For example, most nonlibrary computing centers seldom understand why the library must have its circulation system online and available for use from 7:00 a.m. until midnight, seven days a week. Few computing center staff outside the library understand the complexity of library operations and files. This lack of understanding can result in serious problems for the library and major deficiencies in the effectiveness of the system operations.

COMPONENTS OF THE COMPUTER SYSTEM

A computer system consists of a number of metallic, plastic, magnetic, electric, electronic, and other physical parts referred to as hardware. Each computer system includes different pieces of equipment, in different arrangements and sizes, and with varying capabilities of speed and sophistication. The pieces of equipment that make up a specific computer system are referred to as a configuration. Regardless of its size, capabilities, or cost, a computer system is usually composed of only three basic types of hardware components: a central processing unit, auxiliary storage, and input-output devices (see Figure 2-1).

Figure 2-1. A Block Diagram of the Components of a Computer System.

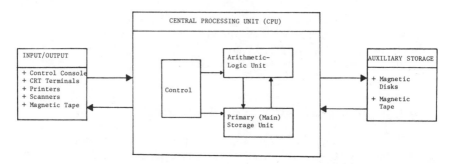

The Central Processing Unit

The actual computer is referred to as the central processor or central processing unit (CPU), which consists of control, arithmetic-logic units, and primary storage housed in a system console (see Figure 2-1). All auxiliary storage and input-output devices such as the control console and cathode ray terminals, or CRTs, are directly connected by electric cable to the central processing unit and operate under its control; that is, they are online to the CPU.

Control Unit. The control unit directs, coordinates, and integrates the step-by-step operations of the computer system. It controls all input and output devices and handles the transfer of information from an input device into primary storage or from primary storage to auxiliary storage. The control unit also selects the applicable instructions from primary storage, interprets them, and directs their execution. This involves routing information from primary storage to the arithmetic-logic unit, directing the operation of the arithmetic-logic unit, and routing information back to primary storage.

ROM ← <u>Arithmetic-Logic Unit</u>. The arithmetic-logic unit contains the circuitry necessary to perform arithmetic and logical operations on the information to be processed, according to the set of instructions that has been provided. Addition, subtraction, multiplication, division, and comparison of information are peformed here; in other words, the actual processing of information occurs in the arithmetic-logic unit of the CPU.

RAM → <u>Primary Storage</u>. Primary storage, which is referred to as main, internal, or high-speed memory, holds information being processed and the step-by-step instructions for processing that information. Due to the relatively high cost of primary storage, it is used only for the temporary retention of information and programs during processing. When other information is ready to be processed, the new information replaces the old. Information not being processed at the moment is retained in less expensive auxiliary storage. In the past, primary storage consisted of heavy metal rings or cores, but current computers usually rely on integrated circuits or microchips for primary storage. The amount of primary storage available to hold information is measured by the number of eight-digit binary numbers, called bytes, that can be stored at any one time.

Auxiliary Storage

Auxiliary storage supplements the primary storage unit of a computer and provides a mass storage capability to the system. When information in an auxiliary storage device is to be processed by the computer, it must first be transferred to the primary storage. Common auxiliary storage devices include magnetic tape and magnetic disk, both of which can store larger amounts of information than can primary storage, at a lower cost.

<u>Magnetic Tape</u>. Computer magnetic tape, which is similar to that used in home tape recorders, consists of a plastic base coated on one side with iron oxide that can be magnetized. The tape is divided horizontally into rows called channels or tracks, which run the length of the tape, and vertically into columns or frames. Alphabetic, numeric, and special characters are recorded on the tape in coded form as invisible, magnetic spots on the oxide coating of the tape's surface. The number of columns of characters that can be recorded per inch of tape is referred to as the tape density. Common tape densities are 800 and 1600 bits per inch (BPI). Tape width is commonly half-inch, three-quarters inch, or one inch, wound on spools called reels. Information recorded on magnetic tape can be read or sensed by the computer as many times as is desired or can be erased and the tape reused indefinitely. The information is automatically erased as new data are being recorded.

<u>Magnetic Disks</u>. Magnetic disks, which resemble phonograph records, are also coated with a metallic oxide which can be magnetized. Information is recorded as invisible, magnetized spots in the

metallic oxide coating on the surface of the disk, within concentric circles called tracks. The disks can be mounted in groups called a disk pack or used singly. Newer, and usually smaller, types of disks are called diskettes, flexible disks, or floppy disks. Hundreds of thousands or many millions of characters of information can be recorded on a disk or disk pack. Information can be read or sensed by the computer as many times as is desired or can be erased and the disks reused indefinitely. As with magnetic tapes, information is automatically erased as new data are being recorded.

Input-Output Devices

Information that is to be processed or utilized by the computer is referred to as input, and information that has been processed by the computer is called output. Input data must be in a machine-readable form or in a form that can easily be converted to a machine-readable form. Machine-readable information is discussed later in this chapter. The devices or hardware that read or sense information for the computer are referred to as input devices, and the devices that present the results of processing are referred to as output devices. Often, the two are combined, and the result is an input-output (I/O) device. Common methods of computer input and output include typewriter terminals, visual display terminals, optical character scanners, barcode scanners, and printers.

Terminals. Typewriter and visual display or cathode ray tube (CRT) terminals provide a fast and easy means by which information can be entered directly into the computer system for processing and storage without first being prepared in a machine-readable form. In addition, the results of the processing by the computer can be returned to a user through these devices.

The typewriter terminal is similar to a standard office typewriter. As an operator depresses the keys, the action creates a coded pattern of pulses representing the characters sent to the computer for processing over cable or a data communications system. As the operator types the information, a hard copy is also produced.

Another type of terminal is the visual display terminal, also called a CRT. This type of terminal has a typewriter-like keyboard for input and a television screen for output. The screen replaces the carriage and paper found in the typewriter terminal. As information is typed into the computer, it is displayed on the screen.

Control Console. A computer usually has an operator or control console, which is a special input-output device used by an operator to communicate with the machine. A keyboard or keyboard and visual display unit combination usually serves as the control console.

Scanners. Optical character and barcode scanners can be used as a means of computer input. Optical characters are human-readable, symbolic characters which also can be sensed or read optically by a machine and converted to a machine-readable form for computer input. Information can also be represented as barcodes, whereby information is in coded form as vertical bars of varying heights, widths, and spacings. Optical characters and barcodes are widely used in automated circulation systems as a means of identifying borrowers (library cards) and materials which will be circulated.

Printers. Documents or reports prepared by a printer online to the computer system are referred to as printouts. A wide variety of printers are available as output devices for use with computers, including hammer character, matrix, thermal, laser, ink jet, electrostatic, printwheel, chain, and drum printers. They may be categorized as either character printers, which print one character at a time, or as line printers, which print one line at a time during a print cycle. Printers that operate at 500 or more lines a minute usually are classed as high-speed printers.

COMPUTER PROCESSING MODES

There are two methods or modes of computer processing that can be used by a library: interactive and batch processing. If required, either mode can be accomplished via remote processing and via timesharing.

Interactive Processing

The most popular means of using a computer is in an interactive mode. In this method, the operator and the computer exchange information or messages in an ongoing, almost conversational manner. Each supplies input to the other via the keyboard or visual display screen. This method of using a computer is fast, enables the operator to obtain immediate feedback from the computer, and enables files to be kept current at all times.

Batch Processing

Another method of using the computer is referred to as batch processing. In this method, the computer performs specified operations during a single machine run on groups or batches of records already stored in an online file. For example, the computer can be programmed to search an online circulation file for records of overdue items, copy the records of delinquent materials which are identified into a work file, and print notices to be sent to borrowers. An operator need only initiate the program, supply the computer with the proper file or files, and set up the printer for preparation of the notices.

Remote Processing

Utilizing data communications technology, a library can use a computer, which may be located some distance away, without physically going to the computing center. This means that the input of information or instructions can be accomplished at any point in the library where computer processing is needed; that is, at the circulation desk or other work station. The transmission of information and commands from a point in the library to a remote computer for processing, then having the results returned to the same point in the library, is referred to as teleprocessing or remote processing. Data communications, which makes remote processing possible, is discussed later in this chapter.

Timesharing

Through a process known as timesharing, a number of users can concurrently and independently share the same computer. Each user will have a remote terminal such as a typewriter or CRT terminal connected to the computer system via cable or a data communications system. Users are independent of each other, acting as if he or she is the sole user of the system. Each user can either share programs and data files or be restricted to only utilize separate ones. The computer will switch rapidly among users, allocating tiny, but frequently repeated, slices or allocations of time to each. There might be frequent interruptions to the processing of a user's information, but if the system is not overloaded with too many users, the interrupts will occur so rapidly that the individual is usually unaware of these time lapses.

COMPUTER SOFTWARE

Computer software are the sets of step-by-step instructions or programs that command the machine to perform operations on information. A string, list, or set of these instructions is called a computer program. The computer follows the program, one instruction after another, in a specified sequence, until a job is completed. A different set of instructions is required for each application or job the computer is to perform. The two basic types of software are system and application software.

System Software

System software, which usually is supplied by the hardware manufacturer, is necessary to operate and maintain a computer system and to facilitate the programming, testing, correction, and running of application software. Examples of system software include, among others, operating systems and utility programs.

Operating Systems. The goal of the library should be to operate a computer system with such efficiency that it is continuously used at or close to its capacity. However, when a human is required to load the input, set switches on the console, start processing runs, unload the output, keep log records of runs, select the next program to be run, and check hundreds of other essential operations, it is unreasonable to expect the computer to be used efficiently. The computer will have to sit idle while the operator catches up with it. To increase the efficiency of their machines, computer manufacturers have developed special operating system software to perform many of the jobs previously done manually by humans.

An operating system, which sometimes is called a supervisory or executive program, is a collection of special programs that supervise and control the running of other programs. The primary function or purpose of an operating system is to increase the utilization of the computer by limiting human intervention in the processing cycle and making all operations virtually automatic. The operating system will:

1. Control priorities of job requests and queues for input-output devices.
2. Provide logs of time utilization for user accountability.
3. Maintain an index of all programs in the system.
4. Coordinate the different areas of storage with program requirements so that space may be used efficiently.
5. Allocate and assign storage space for programs.
6. Keep track of assigned space and reallocate space when it becomes available.
7. React to hardware failures, input or output needs, and program errors.
8. Coordinate input and output between the CPU and the particular devices being used.

Utility Programs. Utility programs are general purpose programs supplied by the computer manufacturer and others to assist in the operation of a computer system. Utility programs include such standardized operations as sorting and merging, clearing storage, loading programs, transferring data from one storage medium to another, and program testing aids.

Application Software

Application software refers to the sets of computer instructions or programs required for specific applications such as library acquisitions, cataloging, circulation, and an online catalog. In most automated library systems, many sets of software might be necessary for particular functions. This type of software is not usually supplied by the hardware manufacturer but must be purchased or leased from a software vendor, shared with other libraries, borrowed and adapted from other libraries, or developed and prepared locally. The software can be written in a variety of programming languages such as FOR-TRAN, COBOL, BASIC, or PASCAL.

One of the most common application programs used on a computer is a database management system or DBMS. It is a software system that manages the organization, location, storage, retrieval, and maintenance of a large volume of information in a collection of related files or database. It can be used effectively, for example, in the management of the file of bibliographic records supporting an online catalog.

MACHINE-READABLE INFORMATION

Information is a very important element of all automated library systems. However, the information that the computer is required to process, store, and retrieve must be in a form that it can accept; that is, in a machine-readable form. This section reviews some fundamentals of machine-readable information, including its definition, computer codes for information representation, information essential to an automated library system, and information organization.

Definition of Machine-Readable Information

Information can be defined as data symbols which have been combined or arranged to represent or convey meaningful facts, ideas, conditions, or knowledge about people, physical items, and other things. Data symbols include the alphabetic letters A through Z, the numeric characters 0 through 9, and special characters such as punctuation marks and signs. While, technically, there is a distinction between the terms "data" and "information," the two are often used interchangeably.

The computer requires that the information it is to process be in a form that it can sense and accept; that is, in a machine-readable form. Machine-readable information is data in the form of electronic or electric signals or pulses or in a form that can easily be converted to electronic signals. Symbolic information is represented in machine-readable form by the presence or absence of electrical signals or pulses. To give meaning to this concept, the numeric symbol "1" has been arbitrarily chosen to represent the presence of an electronic signal or pulse, and "0" to represent the absence of a signal. There are no other conditions possible using this concept—only the two symbols "0" and "1." That is, either a signal is there or it is not there; there is no "in between." For this reason, the electronic signal is said to represent a two-state or binary condition. Each electronic signal condition is called a binary digit or bit, which is a contraction of the two words, "binary" and "digit."

Computer Codes for Information Representation

Groups or patterns of pulses, analagous to dots and dashes in the Morse code, are used to represent alphabetic, numeric, and special characters of information. The common information or computer codes in use today include the Binary Coded Decimal Code, the Extended Binary Coded Decimal Interchange Code, and the American Standard Code for Information Interchange.

Binary Coded Decimal Code. The Binary Coded Decimal Code or BCD code consists of six bits representing each character of symbolic information. Alphabetic, numeric, and special characters are represented as unique combinations of 1- and 0-bits within the six positions. For example, in BCD code, the alphabetic letter "A" is represented as "110001," or "pulse/pulse/no pulse/no pulse/no pulse/pulse."

Extended Binary Coded Decimal Interchange Code. The Binary Coded Decimal Code explained above is not sufficient to provide for both upper- and lower-case letters and the wide range of special characters needed by many computer applications. To permit greater flexibility, an eight-bit code, the Extended Binary Coded Decimal Interchange Code or EBCDIC was developed to permit 256 different characters to be represented. In this code, the alphabetic letter "A" is represented as "11000001," or "pulse/pulse/no pulse/no pulse/no pulse/no pulse/no pulse/pulse."

American Standard Code for Information Interchange. The American Standard Code for Information Interchange or ASCII is a special code developed for use in data communications systems and networks. There are two versions of ASCII: a seven-bit code and an eight-bit code. The alphabetic character "A" in seven-bit ASCII is represented as "1000001," or "pulse/no pulse/no pulse/no pulse/no pulse/no pulse/pulse." It is not important to the user to know what code is being used in a particular computer system. The above explanation is meant to be a help in developing a greater understanding of computer interfacing.

Information Essential to an Automated Library System

There are several types of information that might be required by an automated library system, including bibliographic, copy, transaction, user, textual, and management information.

Bibliographic Information. Bibliographic information, which describes materials for cataloging, indexing, location, and accountability purposes, is required by automated acquisitions and circulation systems and by an online catalog. A standardized format, MARC (MAchine-Readable Cataloging) has been developed by the library community for the transfer or communication of bibliographic information in machine-readable form between libraries. Libraries are being encouraged to adopt MARC as the format for the storage of bibliographic records in their local databases that are to be available by computer access.

Copy Information. Copy information describes each copy of material owned by a library. Typically, copy information might include a copy number, a location within the library, a material type designation, the call number, cost of the item, a barcode or optical character code number, and perhaps the date the item was acquired. This information is required by automated acquisitions and circulation systems and by an online catalog. The MARC format does include a format for copy records.

Transaction Information. Transaction information is contained in the circulation records, selection requests, interlibrary loan requests, purchase requests, invoices and vouchers, overdue and fine notices, and other similar records often needed by circulation, acquisitions, and cataloging systems. There is no standardized format for this type of information. Rather, each automated library system will have its own format which may or may not be similar to others.

User Information. Information about borrowers or users is required by automated circulation and interlibrary loan systems. User records, which contain borrowers' names, addresses, and other personal information, should be brief and well structured, but as yet, there is no standard format accepted by the library community.

Textual Information. The contents of operational and technical guides are stored by some automated library systems as textual information, to be used for online reference or for printing hard copies upon demand. Some libraries are experimenting with the full-text machine storage of journal articles, documents, reports, and even books. Such masses of information can be stored electronically, but with the current cost of storage capacity, it is not yet economically feasible or necessarily desirable, except on a limited scale.

Management Information. A final type of information often generated by and stored in an automated library system for retrieval and dissemination by staff and others is management information. Statistics of system use or activities are gathered by almost all automated library systems. Other management information, such as accounting information, may be required in an automated acquisitions system. Currently, this type of information also has no standardized format recognized by the library community.

Information Organization

Information utilized by an automated library system is organized into records and then combined into files for ease of storage, retrieval, and use.

Records. The basic organizational unit for information is the record, which is a collection of related information about a person, physical item, or transaction. Some examples of library records include bibliographic, circulation, transaction, borrower registration, and personnel records. Abstract, bibliographic, transaction, and management information usually are organized into records, while lengthy textual information generally is not.

A record can contain words, phrases, sentences, and numeric, alphabetic, and special codes, arranged or subdivided into groupings called fields and subfields. A field is a group of related information describing a particular aspect of a person, physical item, or transaction to which the record corresponds. For example, a bibliographic record can be divided into main entry, title, edition, imprint, notes, and added entry fields. Any field of a record can be further subdivided into two or more subfields, which are groups of related information describing particular aspects of a field. For example, an imprint field of a bibliographic record can be subdivided into place of publication, publisher, and date of publication subfields.

The computer can distinguish between fields and subfields of a record in two different ways. The first method utilizes special characters or symbols called delimiters to distinguish fields from subfields. Periods, slashes, asterisks, dollar signs, and extra blanks are among the special characters commonly used as separators or delimiters. The computer can determine where one piece of information ends and another begins if delimiters are used, but it cannot distinguish one field or subfield from another except by their position in the record. This can result in a major weakness in the flexibility of a system that utilizes delimiters. If fields or subfields are omitted or added or if their positional relationships are altered, the computer will not identify them correctly. The second and best method of enabling a computer to identify fields of a record is to assign each a unique numeric or alphabetic identifier called a tag.

The maximum length of fields and subfields can be specified, depending upon the application and the information. A field or subfield containing the same number of characters from record to record is said to be of fixed length. For example, a fixed-length field designated for a ZIP code always will contain five numeric characters, unless an error occurs. As another example, a fixed-length field defined as having a maximum length of 15 characters could contain only "Gone with the W" of the title, "Gone with the Wind." The remainder must be eliminated or truncated and cannot be recorded in the field. On the other hand, the field could contain all of the title "Animal Farm," with four positions remaining blank.

A field or subfield that can contain a variable number of characters from record to record is said to be of variable length. In this case, the length of the field or subfield is dependent upon the information recorded in it.

Files. Related records are organized into groups called files. Some examples of library files include the card catalog, a circulation file, and a personnel file. A group of related files in the library is called a data bank or database.

There are several common types of files used with computers. A master file contains relatively permanent, current-status records, which are the major source of information for a particular application such as acquisitions, cataloging, or circulation. Such a file is updated periodically through the addition, deletion, and modification of records when necessary to maintain its current status. New or modified records are accumulated and recorded in a transaction file and then are used to update the master file. A work file contains records extracted from another file, such as a master file, to be used for special processing or in another application. For example, records of overdue materials can be extracted from a master circulation file to be used in the preparation of overdue notices. A backup file is a total or partial duplicate of another file. A backup file is maintained in case the original is damaged or destroyed and would be used to replace or recreate the original file. A history or archival file contains obsolete or noncurrent records which can be used later in the compilation of management information reports, for legal purposes, or for other reasons.

A file is organized to facilitate later location and retrieval of specific records and to allow routine file maintenance as necessary. Usually, a file will be arranged according to the most often used or most important field of its records. A field upon which records in a file are sequenced is called a control field or file key. This key will determine each record's position or location in the file. For example, the file key for a shelf list catalog might be the classification number, and for an author catalog, the main entry. A minor or subordinate file key also may be used to further sequence records when a number of them have the same primary key. For example, a file with the main entry as its file key would probably use the title as the subordinate file key. In this manner, when more than one record has the same main entry, the minor file key would ensure that works by the same author would be retained in alphabetical sequence. The choice of file keys for records will be dictated primarily by how a file will be searched and, additionally, in an automated system, by the storage device being used. Users will want to search a file by name, title, subject, and so on. These search keys will be compared with the file keys for possible matches and subsequent retrieval of a specific record.

There are two basic methods of organizing records in a file. In a sequentially organized file, records are stored one after the other, in ascending order according to a file key. This is the most common method of arranging records in a file because it is simple to organize and use. The primary disadvantage of this method is that a computer search for a specific record must begin with the first record in the file and proceed, one by one, until the desired record is located. A second disadvantage is that, in order to update the sequentially organized file, new records to be added must first be sorted into sequence before they can be interfiled with old records. A more efficient system uses an indexed file organization. In an indexed file, records are stored either sequentially or randomly in a main file, and one or more separate indexes containing the file keys and addresses or pointers to the records stored in the main file are maintained. To retrieve records, the index is first searched to identify the file key of a desired record. If the key is in the index, the record address in storage will be indicated, and the record can then be retrieved from the main file. This method of file organization provides one of the fastest means of record retrieval when large files are involved.

DATA COMMUNICATIONS

While terminals and other input-output devices can be connected by cable direct to the central processing unit supporting an automated library system, signals sent further than several hundred feet can become so distorted that the information content is lost. In this case, use of a telecommunications or data communications system will be necessary. This section includes a definition of data communications and descriptions of data communication steps, channels, and equipment.

Definition of Data Communications

Data communication is the process of transmitting or transferring computer data or information between a library and a remote computer, through means of data transmission or communications channels and equipment. This process enables the use of a remote computer terminal at any point in the library as long as a communications link can be installed.

Data Communications Steps

In the early days of computing, all information to be processed for a library had to be physically taken in batches to a central computing center, the work placed in a queue, and the results picked up by the library after the input was processed. While this method still is effective and economical, rapid technolgical advances and a convergence of computer and communications technologies make this tedious process unnecessary. In a modern online computer system, information and instructions can be entered into a terminal device located in the library, then transmitted to a remote computer via a communications link, such as an ordinary telephone line. After processing the information, the computer returns the results to the library over the same link.

There are 11 basic steps in the process of using a remote computer via data communications (see Figure 2-2).

Figure 2-2. The Steps of the Data Communication Process.

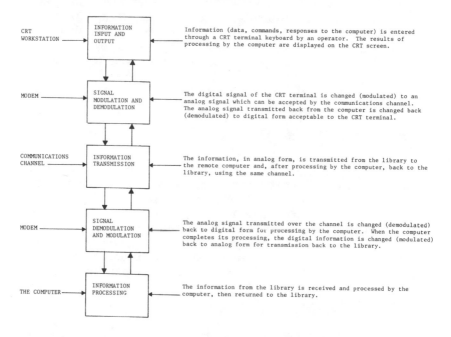

CRT WORKSTATION → INFORMATION INPUT AND OUTPUT

Information (data, commands, responses to the computer) is entered through a CRT terminal keyboard by an operator. The results of processing by the computer are displayed on the CRT screen.

MODEM → SIGNAL MODULATION AND DEMODULATION

The digital signal of the CRT terminal is changed (modulated) to an analog signal which can be accepted by the communications channel. The analog signal transmitted back from the computer is changed back (demodulated) to digital form acceptable to the CRT terminal.

COMMUNICATIONS CHANNEL → INFORMATION TRANSMISSION

The information, in analog form, is transmitted from the library to the remote computer and, after processing by the computer, back to the library, using the same channel.

MODEM → SIGNAL DEMODULATION AND MODULATION

The analog signal transmitted over the channel is changed (demodulated) back to digital form for processing by the computer. When the computer completes its processing, the digital information is changed (modulated) back to analog form for transmission back to the library.

THE COMPUTER → INFORMATION PROCESSING

The information from the library is received and processed by the computer, then returned to the library.

Information Input. Step 1 of a data communications system is accomplished by entering information into a transmitting device such as a CRT or typewriter terminal. The information may be commands or instructions to search a file, update a file, create a record, charge a book, or start a program to print a report; or the information may simply be data to be stored in a file. The terminal device converts the input into a stream of digital pulses representing the characters of information that are keyed.

Signal Modulation. The second step of the data communications process is a conversion or modification of the terminal device digital pulses to high-frequency communications signals which can be transmitted over a data communications channel.

Information Transmission. The third step is the transmission of the information, in the form of the coded, high-frequency signals, from the library to the remote computer over a communications channel. The channel can be an ordinary telephone line or a more expensive coaxial or fiber optics cable (see below).

Signal Demodulation. At the computer end of the communications channel, the signals received from the terminal located in the library are converted or modified back to digital form which the computer can accept and process.

Information Output. In Step 5, the information or commands are received as output of the data communications system in digital form, ready for processing by the computer.

Information Processing. The sixth step of the cycle is the processing of the information by the computer. The computer will process information or execute commands, just as if the user were at the computer site.

Information Input. Once information has been processed or commands have been carried out, the computer will send back to the user, at the remote library terminal, a confirmation or error message, data from a file, a report, or whatever results of processing the user requested. This output of the computer's processing becomes input to the data communications system on the return path.

Signal Modulation. The eighth step is for the processing output of the computer, which is in the form of a stream of digital pulses representing the characters of information, to be converted to high-frequency communications signals which can be transmitted back to the library over the same data communications channel.

Information Transmission. The ninth step is the transmission of the high-frequency communications signals from the computer site back to the library, over the same transmission channel used in Step 3.

Signal Demodulation. The tenth step is the conversion of the high-frequency communications signals back to digital form that can be accepted by the library's output device.

Information Output. In the last step of data communications, the computer's output or response to commands is received by the CRT or typewriter terminal of the user. (Usually, transmitting and receiving are performed in the same terminal device in the library.) The output will be displayed on the screen of the CRT or printed by the typewriter terminal. If the user in the library now wishes to respond back to the computer or enter new information, the data communications process is begun again at Step 1. The steps are repeated endlessly as long as the interactive use of the computer is needed.

Data Communications Channels

Data communications links or channels are the paths over which information is transmitted from the library to the remote computer and back again. Two typical communications channels are the common telephone line and a local area network.

Telephone Lines. For distances in excess of several hundred feet, most libraries use the telephone lines of a common carrier for data transmission to and from a remote computer. A common carrier is a public utility company recognized by an appropriate regulatory agency such as the Federal Communications Commission as having a vested interest in, and responsibility for, furnishing communications services to the general public. Examples of communications common carriers include the American Telephone and Telegraph Company (AT&T), General Telephone and Electronics (GTE), Western Union, a local cable TV company, and others.

These carriers offer two common types of communication lines: dial-up and leased. Public-switched or dial-up telephone lines are widely used for data communications. The ordinary telphone line is the best example of a dial-up facility. This type of line, which requires that a connection be made through an operator or an automatic switching center, is available as long as a connection is made, and the cost of the connection is determined by mileage, time of the day or night, and duration of the connect time. The great advantage of using this type of line is that it can be installed anywhere inexpensively. However, the carrier does not guarantee the quality of transmission over the ordinary voice-grade line. In contrast, a private or leased line remains connected for the duration of a lease, and the leasee has sole, unlimited use of the facility during that time. Special equipment can be added to a leased line to guarantee a higher quality of transmission. A leased line costs more money but may be required to get quality communications.

The grade of a channel indicates its capacity to transmit information, usually measured in terms of bandwidth. Bandwidth refers to the range of frequencies within which a channel can transmit, measured in cycles per second (cps) or hertz. The speed of information transmission is measured in terms of binary digits per second (bps), which is often referred to as the baud rate. Typical transmission speed of the ordinary telephone line is from 300 to 9600 baud.

Local Area Networks. An emerging method of data transmission is the Local Area Network or LAN, which is a data communications system for the interconnection of computers and terminals within a limited area, such as in a building, on a campus, in a city, or within a company. The LAN serves a limited geographic area and a smaller number of users than does the public-switched network. The transmission channels in a LAN may be ordinary cable or coaxial or fiber optics cable. There will be a communications control device, such as a microcomputer or minicomputer, which will allow users to share the same channels and to switch from computer to computer.

Data Communications Equipment

There are a variety of special devices available for data communications tasks, including modems, multiplexors, and concentrators.

Modems. One of the most popular devices used in a data communications system is the modem. In the data communications process, described above, a device called a modulator is used to convert the digital signal to high-frequency signals for transmission, and a device called a demodulator converts the signals back to digital form. Usually, these two processes are performed by a single piece of equipment called a modem, which is a contraction of the terms "modulation" and "demodulation." Modems are available for use with a wide variety of transmitting-receiving terminals. The type selected will depend upon the terminal and transmission channels to be used and the amount of money that the library wants to spend. The most universal types of modems are acoustic couplers and direct-connect modems.

An acoustic coupler is attached directly to a telephone handset. It converts digital signals into audible tones which can be detected by the telephone handset for transmission over the public-switched telephone network. The tones are received at the other end of a channel by another modem and converted back to digital signals. The acoustic coupler, which is not physically wired into the line, is portable and inexpensive but somewhat limited by its low transmission speed.

With a direct-connect modem, no telephone is required. The modem is wired directly into a communications channel. This type of modem is available for a variety of speeds, ranging from 300 to 9600 baud and above. A limited distance modem employing a cable driver or line driver is inexpensive and can operate at high speeds but is limited to a maximum distance ranging from 3 to 50 miles between the terminal and the computer. A radio frequency or RF modem, which transmits information using radio frequencies, may be used in some Local Area Networks, particularly those using fiber optics.

Multiplexors. A multiplexor is a piece of communications equipment that accepts input from several terminal devices, combines their signals, and then transmits them together, simultaneously, over one common communications channel. A similar device at the other end of the communications channel will separate the signals before they are sent to the computer for processing. Multiplexing enables a number of low-speed or low-activity terminals to have economical access to a computer by sharing a single communications channel or line.

Concentrators. A concentrator is similar to a multiplexor but allows only one terminal connected to it to transmit data over the communications channel at any one time. Each terminal has a code address by which it is identified. The computer checks or polls each terminal connected to the concentrator. The first terminal ready to send or receive data gets control of the channel and retains it for the duration of the transaction. Whenever a terminal is using the channel, no other terminal may transmit or receive data.

Part II
Project
Organization and
Management

Chapter 3
Project Organization and Staffing

A variety of people will contribute to the successful completion of any library automation project. Staff who will work directly on the acquisition and installation of the new system might include a project manager and one or more assistant project managers, system analysts, and computer programmers. In addition, a steering committee might be utilized, an automation consultant may be hired, and other resource people may be used during the undertaking. The exact number of people involved in a project will depend upon the nature, size, and complexity of the undertaking and the financial ability of the library to hire additional staff. The number could vary from several persons for a small project to dozens for a large project. These people must be carefully selected and organized to obtain effective results. This chapter includes the following topics:

- Definition of a library automation project
- Project organization
- The project manager
- Other project staff
- The project steering committee
- The automation consultant
- Other project resource people

DEFINITION OF A LIBRARY AUTOMATION PROJECT

An automated library system is developed and integrated into the library operations in an effort referred to as a library automation project. It constitutes a set of resources, including talent, time, and funds and is organized for the purpose of selecting, procuring, and installing an automated system in the library.

PROJECT ORGANIZATION

A library automation project is a significant and costly undertaking which must be organized effectively if the project is to succeed. The project should be placed organizationally outside all existing departments of the library, under direct control of the library director or an assistant or associate director. This will enable the library administration to maintain control over this important work and enable all departments of the library to be served equally, impartially, and free from the control of any one unit. There are several options for organizing people for the library automation project, the two most common being the project team and the matrix approaches.

The Project Team Approach

One approach to organizing people for the project is to select and appoint a project manager, then assign all staff needed to complete the project directly to this person for the duration of the undertaking. The staff would work directly for the project manager. This organizational arrangement is illustrated in Figure 3-1.

Figure 3-1. A Sample Organization Chart for the Project Team Approach to Organizing a Library Automation Project.

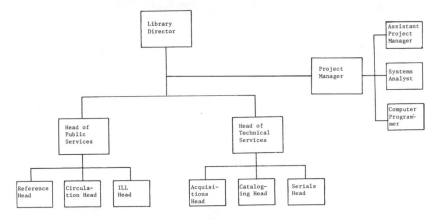

The advantages to this approach are that the project manager might be able to maintain better control over the project because the team would be under his or her direct supervision for the duration of the project; team members would report to only one person and could concentrate solely on the project rather than having responsibilities both to the project and to their normal functional units. The disadvantages are that the functional units might suffer when staff are taken from regularly assigned duties and assigned to the project team, and friction could build between the project manager and the functional supervisor due to the temporary shift of personnel.

Matrix Approach

Probably the best approach to organizing most library automation projects is to select and appoint a project manager and have other staff remain in their functional units but contribute time to the project to develop a new system. This organizational arrangement is illustrated in Figure 3-2.

The greatest advantage to this approach is that disruption in the functional units can be minimized. The greatest disadvantage is the inevitable friction between the project manager and the functional unit managers over the amount of time to be devoted to the project by the team members. Even if a percentage of time is still spent in carrying out regularly assigned duties in the functional unit, the project manager will inevitably take staff away from those responsibilities longer than the unit manager desires, to the possible detriment of the production load of the unit.

The approach chosen is usually a matter of personal preference and is likely to be a function of the size of the organization and the personalities and work habits of the people involved.

Figure 3-2. A Sample Organization Chart for the Matrix Approach to Organizing a Library Automation Project.

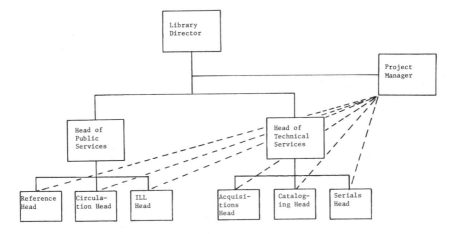

THE PROJECT MANAGER

Responsibility for the successful completion of a library automation project should be delegated to one person referred to as the project manager. Even if an automation consultant is to be used, a project manager is needed to work with and serve as a liaison to the consultant, coordinate the activities within the library, and be responsible for the project in general. This section discusses the qualifications, responsibilities, and selection of the project manager. A sample job description for an automation librarian serving as a project manager is shown in Appendix B.

Qualifications of the Project Manager

The person chosen as project manager should have a broad knowledge of libraries and their operations and staff. Previous experience as a project manager, a systems analyst, or a manager of an operational automated library system will be helpful. Specifically, the manager of a library automation project should have:

1. A creative, systematic, and logical approach to work, with an open mind to new and fresh ideas and an optimistic attitude toward difficult tasks.
2. A firm understanding of systems, computer hardware and software, and telecommunications.
3. Good management abilities.
4. An ability to communicate and work effectively with library staff, governing bodies and officials, purchasing agents, vendors, and others who will be assisting in the development of the new system.

Responsibilities of the Project Manager

The specific duties, functions, or responsibilities of the project manager will depend upon his or her experience and capabilities and the nature of the undertaking. The project manager might be required to:

1. Analyze and plan the activities and tasks that must be accomplished to complete a project successfully.
2. Establish goals and objectives for all phases of the project and its staff.
3. Organize, coordinate, and direct the day-to-day work required to complete activities and tasks within established time schedules and budgets.
4. Analyze and study existing operations in order to determine needs for the new system.
5. Develop hardware, software, and other requirements for the new system.
6. Identify, compare, and evaluate alternative systems and recommend the best system to meet the library's needs.

7. Coordinate the new system installation and solve problems that are encountered.
8. Establish and maintain communication with, negotiate with, and serve as a liaison and resource person to hardware and software vendors, system analysts, computer programmers, and others outside the library or project staff who will be contributing to the successful development of the new system.
9. Serve as a resource person in general to the library staff for information about computer hardware and software and automated library systems in general.
10. Keep the library director and other staff informed about the project's progress and problems.
11. Sell the concept of a new system to governing and funding authorities and to a possibly apprehensive staff who might fear change, loss of prestige, or even loss of their jobs.

Selection of the Project Manager

·   The project manager can be selected from among existing staff of the library, or a new staff member can be hired specifically for project management duties.

In most small libraries, responsibility for managing a project must be assigned to someone already on the staff who will be temporarily relieved of some or all other duties until the automated system has been acquired, installed, and is operating properly. The person might be an assistant or associate director or a staff member in technical or public services, depending upon the type of system to be developed and the background, interest, and experience of the individual. The advantage to this approach is that a new position need not be created, funded, and filled. The obvious disadvantage is that the person will be taken from other duties which might suffer. A second disadvantage is the possibility that no one on the existing staff has the necessary qualifications, experience, inclination, or time for project management.

If an automation project is a large and complex project, which may require several years to complete, a systems or automation librarian can be hired. This person could be responsible for evaluating and improving existing systems, developing new systems, and managing specific projects to acquire and install the new automated systems. An advantage to this arrangement is that the systems or automation librarian could devote the time necessary to a project without interfering with other work which otherwise would have to remain undone. A disadvantage is that an expensive staff position must be created, funded, filled, and housed.

OTHER PROJECT STAFF

If a project is large enough, one or more additional staff members might be required to assist the project manager in the completion of the project. Other project staff might include one or more assistant project managers, systems analysts, and computer programmers.

The Assistant Project Manager

One or more assistant project managers might be required to share some of the responsibilities of project management with the project manager. Qualifications of an assistant manager should be similar to those for the project manager. If assistant project managers are assigned responsibility for specific subsystems, the individuals should also have experience in those functional areas. For example, an assistant project manager for a circulation system should have experience in that area; preferably, this person should be a current employee in the circulation department of the library.

For a very large project, assistant managers could be assigned responsibility for each of the subsystems of the larger system being developed. For example, in a project to develop an integrated library system consisting of circulation, acquisitions, and cataloging functions, an assistant project manager could be appointed for each component subsystem. Other divisions of duties among the project manager and one or more assistant managers are possible, depending upon the qualifications of the individuals involved and the nature and size of the project.

Systems Analysts

One or more system analysts might be assigned to an automation project. A sample job description for a systems analyst for a library automation project is shown in Appendix B.

Necessary qualifications for an analyst might be obtained through a combination of formal course work and experience. The person should have a good understanding of libraries and their organization and operations. In addition, an inquisitive and analytical mind is imperative.

The analyst could be required to:

1. Study and examine existing systems prior to automation to identify and document problems that an automated system might eliminate or solve.
2. Design and document workflow for the new automated system.
3. Identify needs and requirements for the new system.

4. Conduct a cost analysis of the existing system and project costs for a new system for purposes of comparisons between the two.
5. Design forms and reports for the new system.
6. Design and prepare documentation for the new system.

Computer Programmers

If software must be developed as part of the project, one or more computer programmers might be required. A sample job description for a computer programmer for a library automation project is shown in Appendix B.

The programmer could be required to design, code, test, debug, and maintain computer programs for an automated system to be installed in the library. Particularly, programmers might be necessary when an automated system is to be adapted for local use by the library or when software to be acquired must be modified or enhanced before it can be used by the library.

The person selected might be on the library staff, on the staff of a computing center serving the library, or on the staff of another organization under contract to perform programming services for the library during the automation project.

THE PROJECT STEERING COMMITTEE

The formation of a project advisory or steering committee can provide an excellent means of involving staff and ensuring the development of a better automated system. This section discusses the responsibilities and selection of a project steering committee for the library automation project.

Responsibilities of the Steering Committee

The specific duties, functions, or responsibilities of a project steering committee depend upon the nature of the project to be undertaken. Typical duties of such a committee might include involvement in the following:

1. Establishment of project priorities, goals, and objectives.
2. Identifying requirements and specifications for the automated system to be developed.
3. Selection of an automation consultant, if one is to be used.
4. Selection of hardware and software to be acquired.
5. Providing the project team with general advice and guidance during the new system installation process.

6. Providing general support for the project and for the new system to be acquired and installed.

Selection of the Steering Committee

The project steering committee might be composed of key staff of the system soon to be automated as well as representatives from other departments or units of the library. The size of the committee probably should be no fewer than 3 nor more than 10 members; a smaller number would negate the representative committee concept, and a larger number would be too unwieldy. While the project manager can suggest names of prospective committee members, to stress the importance attached to the committee and the project, the library director should make the appointments of those who will serve. The project manager might be an ex officio member of the committee but probably should not serve as its chair.

THE AUTOMATION CONSULTANT

A consultant or consulting firm can be hired for the library automation project. An automation consultant might be needed if no one on the library staff has the specialized background and skills essential to perform all the activities required to complete the project, if no one on the staff can be spared to perform the necessary work, or if it is thought that an outside person would be more objective during some phases of a project. This section includes discussions of the responsibilities and selection of an automation consultant for the project.

Responsibilities of the Automation Consultant

Typical functions or responsibilities of an automation consultant might be to:

1. Conduct a feasibility or preliminary study prior to the acquisition of the automated system,
2. Prepare design requirements for the new system or review and critique requirements prepared by the staff for the new system.
3. Assist in the evalution of alternative systems and selection of the best system for the library.
4. Assist in the installation of the new system.
5. Provide general advice and consultation throughout the project.

The Request for Proposal (RFP) for an Automation Consultant

A Request for Information (RFI), Request for Quotation (RFQ), or Request for Proposal (RFP), hereafter referred to generally as a Request for Proposal or RFP, can be prepared for an automation consultant. Usually, the project manager and the project steering committee jointly prepare this document, which serves as a means for advertising that the library is seeking a consultant, provides prospective consultants with necessary information about the work to be performed, and solicits information from those who submit proposals to perform the work.

A RFP should be brief but clear and concise. Minimally it should include several parts, including the following.

Purpose of the RFP. An introductory paragraph to the RFP can state the reason why the library is issuing the document.

Example: The library is seeking applications from individuals or firms to serve as a consultant who will assist in the selection, acquisition, and installation of an automated, integrated library system.

Description of the Library. A general description of the library and its environment should be included to provide prospective consultants with background information which can assist them in deciding whether they are interested in submitting a proposal in response to the RFP.

Example: The library has holdings of approximately 300,000 volumes divided between the main library and two branch libraries. It serves a population of 150,000 and has an annual book circulation of approximately 450,000 items. The service area of this library is the entire county of Anycounty. The two branches are served by manual circulation systems, and the main library uses a punched card system. The operating budget for FY 198x /xx is $1,234,123, and the staff numbers 40.

Statement of Work. A detailed statement of the work the consultant is to perform should be included in the RFP.

Example: The consultant selected shall perform the following tasks: (1) study the feasibility of automated acquisitions, serials control, cataloging, online catalog, and circulation systems for the library; (2) assist the library in establishing requirements for the integrated system; (3) assist the library in preparing the RFP for the system; (4) assist a library team to evaluate the responses to the RFP and select the best system to acquire; (5) assist in the negotiation of a contract with the successful vendor; and (6) serve as a general advisor during installation of the automated system acquired.

Reports Requirement. If written or verbal reports are required of the consultant, this should be stated, either as a part of the Statement of Work or separately.

Example: The consultant shall make verbal monthly reports to the library's project manager describing the work accomplished to date and any unusual problems encountered.

Proposal Format. A description of the content of applications or proposals expected from prospective consultants in response to the RFP should be included in the document.

Example: A proposal submitted by a prospective consultant to the library must contain the following: (1) the proposed methodology for completing the tasks outlined in this RFP; (2) the name, address, and telephone number of the applicant; (3) the names and resumes of all persons who will be responsible for completing the tasks outlined in this RFP; (4) a list of the libraries, with the names of contact people, for which similar consulting work has been performed; (5) a timetable for expected completion of each activity; and (6) a detailed budget for performing the tasks outlined in the statement of work.

Methodology for Selecting the Consultant. The methodology the library will use in selecting the consultant should be included in the RFP. This statement can be brief or elaborate.

Example: The library's project steering committee will review each response to the RFP. Personal interviews, at the applicant's expense, may be requested. The final decision as to the award of a contract will be made by the library director, upon review of the steering committee's recommendation.

Example: The library's project steering committee will review each response to the RFP and select those consultants to be interviewed. A combination of criteria will be used in selecting the consultant, including (1) the best proposed methodology for completing the work within the expected timeframe; (2) the best qualifications for completing the work; and (3) the proposal which will result in the least cost to the library. Upon completion of the interviews, the steering committee will select the consultant to be hired.

Contract Calendar. The anticipated calendar for the project, including deadlines for submitting proposals to the library and the day the library expects to select the successful bidder should be included in the RFP.

Example: The library expects a nine-month contract, beginning January 1, 198x. The following calendar is expected:

1. Proposals from prospective consultants due by 4:30 p.m., January 1, 198x.
2. Begin interviewing prospective consultants, January 15, 198x.
3. Award contract to the consultant selected, January 20, 198x.
4. Consultant will begin work, February 15, 198x.

5. Report including recommendation of consultant for circulation system to be developed due in the library, April 1, 198x.
6. RFP document for acquiring hardware, software, and other vendor services due in the library, May 15, 198x.
7. Library will issue the RFP to prospective vendors, June 1, 198x.
8. Bid documents due in library by 4:30 p.m., July 1, 198x.
9. Report of evaluation of the bid documents by the consultant due in the library, August 1, 198x.
10. Contracts awarded for hardware, software, and other vendor services, August 15, 198x.
11. Final report of the consultant due in the library, September 30, 198x.

Procedure for Submitting Responses to the RFP. Procedures which prospective consultants should follow in submitting responses to the library's RFP should be included in the document.

Example: Five copies of a proposal and any supporting documentation should be sent to Jane Doe, Project Manager, Anytown Library, P.O. Box 123, Anytown 123456, no later than 5:00 p.m., CDT, February 21, 198x. Envelopes containing proposals should be clearly marked on the outside as "Automation Consultant Proposal."

Right Not to Award Contract. A statement that the library may choose not to award a contract to any consultant should be included in the RFP.

Example: The library reserves the right to reject any or all proposals if it feels applications received do not meet its needs or if the costs proposed are in excess of budgeted funds.

Contact Person. The name, address, and telephone number of the person in the library or its purchasing department who can be contacted for additional information about the RFP should be included in the document.

Example: James Doe is the prime contact person for prospective consultants, and all inquiries regarding this RFP and the resulting contract should be directed to him at the Anytown Library, 123 Anyway Drive, Anytown 123456. Telephone (123) 456-7890.

Solicitation of Proposals

Once an RFP has been prepared and approved by the project steering committee and others, copies must be distributed to solicit proposals from prospective consultants. There are several methods of identifying consultants to whom the RFP can be sent. The American Library Association, other professional organizations, or the library's state library agency can usually provide a list of possible consultants. Notices can be placed on bulletin boards at local, state, regional, or national professional meetings, or advertisements can be placed in professional library journals.

> *Example:* An RFP for a consultant to assist the Anytown Library in selecting, acquiring, and installing automated acquisitions, serials control, cataloging, online catalog, and circulation systems is now available. Consultants and other interested parties are invited to respond. Contact James Doe, Anytown Library, 123 Anyway Drive, Anytown 12345 for copies. RFP deadline: January 1, 198x.

Other methods include asking colleagues and friends if they can recommend one or more consultants, advertising by word of mouth, and reading the professional literature to identify consultants or writers on automation in the area of the library's project who potentially might serve as a consultant. A combination of approaches might be necessary to compile a mailing list for solicting bids. A brief cover letter explaining why the RFP is being sent to a prospective consultant can be included.

Selection of the Consultant

Once proposals have been received from prospective consultants, the best individual or firm for the project can be selected and hired.

The project manager, steering committee, and others should examine, compare, and evaluate the proposals received from prospective consultants. Additional or clarifying information can be requested from a bidder if necessary, and telephone or in-person interviews may be held with several of the best candidates before a final decision is made. Inquiries should be made to several or all of the libraries that have used a prospective consultant's services in the past, and on-site visits might be made to several or all of these libraries. If possible, reports and other documentation produced for these libraries should be examined.

After the best proposal has been selected and the successful bidder has been notified, a simple contract should be drawn up and signed by the consultant and a legal representative of the library. As a courtesy, the consultants not selected should be notified of the bid award and thanked for submitting proposals.

OTHER PROJECT RESOURCE PEOPLE

The talents of many other people might be required during a library automation project. Many will not be on the library staff.

Those who may play important roles in a project include the library director, the staff of the system to be automated, vendor representatives, staff in other automated libraries, staff of a computing center serving the library, and miscellaneous resource people.

The Library Director

The role of the library director in the automation project should be that of an overseer, a critic, an advisor, an encourager, and an enthusiast. The director should:

1. Provide continuing support for the project and its team.
2. Give approval when necessary to actions or requests of the project manager and steering committee.
3. Keep governing and funding authorities apprised of progress being made in developing the automated system.
4. Secure approval and funding for the new system from governing and funding authorities.

The director might initiate the project and appoint its manager and advisory committee, but he or she will not normally be directly involved in the day-to-day activities of the endeavor; that is the function of the project manager and others on the project team.

Staff of the System to Be Automated

While the project steering committee might provide most of the guidance for development of the new system, the advice of other staff of the system to be automated should be solicited when necessary to learn more about operations as they currently are being performed and to acquire suggestions for improvement. These people can provide valuable information about the present system and the projected needs and demands on a new one.

Since the ultimate success of a new system depends to a great extent upon the support and interest given it by those who will operate and manage it, these people will be more prone to accept a new system if they feel personally involved in its development and if they can see tangible benefits to them and to the library. Their continuing involvement in the project can facilitate their support and approval of any new or improved system which will be implemented. A new system suddenly imposed upon the rank and file staff without their prior knowledge or involvement may not be easily and readily accepted.

Vendor Representatives

Representatives of hardware and software vendors and networks can provide valuable assistance during an automation project by supplying information about systems and services which the library is considering for acquisition and installation. It must be remembered, however, that these representatives are trying to sell products, and their views will be biased in favor of their own systems and services.

Vendor representatives usually are pleased to provide descriptive brochures and other information about their products, and if requested, most will visit the library at no obligation in order to provide additional verbal and visual information and perhaps demonstrate their products. Also, most vendors attempting to reach the library market will exhibit regularly at national, regional, and state library conventions. On such occasions, the librarian can talk with the vendor representatives, see products and systems, have them demonstrated, obtain informational brochures, and possibly talk with other librarians who use the products and services.

If an automated system is to be shared with others through a national, interstate, or intrastate network, representatives of the network's organization can supply promotional literature, technical information, and demonstrations to assist in the decision as to whether the system should be acquired and installed in the library. If the shared system is selected, the network representatives can assist in integrating the system into existing operations in the library and can provide some or all of the staff training essential to use the new system.

Staff of Other Automated Libraries

The staff of other libraries with automated systems can be helpful by demonstrating their systems, sharing experiences encountered during their automation projects, and providing encouragement to the library just beginning to develop its first computer-based system. Advice about system development and potential problems which might be encountered or situations to be avoided can be helpful to the library that does not yet have experience with automated systems or with particular vendors.

Staff of a Computing Center Serving the Library

Most libraries are served by a central data processing or computing center in their host institution or organization. This center might have one or several computer systems, communications equipment for distributing computing power to remote locations, data conversion equipment, and other peripheral hardware essential to maintain and operate the installation.

Staff of the computing center might include systems analysts, computer programmers, computer operators, data entry staff, database managers, telecommunications specialists, hardware maintenance engineers, and many others. This specialized staff who operate and manage the center could be helpful in providing and interpreting information about computer hardware, software, and systems and assisting the library in planning, designing, implementing, and operating a computer-based system. Even if it does not plan to use the center's services, the library can benefit from the knowledge, advice, and political weight of its staff.

Miscellaneous Resource People

Dozens of other people might be utilized, however briefly, during an automation project. These people could include purchasing agents, legal advisors, communications experts, carpenters, electronics engineers and technicians, air conditioning and heating experts, painters, hardware and software installers and maintenance staff, typists and clerical staff to prepare requests for proposals or quotations, data entry staff for file conversion projects, training staff for teaching the staff to operate and manage the new system, and many others. Each will play a vital role in the process of planning, designing, and implementing an automated library system.

Chapter 4
Project Planning and Control

There is a direct correlation between the amount and quality of planning preceding and during the acquisition and installation of an automated library system and the later success of that system. Good planning can increase the chances that a system will be installed with minimum problems and maximum efficiency and that it can be operated effectively thereafter. Inadequate and ineffective planning of a project could delay the installation, waste financial resources, reduce the acceptance of the system by staff and users, and possibly do long-term damage to the organization through the generation of ill will and loss of credibility.

This chapter addresses some of the planning that is necessary before and during a library automation project. Specifically, this chapter includes:

- The long-range automation plan
- Project justification
- Project goal
- Project constraints
- Project outline
- Project schedule
- Financial and cost planning
- Project approval
- Progress reports

THE LONG-RANGE AUTOMATION PLAN

It behooves library management not to allow any automated system within its organization to be developed in isolation from other automated and manual systems currently in use within the library, since each is interacting and interdependent. A well-defined master or long-range plan for automation can assist in avoiding this problem by providing general guidelines for the orderly development of all automated systems throughout the library. The plan also can be used as a public relations or informational document for governing boards and other interested individuals and groups and as a means of obtaining funds for automation.

If a long-range automation plan does not exist, one should be prepared before a project to develop the first automated system in the library is undertaken. The plan, which should be reviewed and revised periodically to reflect new ideas and changing conditions within the library and its environment, might include the library mission statement, general automation goals, specific automation goals, and a long-range implementation strategy as a minimum. If desired, a general statement for funding automation can also be included.

The Library Mission Statement

The long-range automation plan might begin with a statement of the role or mission of the library in its academic environment, parent organization, community, or in society as a whole. The mission statement will provide a focus for the planning of individual automation projects and can minimize deviations from the library's reason or reasons for being. The statement, which identifies the goal, purpose, or reason why the library exists as an organization, should be open-ended, ideal, and not subject to change over time. It should be clearly defined and truly reflective of the reason for the library's existence.

Example: The mission of the library is to support education and research in the university through the selection, acquisition, organization, and dissemination of a collection of informational materials and through the provision of access to information and materials not owned by the library.

Example: The role of the library is to provide its users with access to the recorded knowledge of humankind.

Example: The goal of the library is to provide access to educational, cultural, and recreational materials and information to all within its community of users.

Example: The purpose of the library is to assure citizens equal access to the recorded knowledge of humankind through the provision of library materials upon which all may draw for their information needs.

General Automation Goals

The long-range automation plan might include a set of general goals which will provide the project staff with guidelines to follow when planning, acquiring, installing, and operating specific automated systems. General automation goals usually focus on improving the quality of services, producing additional output, or reducing the costs of producing output or providing services. These general automation goals, which will provide overriding or umbrella guidelines for any automated system to be developed for the library, must be supportive of the mission of the library, or else conflict and wasted resources could result.

Example: Automation should enable the staff to select, acquire, organize, store, preserve, locate, retrieve, and disseminate or lend information to library users more accurately, rapidly, and inexpensively than with a manual system.

Example: The goal of automation is to reduce or stabilize the costs of providing library services.

Example: The goals of the library automation program are to increase the volume of work that can be performed, expand services without need for additional staff, free staff from as much routine work as possible, speed up the processing of materials or the provision of services, improve the quality of existing services, and provide better control over services and materials.

The goals may also be of a constraining nature and may place limits or conditions on automation.

Example: The computer is to be a tool of the library staff and, ultimately and indirectly, of the user. At no time are humans knowingly to be subjugated to the machine. Rather than humans having to bend to the ways of the computer, the computer must bend to the ways of the humans; the machine is flexible enough to do this, given the perseverence of humans.

Example: Specific conditions on automation are that all automated systems developed must be compatible with each other and with all existing manual systems in the library.

Example: No automated system that requires computer programmers to be added to the library staff shall be developed.

Specific Automation Goals

Specific automation goals define exact areas or functions where future automation efforts will be concentrated. These goals also must be supportive of the mission of the library or else conflict and wasted resources could result. All functions in the library thought likely to be automated should be included in the plan.

Example: A goal of automation is to provide online access to bibliographic and availability information for the library's resources via an online public catalog widely available in locations throughout the city.

Example: A goal is to serve as a center for computer-stored textual information, such as the contents of documents and journals, and provide for their online retrieval and subsequent electronic dissemination for viewing and copying to remote points on campus and elsewhere.

Example: A goal is to select and acquire an automated circulation system for the library.

Example: A goal is to serve as an electronic switching center to the resources of other libraries and information centers in the area, region, and nation.

Further narrative comments can be added to each goal as a rationale for including a specific function in the list or simply for descriptive purposes.

A Long-Range Implementation Strategy

A long-range implementation strategy might be included in the automation plan. This strategy can provide guidance through the years as various automated systems are developed in the library.

Adapting an integrated systems approach to library automation can be more economical and efficient for a library than having separate, stand-alone systems operating in isolation from each other. This long-range planning approach implies that several automated systems, such as acquisitions, cataloging, circulation, and an online catalog are designed to interrelate with each other, share some or all of the same information files, and share the same computer.

Implementation of individual automated systems in the library can proceed one at a time as time and funding permit, and assigning each function to be automated a priority for implementation can be very helpful in planning future projects. The priorities should be reviewed periodically, particularly before any new project is begun.

A long-range implementation calendar or schedule for developing automated systems in the library might be helpful, either included as a part of the list of specific automation goals described in the above section, or separate. The schedule will give tentative dates when specific functions are expected to be automated.

Example: Project 1: Cataloging. Project to begin in the Fall
of 19xx.
Project 2: Circulation. Project to begin in the Fall
of 19xx.
Project 3: Acquisitions. Project to begin in the Spring of
19xx.
Project 4: Online Catalog. Project to begin in the Summer
of 19xx.

This schedule can provide library management and others with an idea when funds must be obtained and when other resources must be made available.

PROJECT JUSTIFICATION

Most libraries are required to justify the need for an automated library system. The necessity for an automated system should be identified and the justification developed before an automation project is begun, or as a first step of the undertaking. This activity requires a problem identification phase and problem statement preparation.

Problem Identification Phase

The fact that a computer is available or that free computer time is offered to the library, that someone thinks using a computer will make the library appear more progressive, or that other libraries use computers, are not legitimate reasons for developing an automated system; each of these is the equivalent of saying: "Here's a solution—now let's find a problem that fits it."

Typically, the library will be faced with a number of problems which point to the need for an automated system. These problems are usually identified through personal observations and knowledge of situations, reports from other staff, results of studies of the library and its operations, or suggestions and complaints from users. Some problems which could cause a library to seek an automated system might be that:

1. The workload within an existing manual system is expanding so rapidly that the increased volume cannot be handled effectively unless the staff is doubled or tripled.
2. The costs of operating an existing system are increasing so rapidly that the library can no longer afford to provide the service by manual methods.
3. Pressures are mounting from library management, governing and funding officials, taxpayers, and others for the library to be able to produce more in the future with fewer staff members and to provide better accountability for materials and services.
4. An existing system needs improvement or upgrading in general. The system may be operating satisfactorily but is limited in what it can do and is unable to provide, for example, adequate administrative reports and statistics.
5. The library needs to provide a new service but cannot do so with a manual system.

Symptoms of problems often are more apparent at first than the problems themselves. Some observable symptoms of problems might be:

1. Increased time required to process materials.

2. Long queues at service desks.
3. An increasing number of errors in a system or service.
4. A decline in the quality of a service.
5. A high number of complaints from users.
6. An awareness that users are turning more frequently to other organizations for information services.
7. A continual need for more funds to operate a system.
8. A necessary curtailment of services due to lack of staff, time, or funds.

Once symptoms are identified, their causes can be explored to determine the problems. A general systems study may be required to identify and document a problem fully.

Problem Statement Preparation

Problems which are identified should be translated into clear statements that can be used to justify the initiation of a project to acquire and install an automated system. A problem statement should include, as a minimum, a description of the problem, effects of the problem, and supporting data.

A Description of the Problem. The problem statement should begin with a brief but clear description of the problem or problems that have been identified.

Example: Because of increased use of the library and the resulting increased number of loans to borrowers without a corresponding increase in personnel, the circulation staff must spend almost its entire time charging and discharging materials.

Example: Because of the increased number of materials purchased and a mandated reduction of staff, the catalog department staff can process only 60 percent of the library's new acquisitions each year.

Example: The acquisitions department must begin reporting to the library committee each month the number and cost of titles acquired by the requesting agency or department. Also, a new accounting system to meet new fiscal requirements mandated by the city (or county or state) must be installed.

Results of the Problems. What has happened as a result of the problems identified should be described.

Example: As a result of the problem, long queues form at the charge station, long delays in discharging materials occur, all except first overdue notices have had to be eliminated, large backlogs of records awaiting merging into the circulation file are frequent, and staff morale has deteriorated because of complaints from borrowers about slow service.

Example: As a result of the problem, the backlog of materials awaiting processing is increasing rapidly, users are unable to have rapid access to new materials, the number of processing errors has increased due to the pressures to handle more materials, and low morale of the staff resulting from complaints from users about the slow processing times has developed.

Example: The present system cannot report the new statistics required by the library governing body without additional staff or an elimination of other services, due to the time-consuming nature of gathering, compiling, and reporting the desired information. Also, integrating the new accounting system into the existing system will necessitate a complete overhaul of all procedures from submission of requests for purchase through receipt and payment of invoices.

Supporting Data. Supporting costs, work measures, and other quantitative facts and statistics should be included, if possible, in each problem statement. Figure 4-1 illustrates data supporting a problem identified in an existing system.

Statistical and accounting reports and other budgetary information can be studied and analyzed to obtain the supporting data. The inclusion of quantitative facts and statistics provides a means by which the need for a solution to a problem can be easily assessed. Including cost or other supporting data for a period encompassing several years is preferable to including only current costs. Administrators need to be able to relate current costs to earlier costs and to projected costs under the current systems. Actual cost figures need to be presented, rather than stating vaguely that the cost of providing a service is increasing too fast. For example, if the cost of circulating an item was $2.75 per transaction two years ago and is currently $3.78 with a projected cost of $5.00 next year, using the current manual system, an effective argument can be made for automating the circulation process.

Figure 4-1. A Sample of Data Supporting a Problem Identified in an Existing System. In this Case, the Number of Users and Loans, but not Staff, Have Increased Dramatically.

Year	Persons Using Library	Number of Loans	Staff
1981	40,000	110,980	4.0
1982	65,500	156,777	4.0
1983	91,900	209,080	4.5
1984	111,500	224,523	4.5
1985	124,800	260,129	4.5

PROJECT GOAL

While the purpose, mission, or goal of a specific library automation project might appear obvious, a statement should be prepared to eliminate any ambiguity or uncertainty and to provide a written reference and focal point for the work to be undertaken. The project goal outlines the specific end results toward which achievements should be directed and clearly defines what is expected to be accomplished upon completion of the project. The goal statement for a project should be clear and specific.

Example: The purpose of this project is to identify alternative automated circulation systems available to the library, analyze and compare the options, then select, acquire, and install the most feasible system.

Example: The goal of the project is to upgrade and improve the present acquisitions, cataloging, and circulation systems by developing an online, integrated system encompassing acquisitions, cataloging, circulation, serials control, and an online catalog.

Example: The project goal is to develop an online, automated acquisitions system to serve the main library and its three branches.

The goal of a project must not be in conflict with those established in the library's long-range automation plan.

PROJECT CONSTRAINTS

Constraints may be placed on a library automation project by library management, the library's governing or funding agency, or others, and these constraints will limit or place conditions on the undertaking.

Example: The project must be completed by August 31, 19xx.

Example: The project must be completed within the budget authorized by the library board and the library director.

Example: A written report must be submitted to the library director after each phase of the project is completed, and approval by the director must be given before the next phase is begun.

These constraints should be identified before the project is begun to avoid wasted efforts and to guide the development of requirements for the automated system that is to be acquired and installed.

PROJECT OUTLINE

A project is started and completed in broad stages or phases. Each phase contains a number of subdivisions or activities, and each activity comprises a number of tasks or steps. The exact number of events in a project will depend upon the nature and complexity of the anticipated system to be developed and the implementation process that will be used.

The plan for completing a project should begin with an outline of the phases, activities, and steps that are expected to be accomplished to complete the endeavor successfully. The first level headings of the outline represent the phases of the project; the next level, the activities; and the third level, the steps of each activity. A list of phases, activities, and steps for a typical project to develop an automated system is shown in Appendix A.

The plan should be dynamic; that is, the outline can and must be altered as work on the project progresses and as new conditions and situations arise. For example, if after a preliminary evaluation it is decided that the computer supporting the system to be installed will reside in a remote computing center rather than in the library, then the outline must be revised to eliminate the now unnecessary computer room design and construction activity.

PROJECT SCHEDULE

A schedule for completion of the events in the plan for a project should be prepared. Either a simple calendar, a Gantt chart, or a more complex network chart will be sufficient for this purpose.

The calendar of events is one of the simplest scheduling tools for a project (see Figure 4-2). The activities to be completed are merely listed, with completion dates beside each event. The calendar can be highly detailed or can include only major events. It is easily prepared, easily revised, and universally understood.

The Gantt chart is another simple and effective scheduling tool (see Figure 4-3). To prepare this chart, the phases and /or activities taken from the project outline are listed along the left side of the chart. Time in days, weeks, or months is represented along the top. The expected or scheduled beginning and completion times of each event are indicated by *Xs* or a solid bar within the appropriate time frame. If desired, the actual beginning and completion times of each event can be shown beneath the planned times of each event. If this is done, those events that were started on time and are ahead or behind schedule can be quickly determined at a glance. A disadvantage to this type of chart is that it does not effectively indicate relationships among the different events of a project. In addition, each time any one part of the project outline is changed, the chart also must be revised to reflect the changes.

Figure 4-2. A Sample Calendar of Events for a Library Automation Project.

May 30, 198x	Request for Proposal sent to vendors
July 30, 198x	Bid responses due; bid opening
August-November 198x	Evaluation of bids; vendor selection; contract negotiations
December 198x	Planning for preparation of database tapes
February 198x	Delivery and installation of hardware and software
March 198x	Hardware testing
April 198x	Delivery and installation of software for circulation and online catalog; begin database loading
May 198x	Begin building borrower files; begin applying barcodes/OCR labels to materials
June 198x	Load additional OCLC tapes; database editing
July 198x	Delivery and installation of software for acquisitions system
August 198x	Bring circulation system up
September 198x	Begin building acquisitions files; install CRTs for public use
November 198x	Bring Online Public Catalog up
January 198x	Bring Acquisitions System up

The network chart is the most difficult scheduling tool to prepare, but it does graphically illustrate the interrelationships of events required to complete the work to be performed in a project. Part of a network chart for a project is shown in Figure 4-4. To prepare the chart, the activities of a phase are numbered and lincs drawn between circles representing activities. A left-to-right sequence represents the order in which activities should or must be completed; in most cases, an activity cannot be started until a previous one has been completed. If two or more activities can be completed simultaneously, separate lines emanating from the same circle are drawn.

The network chart can be improved further if beginning and completion times are estimated and added to the activities, as in the Program and Evaluation Review Technique (PERT) and Critical Path Method (CPM). While these are not described here, references to other literature can be found in the bibliography to this book.

Figure 4-3. A Sample Gantt Chart for Preliminary Events in a Library Automation Project.

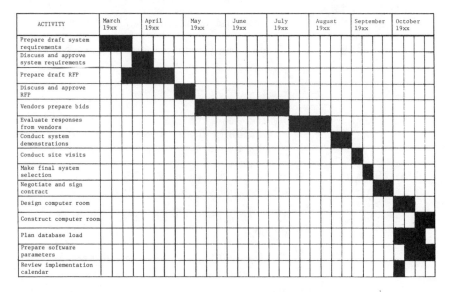

ACTIVITY	March 19xx	April 19xx	May 19xx	June 19xx	July 19xx	August 19xx	September 19xx	October 19xx
Prepare draft system requirements								
Discuss and approve system requirements								
Prepare draft RFP								
Discuss and approve RFP								
Vendors prepare bids								
Evaluate responses from vendors								
Conduct system demonstrations								
Conduct site visits								
Make final system selection								
Negotiate and sign contract								
Design computer room								
Construct computer room								
Plan database load								
Prepare software parameters								
Review implementation calendar								

FINANCIAL AND COST PLANNING

No library should undertake an automation project without understanding the fiscal implications of the endeavor. An automated library system is expensive to acquire, and its benefits may not become evident until several years after its successful installation and operation. Both developmental and operating costs are pertinent to an automated library system.

Developmental Costs

Developmental costs are those one-time expenses necessary to initialize or start-up an automated library system. These costs are not expected to be repeated once a system has been implemented and is operational and are therefore referred to as nonrecurring costs. There are at least eight categories of developmental costs.

Design Costs. Design costs include those expenses necessary to translate the library's requirements into a detailed plan or set of specifications for an automated system. Costs of this creative process, in which a completely new scheme for handling work in the library is devised, usually include:

1. Salaries and wages of systems analysts, consultants, and other staff who will plan and design a system.
2. Travel for visits to other libraries if necessary.
3. Supplies such as flowcharting templates and forms and specification binders.
4. Miscellaneous expenses such as reproduction services necessary for design documentation.

While design costs will be included in the purchase price of a turnkey system, the library may be required to pay for the design of a system developed locally from scratch.

Figure 4-4. A Sample Network Chart for Part of a Library Automation Project.

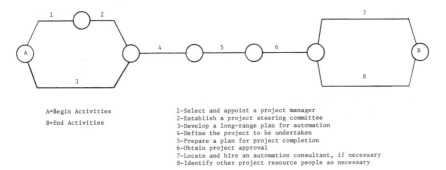

A=Begin Activities
B=End Activities

1-Select and appoint a project manager
2-Establish a project steering committee
3-Develop a long-range plan for automation
4-Define the project to be undertaken
5-Prepare a plan for project completion
6-Obtain project approval
7-Locate and hire an automation consultant, if necessary
8-Identify other project resource people as necessary

Hardware Costs. Hardware costs include the purchase of any equipment such as the central processing unit, magnetic disk drives, disk packs, magnetic tape units, printers, modems, CRT terminals, scanning wands, and other electronic and electro-mechanical devices necessary for an automated system. If hardware for a system is to be leased rather than purchased, the costs are considered annual operating expenses and are not included as developmental costs.

Software Costs. Software costs are the expenses necessary to design, code, test, correct, and document the computer programs for an automated library system. These costs will be included as part of the cost of a turnkey system package. If a system is to be developed locally from scratch or adapted from another library, expenses will be incurred for the systems analysts, programmers, and other staff who will prepare the software, the computer time necessary to test and correct the programs, supplies, and miscellaneous costs such as system documentation. The cost of system software usually will be included in the cost of the hardware package but may be separate.

Site Preparation Costs. Site preparation costs might be necessary to modify the library building, install electrical circuits, plugs, and cables, and alter or install heating, air conditioning, and humidity control systems prior to installation of an automated system.

Data Conversion Costs. If a library does not already have the records required by an automated system in machine-readable form, the cost of converting essential files will be necessary. Data conversion is discussed further in Chapter 9.

Staff Training Costs. Training costs may be included as part of the software package of one turnkey system vendor, while others charge separately for such services. If not provided by a vendor or a network operations office, staff training must be supplied by the project manager, other members of the library staff, or a consultant.

Equipment Costs. Capital costs for equipment other than computer system hardware can include the purchase of furniture or equipment necessary to operate a system, such as tables, shelves, cabinets, desks, chairs, and the like. A list of typical equipment for an automated library system is included in Appendix C.

Miscellenous Costs. Some miscellaneous developmental expenses may be necessary for an automated library system. Shipping and installation of hardware, software, and other equipment, if not already included in other cost estimates, may be an expense to the library. Another cost that may be required before a circulation system can be operated is the expense for attaching barcode or optical character labels to materials. In this case, salaries and wages of staff who will prepare and apply the labels, as well as the costs of the necessary supplies, must be estimated. Costs of adding barcodes or OCR labels to newly acquired materials after system implementation is usually considered an annual operating expense.

Operating Costs

While developmental costs are not expected to recur once a system has been implemented and is operational, other costs will be repeated year after year for the lifetime of a system. Operating costs are those expenses necessary to make a system work or perform on a day-to-day basis after its implementation. Usually, operating costs are computed on an annual basis and therefore are usually referred to as annual operating costs or sometimes simply as recurring costs. There are at least seven categories of annual operating costs.

Salaries and Wages. Salaries and wages include the costs for all staff required to manage and operate the automated system on a daily basis after system start-up. If desired, fringe benefits can be included in this category.

Supplies. In addition to the usual paper, pens, paper clips, and other office supplies, an automated library system might need customized forms, printer paper, ribbons, magnetic tapes, bar codes, and other specialized consumables necessary to operate a system each year of its projected life. A list of typical supplies for an automated library system is included in Appendix C.

Communications Costs. If an automated system uses leased communications lines to connect CRT terminals and other input-output devices to a remote computer, the cost of these channels are an annual operating expense which must be considered.

Hardware Maintenance. Hardware must be maintained after the automated system has been installed, whether the equipment is owned by the library or leased. Contracts must be made with the hardware vendor or other firms to keep the hardware in good operating condition.

Software Maintenance. Software, like hardware, must be maintained in good operating condition, and the cost of this maintenance is considered an annual operating expense for an automated library system. Contracts can be made with the vendor, another firm, or the computing center serving the library to maintain the software, depending upon the system.

Transaction Fees. Systems shared through networking usually require that the library pay a fee for each transaction completed in the system. For example, OCLC (Online Computer Library Center) charges a fee each time a record in its database is used for local creation of a cataloging record. These costs, if applicable, must be included in the operating costs of a system.

Miscellaneous Costs. Any miscellaneous costs for a system must be identified. Some examples include purchase of catalog card sets, access fees to a bibliographic utility such as OCLC, and energy to power a special air conditioning unit required for a computer. If desired, any or all of these can be treated as a separate cost element rather than grouped together as a miscellaneous expense.

PROJECT APPROVAL

While the library director will have either formally or informally authorized preparation of preliminary plans for the automation project, higher governing or funding authorities may or may not have been involved up to this point. Before further work is performed, formal approval to initiate the project will usually be necessary.

A project proposal document can be prepared for submission to the library director and others for initial approval of the project. The document should be brief yet complete and clear enough for easy assessment of the merits of approving the project. Information in the document should include as a minimum:

1. A justification for a library automation project.
2. The goal of the project.
3. A statement of any constraints on the project.
4. A summary outline of the plan for completing the project successfully.
5. The project calendar or schedule.
6. An explanation of how the automated system is to be funded.

Other pertinent background or explanatory information considered necessary to improve the report, such as the library's long-range automation plan, can be included or appended. The project manager, the project steering committee, the automation consultant, if one is used, and other project staff also can be identified.

A draft of the project proposal can be circulated widely before it is submitted for approval, in order to inform the library staff of the request, solicit their suggestions for improving the document, and gain their vital support for the endeavor and the automated system which will result. Formal or informal meetings and discussions can be held to gain input from as many of the staff as possible. Their suggestions and comments should be evaluated carefully and, if possible, incorporated into the document before it is submitted for approval.

After the proposal has been approved by the library director, authorization to proceed may also be necessary from a city manager, mayor, president, board, council, or other group advising or governing the library. Even if persons or groups have advisory powers only, their approval should be sought and obtained before work on a project continues. These people may be instrumental later in obtaining needed funds for an automated system.

PROGRESS REPORTS

A means of reporting regular progress being made toward completion of the project should be established. These progress reports should be presented to the library director, the project steering committee, and other interested parties. Wide distribution of the project plan or outline and the current project schedule provides an excellent method of informing others about the endeavor. In addition, every opportunity should be taken to discuss the project informally with interested parties and to present verbal reports at meetings with the library director, governing and funding authorities, and others. Progress reports should include short descriptions of work completed to date compared with estimated completion times and any unexpected problems encountered since the last report.

Still another way of reporting progress is to issue a newsletter to all interested persons. The publication can be short or lengthy and formal or informal, depending upon personal preferences. It can be typed or photocopied or reproduced by other methods.

Part III
System
Procurement

Chapter 5
Requirements for an
Automated Library System

A critical part of a library automation project is the establishment of a set of requirements for the system to be acquired and installed. This activity should be completed before alternative systems are identified, evaluated, and compared and as a prelude to the preparation of the Request for Proposal, discussed in Chapter 6. This chapter includes:

- The definition of a system requirement
- The need for system requirements
- A focal point for developing requirements
- The task force for developing requirements
- Common types of system requirements

A complete set of system requirements for an automated library system is included in the sample Request for Proposal in Appendix D.

THE DEFINITION OF A SYSTEM REQUIREMENT

A system requirement is a statement which defines some desirable aspect of an automated system or specifies what the system must do, how it must perform, or how it is to be operated and maintained. It is a specific need, desire, or demand to be placed on an automated system to be acquired. Additional requirements also may specify constraints or limits on the system's design, operation, performance, or maintenance.

Example: The system shall inform the user of how many records will be retrieved by a search term.

Example: The system shall share bibliographic records with the circulation and acquisitions systems.

Example: The system shall exhibit an average response time not exceeding six seconds for data input and edit.

Requirements can be either mandatory or optional. A mandatory requirement is one which absolutely must be met by the automated system, while a desirabie or optional requirement may enhance the system but need not necessarily be met for a system to be acceptable. Usually, a requirement is considered to be mandatory unless it is specifically labelled as being optional.

THE NEED FOR SYSTEM REQUIREMENTS

Selecting an automated library system is a confusing and complex activity made more difficult by the number of similar systems available and the conflicting and often incorrect or overstated claims made by vendor representatives for their products. A set of requirements developed by the library will enable it to obtain a clear picture of the system wanted before the available alternatives are examined and a system is selected. This will provide an objective "shopping list" which, if adhered to, could assist in identifying the one system among the many alternatives that most closely matches the library's model of the best system to meet its needs. Once established, system requirements are used to:

1. Formulate a Request for Proposal or RFP for an automated system (see Chapter 6).
2. Systematically and objectively compare and evaluate the alternative systems that possibly might meet the needs of the library (see Chapter 7).
3. Guide the installation of the automated system after it is acquired (see Chapters 8-11).
4. Evaluate the automated system, once it is installed and operational, to determine if it actually meets the needs that were established at the beginning of the project (see Chapter 11).

Without a set of requirements, the exact needs and desires of library management and staff for an automated system will not be known, and a system could be acquired which will not be acceptable upon installation. Wasted time and money, an unsuitable system, and a possible loss of credibility on the part of the library could result. An analogy might be a contractor who is told to begin building a house without a set of blueprints and that specifications will be provided as construction progresses or after the house is built. A poorer house—or automated library system—will result unless the expected end product of a project is envisioned and planned before construction begins.

A FOCAL POINT FOR DEVELOPING REQUIREMENTS

A focal point should be established for the process of developing requirements for an automated system. Otherwise, those who will be preparing the specifications could lose sight of the end result wanted upon completion of the project. The focal point for developing requirements for an automated library system could be the goal of the library automation project, the goal of the system to be automated, or the general automation goals established by the library.

The Goal of the Library Automation Project as a Focal Point

The goal of the library automation project itself, discussed in Chapter 4, can serve as a focus for developing system requirements.

Example: The goal of the project is to acquire and install an automated circulation system for the library. The system shall include a means of creating and maintaining the bibliographic records necessary to support the system.

Example: This project is being undertaken to develop a state-of-the-art, automated acquisitions system for monographs and serials, including serials check-in.

Example: The goal of this project is to acquire and install an automated, integrated library system, consisting of an acquisitions system, a circulation system, and an online catalog.

The Goal of the System to be Automated as a Focal Point

The goal, mission, reason for being, or purpose of the system to be automated, discussed in Chapter 1, might provide an even better focal point for developing requirements.

Example: The goal of the circulation system is to loan informational materials to registered borrowers in good standing and provide accountability for the successful return of the loans.

Example: The goal of the cataloging system is to control the process of creating, storing, and maintaining bibliographic and copy records of the library's holdings.

Example: The goal of the acquisitions system is to acquire informational materials efficiently for the library's collections through purchases, gifts, and exchanges and provide a reliable means of controlling and reporting the expenditure of acquisitions funds.

General Automation Goals Established by the Library as a Focal Point

Additional guidance can be given to those who will be writing the requirements by stating any general automation goals established by the library prior to initiation of the specific automation project. General automation goals are discussed in Chapter 4.

Example: Goals for automation are to eliminate all manual files, speed up the processing of materials, and provide better control over services and materials.

Example: The library wishes to use automation to increase the amount of work that can be performed without additional staff and to be able to offer new services within existing staffing levels.

Example: A primary goal for any automated system to be installed in the library is to reduce the cost of operating that system.

In addition, very specific automation goals can be established for the system to be acquired and installed.

Example: The automated system shall enable the staff to process 98 percent of the library's new acquisitions within three weeks of receipt.

Example: The automated system shall eliminate all manual filing and files.

Example: The automated system shall provide a full range of overdue and other notices and reports that will improve services to citizens.

THE TASK FORCE FOR DEVELOPING REQUIREMENTS

A task force should be established to compile the list of requirements for the automated system to be acquired. An automation consultant with experience in writing requirements for and using automated systems can be very helpful in providing guidance and assistance to the library during this activity. However, the library staff should actually write the system requirements. The process of developing the requirements will be beneficial to the staff. Their involvement will be educational and will be helpful in gaining their interest and support for the new system. This section discusses task force establishment and a methodology for developing requirements.

Task Force Establishment

A task force should be established to develop the requirements for an automated system to be acquired and installed. This group need not be large; its size will depend upon the size and scope of the automated system to be acquired and the availability of staff to serve. Staff from several units or departments of the library should be included on the task force to provide a variety of backgrounds and opinions. Members of the task force can be identified or recommended by the project manager, then appointed by the library director or identified and selected by the project manager or the project steering committee. There is no reason why members of the project steering committee should not also serve on the task force established to develop requirements for the system to be acquired.

Methodology for Developing Requirements

A methology for developing the requirements should be established to make optimum use of the task force's efforts. A five-step methodology is suggested.

Subdivide the Requirements. A good approach to preparing the set of requirements is first to identify the categories of requirements that should be written, then assign each category to one or more task force members for development. The charge to each group should be the same: compile a list of requirements for an automated system in the assigned area or areas of responsibility. Sets of requirements for automated systems developed by other libraries should be gathered to be used as models. Most libraries are pleased to share their requirements or Requests for Proposals containing system requirements, either free of charge or for the cost of reproduction and mailing.

Prepare Draft Requirements. Next, the task force groups should prepare a draft set of requirements for their assigned aspects of the automated system to be acquired. The automation consultant, if one is used, and other project resource people should be used as needed during this activity to assist in identifying requirements needed and in writing the specifications accurately and clearly. A starting point in the drafting process might be to study the sample lists of requirements collected from other libraries. Each requirement in the lists can be discussed, then rewritten if necessary, and incorporated into the library's list or rejected. Others can be added as the drafting process progresses. Each requirement drafted should be clear and unambiguous and should convey only a single idea or concept. Vague statements tend to lead to misunderstanding.

The task force groups should be given a reasonable length of time to prepare their draft requirements, but a specific deadline should be clearly stated for completion of the work. The preparation of requirements might take several months, depending upon the size and complexity of the system to be acquired and the time that can be devoted to the activity. It may be helpful for the task force to meet as a whole from time to time during the drafting process to compare ideas and to review progress being made.

Study the Draft Requirements. The draft lists of requirements should be collected from the task force groups, edited for consistency and style, and consolidated into a master set by the project manager or by an editor selected by the project manager, the project steering committee, or the task force itself. The consolidated draft set of requirements should be circulated for study to the task force members, the project manager, the project steering committee, the library director, other project resource staff, and any other interested persons. The task force should meet to review and discuss the draft. Open meetings or hearings for other library staff and other interested persons should be held, if possible. The automation consultant should critique the draft and meet with the task force to discuss the proposed requirements.

Rewrite the Draft Requirements as Necessary. The draft list of requirements should be rewritten to incorporate the comments, suggestions, and ideas received as a result of study and discussion of the draft. It might be necessary to draft, edit, circulate, and discuss several versions until a realistic, clear definition of the system wanted for the library emerges and a final working set of requirements is acceptable. Further refinements and changes can be made to the list as work on the project progresses.

Approve the Set of Requirements. The final step of the process is to approve a set of requirements for the automated system. The final set of system requirements should have either consensus or formal acceptance and approval of the task force, the automation consultant (if one is used), the project manager, the project steering committee, the library director, and other concerned persons.

COMMON TYPES OF SYSTEM REQUIREMENTS

There are no standard categories of requirements that should be developed for an automated system. Those selected will depend upon the nature and size of the automated system to be acquired and the scope of the project to be undertaken. Common types of system requirements include functional, database, management report, workload, performance, hardware, software, documentation, training, hardware maintenance, and software maintenance requirements.

Functional Requirements

The bulk of the requirements to be established for an automated system will be of a functional nature, defining specifically what the system must be able to do and how it must operate.

The system first should be broken into its component subsystems, to facilitate preparation of its functional requirements.

Example: A circulation system can be divided into borrower control, charges, renewals, discharges, blocks, holds, recalls, fines and fees, overdues, reserves, material booking, and interlibrary communication subsystems.

Example: An acquisitions system can be divided into selection entry and review, verification and searching, purchase order preparation, receiving, claims and cancellations, vendor records maintenance, and fund accounting subsystems.

Example: An online public catalog system can be divided into database creation and maintenance, authority control, searching/inquiries, search results, and index creation and maintenance subsystems.

This approach can greatly facilitate the writing of requirements, because the smaller parts can be more easily visualized, examined, and understood than can the system as a whole. Also, the process can provide clearly delineated parts which can be assigned to different members of the task force for preparation of requirements.

Once the system is divided into its component subsystems and the parts assigned to various staff, detailed requirements for each can be prepared.

Example: Some requirements for the charge activities of an automated system might be as follows: (1) the system shall notify the terminal operator if a borrower is not registered; (2) the system shall check borrower status for any exception condition, including excessive number of books charged, fines or fees owed, etc.; (3) the system shall verify that material is not on hold for another borrower; (4) the system shall notify the terminal operator if the items have been designated as noncirculating, such as reference books or bound journals; (5) the system shall associate a unique material identifier with a unique borrower identifier and store the record in a circulation file; (6) the system shall allow "on-the-fly" circulation of materials; (7) the system shall permit charges to library units and collections such as Interlibrary Loan, Reserves, etc., and subsequent charges from those units and collections to borrowers or other libraries; (8) the system shall calculate loan periods and due dates according to the type of borrower, type of material, and library service hours, allowing for holidays; (9) the system shall allow due dates to be changed online; (10) the system shall display due dates on the terminal screen; and (11)(optional) the system shall print at the charging location a date due slip to be inserted in charged items.

Database Requirements

Considerable thought should be given to the database that will support an automated system. The database can consist of one or several related files.

A first step in developing database requirements is to identify those files necessary to support the automated system to be acquired.

Example: The database necessary for the automated circulation system shall be a file of borrower records, a file of bibliographic records of titles which will be circulated, a file of item records representing copies of titles which will be circulated, and a file of circulation transactions.

Example: The database for the automated acquisitions system shall be a file of acquisitions records, a file of fund accounting records, and a vendor file.

Example: The database for the online catalog shall be a file of bibliographic records being cataloged or edited and another file of bibliographic records fully cataloged and edited.

Once the essential files have been identified, detailed requirements for each can be written. Types or categories of requirements to be written might include general characteristics of files, data field requirements of records, file sizes and growth rates, and conversion needs.

General Characteristics of Files. General characteristics of files expected in an automated system to be acquired can be specified.

Example: The system shall accept and differentiate between all existing MARC (Machine-Readable Cataloging) bibliographic formats (monographs, serials, audiovisual media, sound recordings, machine-readable data files, scores, maps, and manuscripts).

Example: The system shall provide consolidated fine and fee records for all agencies or branches within the library system.

Example: The fund accounting file shall contain a record for each fund established for the purchase of materials.

Data Field Requirements of Records. The data fields to be included in each record of a file can be specified.

Example: The borrower file shall contain data fields for borrower identification (borrower number, surname, first name, and middle initial), address (street, city, state, and ZIP code), expiration date of authorization to borrow, and academic class code.

Example: Vendor records shall have fields for vendor name (variable length), vendor address (variable length), city (variable length), state (two alphabetic characters), ZIP code (five numeric characters), telephone number (10 numeric characters), vendor account number for the library (10 numeric characters), a library-specified number of days which shall lapse before claims are made for orders to the vendor (three numeric characters), and a counter containing the average delivery time in days for the vendor (three numeric characters).

Example: The bibliographic record shall accommodate all fields of the MARC II formats defined for each type of material. Fields can be added, deleted, or changed as the formats evolve.

File Sizes and Growth Rates. The number of records expected to be in each file should be specified (see Figure 5-1). For files that will expand continuously, a minimum of five years of expected growth rate should be specified.

Example: The system shall accommodate a minimum of 35,000 borrower records.

Example: The system shall accommodate a minimum of 400,000 full MARC records in the initial load, plus an additional 30,000 records each year over the next five years (550,000 bibliographic records total), without additional need for disk storage or processing capabilities beyond the initial hardware and software installation.

Example: The system shall accommodate a minimum of 8,000 vendor records.

Figure 5-1. Typical Files with Sample Sizes and Growth Rates.

File	Size Year 1	Growth Year 2	Growth Year 3	Growth Year 4	Growth Year 5	Size End of Year 5
Bibliographic File (Titles)	500,000	25,000	28,000	28,500	30,000	611,500
Bibliographic File (Copies)	600,000	30,000	35,000	36,000	40,000	741,000
Borrower File	25,000	3,000	2,000	2,000	4,000	36,000
Circulation File*	100,000	10,000	20,000	30,000	40,000	200,000
Vendor File	2,000	500	800	900	100	4,300

*Items in circulation at any one time.

Conversion Needs. If the library has special requirements for loading records into a file of the automated system or in converting records from one system to another, these needs should be identified and defined.

Example: The system shall accommodate the batch loading of borrower records using data supplied by the university registrar and academic records office.

Example: The system shall accept and convert data from the library's existing automated system to the new system's record format.

Example: As archival tapes are loaded, the system shall convert the holding symbols in records to library-specified agency/branch location designations.

Management Report Requirements

An automated system should be expected to yield or produce statistical and other management and output reports which can be used to evaluate the use of the system or the performance of the staff operating the system or of the hardware and software itself.

Reports requested for each subsystem should be identified and the library's requirements for each specified. Reports may be presented as an online display, as a printed document, or as both, at the option of the library.

Example: Some requirements for a printed statistical report might be as follows: (1) the report shall include charges, discharges, and renewals; holds placed, filled, and cancelled; and fines and fees levied and collected; (2) the statistics shall be reported by agency/branch and location within agency/branch, with subtotals for each and a grand total for all; (3) cumulative week-to-date, month-to-date, and year-to-date statistics shall be provided for each agency/branch, including grand totals for all; (4) for ease of distribution, statistics for each agency/branch shall be printed on a separate page, with the grand totals on another page; and (5) the report shall be produced on a daily basis.

Workload Requirements

Workload requirements establish the expected amount of work to be handled by an automated system during a period of time such as a year (see Figure 5-2). Such requirements are important because they will define the impact the automated system will have on the effectiveness of the functions to be performed. They also are essential to judge, in conjunction with the file sizes, the amount of internal memory and auxiliary storage capacity and the number of terminals and other equipment that will be necessary for the automated system. Past statistical records generated by the existing system can be analyzed to obtain the types and volume of work to be performed.

Example: The system shall be able to handle 400,000 charge transactions each year.

Example: The system shall be able to process 300,000 overdue notices each year.

Example: The system shall accommodate 50,000 orders placed each year.

Performance Requirements

Performance requirements establish how rapidly or accurately an automated system should process data or perform operations. Performance or response time is the amount of time between a request for information or the initiation of a transaction and the delivery of the data or the completion of the transaction.

Example: The system shall have an average response time of six seconds or less for data input and edit operations.

Example: The system shall have a maximum average response time of six seconds for file inquiries by subject.

Example: The system shall complete each step of charge, renewal, discharge, and other circulation functions within two seconds after entry of the required data.

Figure 5-2. Sample Work Loads for Automated Library Systems

Activity	Transactions per Year	Growth per Year over Past 5 Years
Bibliographic Records Added	40,000	2%
Copy Records Added	47,000	3%
Bibliographic Records Deleted	590	1%
Copy Records Deleted	700	1%
Borrower Records Added	5,000	10%
Charges, Discharges, Renewals	255,000	12%
Holds and Recalls Placed	5,400	2%
Overdue Notices Prepared	55,000	5%
Billing Notices Prepared	8,000	1%

Figure 5-2. Sample Work Loads for Automated Library Systems (continued).

Activity	Transactions per Year	Growth per Year over Past 5 Years
Availability Notices Prepared	3,000	8%
Orders (Titles) Placed	30,000	2%
Order Claims Made	8,000	15%
Cancellations Made	1,000	12%
Volumes Received	50,000	3%
Issues Checked In	75,000	4%
Issues Claimed	2,500	3%
Issues Routed	2,250	25%
Volumes Bound	8,000	-2%

Hardware Requirements

Detailed requirements should be established for the hardware needed for an automated system. An automation consultant, if one is used, the staff of a computer center serving the library, or other resource persons can assist in developing hardware requirements. The RFPs of other libraries can be invaluable as models when writing hardware requirements.

A first step in writing hardware requirements is to identify the various pieces of equipment that must be acquired. Typical pieces of hardware for automated library systems are shown in Appendix C. Once the pieces have been identified, requirements for each can be written. The type, size, quantity, and capabilities of the hardware needed, will of course, depend upon the size and nature of the automated system to be acquired.

Central Processing Unit. The central processing unit or CPU is the workhorse of any automated system. In preparing requirements for the CPU, the task force should make certain that sufficient internal memory is available to hold essential system software such as the operating system, plus software for the functions to be performed. It also should be sure that the channels over which data are transmitted or distributed to and from the CPU and its peripherals, such as magnetic disk drives, printers, and CRT terminals, can handle the volume of work or data traffic anticipated by the library without significant wait times. The library should also require that the CPU be able to be expanded without completely replacing it with a new and larger one.

> *Example:* The CPU shall have sufficient internal memory to perform the library's expected workloads and to allow concurrent operation of the required peripherals within the required response times.

> *Example:* The CPU shall have ports for a minimum of 48 terminals, expandable up to 64 terminals.

> *Example:* The CPU shall be capable of accepting modular additions to memory up to twice the installed memory without reprogramming.

Control Console. The operator or control console provides a means by which an operator can communicate with the CPU and monitor the system. The console can be a printer, but a CRT terminal is more desirable.

> *Example:* The CPU shall have a console with keyboard and a visual display unit (VDU) or CRT.

> *Example:* The operator console shall have a minimum display capacity of 1,920 characters, with a screen display image of at least 24 lines vertically and 80 characters horizontally on each line.

> *Example:* The console shall have at least a 12-inch diagonal screen.

Disk Drives. Automated library systems usually require a minimum of two magnetic disk drives to provide auxiliary or mass storage capabilities to the computer system. The disks may or may not be removable from the drives. The task force should make certain that sufficient disk storage is available to store all of its files and software needed to support the functions to be performed. It also should be certain that sufficient extra disk storage space is available for the growth in the files expected during the lifespan of the system.

> *Example:* Sufficient disk storage shall be available to store the initial files described in Database Requirements and to store the additional records expected to be added for five years after the initial installation.

> *Example:* The system shall be expandable in the future to at least double the disk storage capacity without need for additional disk controllers and without changing the basic hardware or software, except for adding new disk drives.

> *Example:* All disk packs shall be error-free and formatted.

In most modern computer systems, a magnetic tape unit or drive is used primarily to bulk-load records onto magnetic disk or to store back-up copies of files. The primary specifications for magnetic tape drives are the tape density, the speed of the unit, checking capability, and the tape that can be used.

> *Example:* The magnetic tape drive shall accept half-inch tape, recorded in nine tracks, at 1600 bits per inch (BPI).

> *Example:* The tape drive shall operate at speeds of 20-25 inches per second (IPS).

> *Example:* The tape drive shall be able to read and write, with read-after-write error check capability.

Printers. A line or other relatively high-speed printer is usually attached directly to the CPU for batch printing of reports, notices, and other documents. Besides dependability, the task force should be interested in requirements for speed, quality of print, ease of use, and flexibility.

> *Example:* The printer shall have a rated speed of not less than 200 lines per minute (LPM) when printing full 132-character lines.

> *Example:* The printer shall have high-quality print on at least four-part paper.

> *Example:* The printer shall have a manual forms eject capability.

> *Example:* The printer shall be adjustable to accept paper or forms from 4 inches to 14 7/8 inches in size horizontally.

An automated system potentially could require the use of several other types of printers, including printers attached to CRT terminals to copy information displayed and remote printers to print various reports and documents upon demand. Some libraries even want a small printer at the circulation desk to print date due slips and other related circulation data. The task force should look for speed, quality of print, ease of use, and flexibility, depending upon the use to be made of the printer.

> *Example:* The printer shall have an adjustable pin-feed and continuous forms tractor feed capability.

> *Example:* The printer shall be RS-232C compatible to the printer or I/O port of a CRT terminal.

> *Example:* The printer shall have a buffer for a minimum of 1,920 characters of data.

CRT Terminals. The CRT terminal provides input and output capabilities to the automated system. Some features to specify for CRT terminals include the screen size, resolution, and the keyboard.

> *Example:* The CRT terminal shall have a minimum display capacity of 1,920 characters with a screen display image of at least 24 lines vertically and with 80 characters horizontally on each line.

Example: The CRT terminal shall have at least a 12-inch diagonal screen.

Example: The CRT terminal shall have keys designated for special functions such as charge, discharge, renewals, etc.

Example: The terminal's display resolution shall equal or exceed that obtainable with a dot matrix five dots wide by seven dots high.

Other general characteristics of the CRT terminal expected for the automated system can be specified.

Example: The CRT shall display both uppercase and lowercase characters.

Example: The terminal shall have an audible bell or alarm.

Example: The terminal shall operate properly at standard data transmission rates using standard serial asynchronous communication line protocol.

Example: The terminal shall use American-English block-style alphabetic and numeric characters with true descenders.

Optical Scanning. If optical scanning will be essential in a system, there might be a choice between Optical Character Recognition (OCR) or barcodes. OCR labels are somewhat less expensive and can be produced on office typewriters with appropriate type fonts, while barcodes require special printers or a photo-offset method of production. There are a dozen or more types of barcodes, most of which are not compatible or interchangeable with one another. Some characteristics to require are audio or visual feedback to the operator after scanning and error checking.

Example: The scanner shall emit an audible "beeper" tone when a label is read correctly.

Example: The scanner shall be capable of automatic error checking.

Data Communications. If CRT terminals and other devices are to be located more than approximately 1,000 feet from the CPU, some data communications equipment such as modems or multiplexors may be required to prevent data distortion. A modem will convert the digital signals of the computer to analog signals which can be transmitted over telephone lines to remote locations. Another modem is required at the CRT end to convert the analog signals back to digital signals. A multiplexor accepts input from several terminals, combines their signals, and then transmits them together over one communications line. The task force should make certain that the transmission speed is sufficient and that an adequate number of devices are provided.

Example: The modems used shall operate at 4800 baud.

Example: The multiplexor used shall have a minimum of four channels for transmission.

Example: Sufficient modems shall be provided to connect all terminals located in the remote sites specified.

Software Requirements

Requirements for application software for an automated system are inherent in the functional, database, workload, performance, and management report specifications. Some additional software requirements may still be necessary for the operating system, system security, and database integrity.

The operating system, the collection of special programs that supervises and controls the running of other programs, limits human intervention in the processing cycle of the computer by making all operations virtually automatic. The task force should make certain that the operating system being considered can handle multiple tasks at the same time, automatically schedule and load programs into memory, establish priorities, and handle messages and errors from peripherals.

Example: The operating system shall allow concurrent operation of more than two tasks.

Example: The operating system shall provide for the automatic scheduling and loading of programs into memory. It should be capable of coordinating transfer of control between programs or tasks after completion of external events, waiting on one program or task, starting another, and later restarting the first program or task without loss of program or task integrity.

Example: The operating system shall provide for the processing of jobs in accordance with established priorities, by scheduling jobs, overlapping jobs requiring no external intervention, and issuing messages to the operator as needed.

The task force should include requirements for the protection of all data and files from unauthorized persons.

Example: A system of passwords and/or other security mechanisms shall be provided.

Example: The library shall be able to specify individually which functions can be performed at each terminal.

Example: A method of preventing outside determination of user passwords shall be provided.

Requirements should also be included for backups of files and recovery from hardware and software failures.

Example: Software shall be provided which will perform back-ups of all application and system software and all data files and transactions onto some removable magnetic storage medium.

Example: Procedures and software shall be provided which will enable fast recovery from hardware and/or software failure.

Requirements for software utilities and programming languages can also be added.

Documentation Requirements

Documentation refers to the written descriptions of various aspects of the automated system. Documentation is used by library staff and others for instructional and reference purposes while installing, operating, and maintaining the system. A set of documentation requirements should be established and put in a form that can be presented to the system vendor. Types of documentation necessary for an automated system include application, system, and hardware manuals or guides.

Application documentation includes overviews, background perspectives, and detailed descriptions of the automated system, including step-by-step procedures for using it.

Example: An orientation manual describing the general capabilities and limitations of the circulation system shall be provided to the library.

Example: A training and reference manual giving step-by-step procedures on how to operate and manage the acquisitions system shall be provided to the library.

Example: Modifications or enhancements to the manuals, or completely revised manuals, shall be provided to the library on a continuing basis.

System or operations documentation includes descriptive guides and manuals for use by computer operators or computer room personnel when installing, operating, monitoring, and maintaining the automated system.

Example: Manuals which describe how to start up and shut down the system, monitor and operate the system on a day-to-day basis, handle emergencies with the system, and troubleshoot and solve simple problems with the system shall be provided to the library.

Example: Manuals which instruct the staff in loading software enhancements, loading records from magnetic tape, and running file backups shall be provided to the library.

Example: Manuals for using each system utility such as clearing files, transferring records from disk to tape, sorting routines, etc., shall be provided to the library.

Hardware documentation includes technical manuals and guides describing each piece of equipment and how to operate and maintain each.

Example: A descriptive and operational manual shall be provided for each separate equipment model.

Example: Schematic drawings for the CRT terminals shall be provided.

Example: Technical and environmental specifications for each separate equipment model shall be provided.

Other documentation describing the operating system, a database management system, and the programming language or languages used may also be required.

Training Requirements

Training of staff to operate and manage an automated system can be required of a vendor. Different training can be specified for several levels of staff, such as managers and supervisors, operations staff, and basic level clerks and operators.

Example: Managers and supervisors shall be trained to manage the system on a day-to-day basis, with expected competencies including abilities to: (1) use each functional component of the system; (2) start up, shut down, monitor, and operate the equipment supporting their respective functional systems; (3) train other staff members in daily operation and use of their systems; (4) handle emergencies which might arise before computer room supervisors or vendor maintenance staff can arrive; and (5) troubleshoot and solve simple problems in lieu of calling computer room supervisory personnel or vendor maintenance staff.

The number of staff expected to be trained can be specified.

Example: A minimum of 3 computer room supervisors, 5 functional system supervisors, and 10 data entry operators shall be trained by the vendor.

The time and location of the training usually is negotiated after the best system has been selected and a contract has been signed with the vendor.

Hardware Maintenance Requirements

The various pieces of equipment of an automated system will require repair and maintenance from time to time. Requirements for both remedial and preventive maintenance of the system's hardware should be established, in addition to general maintenance requirements.

Remedial or corrective maintenance refers to unscheduled repair of hardware necessary to correct identified malfunctions or problems. The task force should establish, as a minimum, requirements for the period of maintenance coverage, the equipment covered, availability of spare parts, and responses to requests for corrective maintenance.

Example: All-expense, flat-rate remedial maintenance shall be provided at the equipment site Monday through Friday, 8:00 a.m. through 5:00 p.m.

Example: Remedial maintenance shall be provided for the CPU, control console, the disk drives, the line printer, and all CRT terminals.

Example: An adequate supply of repair parts shall be maintained locally to repair a minimum of 85 percent of all hardware failures during a calendar year.

Example: Responses to requests for corrective maintenance shall be made within four hours, 90 percent of the time, for the computer equipment and major peripherals and within 48 hours for terminal equipment.

Preventive maintenance is performed to maintain pieces of hardware in good working condition and to reduce the probability that malfunctions and problems will occur. The task force should pay particular attention to requirements for scheduling preventive maintenance.

Example: All-expense, flat-rate preventive maintenance for the equipment shall be provided at the equipment site, at times mutually agreed upon by the library and the maintenance staff.

Example: Preventive maintenance shall be performed outside normal operating hours of the library, if at all possible.

Example: A schedule for preventive maintenance shall be established each year for each piece of hardware in the system.

Other general maintenance requirements may be added, such as for spare terminals, maintenance logs, charges for maintenance, and payment for services.

Example: Two terminals shall be provided, free of charge, as spares to be located at a site designated by the library. The library shall replace defective terminals with the spares and not use the spares as additional terminals. The spares shall remain the property of the vendor.

Example: The library shall keep a log of operations, including reference to faults, symptoms, and the like, in a manner reasonably required by the vendor and shall make this log available upon request.

Example: The maintenance charge shall include all labor and parts used by the vendor in performing preventive and corrective maintenance on the equipment.

Example: The charge for coverage during the principle periods of maintenance shall be paid annually in advance by the library.

Software Maintenance Requirements

Software, like hardware, requires remedial maintenance, and the library should establish requirements for this service for the automated system to be acquired.

Example: All-expense, flat-rate maintenance of all application and system software shall be provided Monday through Friday, 8:00 a.m. to 5:00 p.m., upon the library's notification that the software is not operative.

Example: The vendor shall respond to requests for corrective maintenance for the software within four hours 90 percent of the time.

Example: A cost-free telephone number for software maintenance calls shall be provided.

Example: Software maintenance shall be performed by a dial-in arrangement using the public switched telephone network. Additional corrective maintenance can be performed by sending corrections and enhancements on magnetic tape to the library for loading.

Example: The vendor shall systematically inform the library of ongoing software enhancements as they are developed and shall solicit library input when critical system changes are being contemplated and stipulate the cost to the library, if any, for software enhancements.

Chapter 6
The Request for Proposal

Most libraries are required to acquire the hardware, software, and vendor services for an automated system through a competitive bidding process or at least through a process wherein proposals or quotations are gathered from a number of prospective vendors and the best and/or least expensive system is selected for acquisition. This chapter includes the following topics:

- The definition of a Request for Proposal
- The need for a Request for Proposal
- Developing the Request for Proposal
- Typical parts of the Request for Proposal

A complete sample RFP is shown in Appendix D.

THE DEFINITION OF A REQUEST FOR PROPOSAL

The Invitation to Bid (ITB), Request for Quotation (RFQ), and Request for Proposal (RFP) are common terms for documents used by libraries to solicit quotations or bids from vendors to supply automated systems which will meet their defined needs. The Request for Proposal or RFP, which is used most often, will be discussed in this book. The RFP contains detailed requirements and pertinent system acquisition information for the automated system wanted by the library. In response to the RFP, suppliers of automated systems indicate how closely their products meet the library's defined requirements, what hardware and software will be required to support their systems, and the costs of the various components and services they are prepared to provide.

THE NEED FOR A REQUEST FOR PROPOSAL

Using the RFP enables the library to minimize the problems encountered during the crucial process of selecting and acquiring an automated system. Specifically, the RFP can be used by the library to:

1. Convey to prospective vendors the exact needs and requirements of the library for an automated system.
2. Obtain exact information and costs or bids from vendors who would like to supply an automated system to the library.
3. Provide a means of fairly and objectively comparing and evaluating responses to the RFP from the several vendors.
4. Form the basis of a contract with the successful bidder for acquiring and maintaining the automated system.

It usually is in the best interests of the library to develop a Request for Proposal document to which several vendors will have a reasonable chance of responding with good bids. Through competitive bidding, the library can gain better prices for a system and retain a sense of fair play in the process. A set of closed specifications—that is, specifications written so that one and only one vendor can meet them—eliminates competitive bidding, stifles competition, could easily result in higher prices for a system, and is illegal in some situations.

DEVELOPING THE REQUEST FOR PROPOSAL

The RFP usually is prepared through the combined efforts of the project manager, the automation consultant, if one is used, the project steering committee, the library's purchasing agent or department, and other resource people available to the library. Several months may be required to prepare this document, depending upon the size and complexity of the system to be acquired, the requirements for the contents of the RFP, and how fast the library can complete the work. A suggested methodology for developing the RFP is to prepare a draft of the RFP, study and discuss the draft, rewrite the draft until it is acceptable, and approve the RFP.

Prepare a Draft of the RFP

The first step in developing the RFP is to prepare a draft document for study and discussion. An individual should be selected and appointed to prepare the draft RFP in consultation with others. One person, rather than a committee, should be able to prepare the document, because the process usually requires only gathering the already developed facts and arranging the information into the prescribed format. A logical choice for the person is the project manager, who will already have been working with the requirements for the system and will be in a good position to work with other resource people during development of the document. The RFPs for automated systems from other libraries, acquired during the development of system requirements, can be used as models.

Study and Discuss the Draft

The second step of developing the RFP is to study and discuss the draft document that has been prepared. The draft RFP should be circulated for review by the project steering committee, the library director, and other resource people. The automation consultant, if one is used, should critique the draft and meet with the project manager and other staff to discuss the document. If possible, open meetings or hearings with the library staff as a whole should be held to discuss the proposed requirements.

Rewrite the Draft until It Is Acceptable

The third step in developing the RFP is to rewrite the draft until it is acceptable. The RFP should be revised to incorporate the comments, suggestions, and ideas received as a result of study and discussion of the draft. It might be necessary to draft, circulate, and discuss several versions before a final document is acceptable.

Approve the RFP

The fourth and final step in developing the RFP is to approve the draft document. The final version of the RFP should have either consensus or formal acceptance and approval of the project manager, the automation consultant, the project steering committee, the library director, the library's purchasing agent or department, and other units or agencies which must approve the document before it is sent to prospective bidders.

TYPICAL PARTS OF THE REQUEST FOR PROPOSAL

While the format of the RFP varies from region to region and from organization to organization, it typically consists of several parts or sections. A sample outline for a RFP is illustrated in Figure 6-1. The library's purchasing agent or other regulatory unit might already have a format used for RFPs, in which case information must simply be written in a format that follows those prescribed guidelines.

Figure 6-1. A Sample Outline for a Request for Proposal.

    I. Introduction
       A. Purpose of the RFP
       B. A description of the library

      C. An overview of the existing system
      D. An overview of the planned system
  II. Administrative Rules for the RFP
      A. Inquiries about the RFP
      B. RFP expenses
      C. Alternate bids
      D. Delivery of bids
      E. Modification of bids
      F. Withdrawal of bids
      G. The bid opening
      H. Evaluation of bids
      I. Disputes
      J. Award of contract
      K. Calendar of events
 III. General Requirements
      A. Firm bids
      B. Demonstration of systems
      C. Contract expectations
      D. RFP responses as part of contract
      E. Performance bond
      F. Delivery of system
      G. Installation of system
      H. Liquidated damages
      I. Guarantees/Warranties
      J. Payment
      K. Title to hardware and software
      L. Acceptance tests
 IV. Vendor Response Requirements
      A. Vendor profile
      B. Proposal summary
      C. Responses to the system requirements
      D. A list of system components and their costs
      E. Environmental and physical specifications
      F. Special conditions and terms
      G. Vendor user list
  V. System Requirements
      A. Public online catalog
      B. Circulation system
      C. Acquisitions system
      D. Hardware
      E. Software
      F. Documentation
      G. Training
      H. Hardware and software maintenance
 VI. Appendices
      A. Workload tables
      B. Desired equipment
VII. Response Forms
      Requirement Response Forms

Cost Response Forms
List of operational installations

The Introduction to the Request for Proposal

Introductory information should be provided in the RFP to orient prospective bidders to the document and to the library. This information can include the purpose of the RFP, a description of the library, an overview of the existing system, and an overview of the planned system

The Purpose of the Request for Proposal. A statement of the purpose of the RFP should be included in the introduction to the document. This statement should indicate clearly what the library is seeking to acquire.

Example: The intent of this Request for Proposal (RFP) is to solicit bids for the hardware, software, and hardware and software maintenance for an automated library circulation and acquisitions system.

Example: The purpose of this Request for Proposal (RFP) is to request bids or quotations from prospective vendors for an automated circulation system for the Library.

Example: The purpose of this request is to procure equipment, software, and vendor support that will provide the Library with computer-based acquisitions, cataloging, and online catalog systems.

A Description of the Library. A second part of the introduction to the RFP might be a description of the library and its environment. Because most, if not all, the vendors who might wish to respond to the RFP will not be familiar with the library, some background information might assist them in preparing their proposals. A brief description of the library and its history and setting or environment may be helpful.

Example: The Library provides services to its 500,000 users from a central research library of 800,000 volumes, 5 suburban branches, and 10 bookmobiles for outlying areas. It has a highly qualified staff of librarians, information specialists, and others to provide a full range of services supporting the research and recreational needs of its users. The Library began studying automation of its services five years ago and has developed a long-range plan for all projects to develop automated systems. Growing pressures of an expanding and increasingly complex information base, demands for new and sophisticated approaches to information access and dissemination, and rising costs are forcing the Library to take advantage of appropriate technological advancements within the information and data processing industry to address these and other problems. The hardware and software products that are explicity identified within this RFP are intended to alleviate somewhat these and other problems in the circulation system and, eventually, in other functions of the Library.

An Overview of the Existing System. The third part of the introduction to the RFP might be a brief overview of the existing system that the automated system will replace or supplement. This can be helpful to the vendor in preparing a proposal in response to the library's RFP.

Example: The existing circulation system is a manual Gaylord charging system. Data for unique identification of items to be circulated are typed on cards placed in pockets inside materials. Eligible borrowers are issued library cards bearing unique numbers embossed in metal tags affixed to the cards. When a borrower wishes to check out an item, the individual's library card and the book card are inserted into the charging machine, which imprints both the date due and the borrower number onto the book card. The date due is stamped on a slip in the item as a reminder of the loan. The book card then is filed manually by date due in a circulation file. As items are returned, the book cards are pulled from the circulation file and placed back in the pockets of materials. Overdues are handled by checking the file for unreturned materials past the date due.

An Overview of the Planned System. Finally, a brief description of the planned system can give vendors an idea of how the library envisions the use of the automated system.

Example: In the planned system, a number of circulation stations, each consisting of a CRT display terminal and an optical scanner, will be connected online to the computer. A borrower wishing to check out materials will go to a circulation station and present the material and his or her identification badge to the operator. After the badge has been scanned, the system automatically will check the borrower file for clearance to loan materials to the borrower. Then the scanner will be passed over a machine-readable label containing a unique identifier on the material to be checked out; information encoded in the label will be read and recorded automatically in a circulation file and printed on a slip which will be given to the borrower. As items are returned from circulation, the scanner will be passed again over the label in the material, with the system in a discharge mode, and the record of the loan will be removed from the circulation file. The system will automatically calculate and record any charges for overdue materials. Any holds or personal reserves previously placed in a hold file will be detected and notices printed informing a waiting borrower of the availability of the materials. Other programs will be provided for logging transactions for file recovery; for searching and displaying individual borrower and circulation records; for entering, modifying, and deleting records; and for recording statistics. A medium-speed printer will be used to print overdue, fine, and availability notices, lists of overdues, and statistical and other managerial reports.

Administrative Rules for the Request for Proposal

General ground rules concerning the administration of the RFP and the bidding process should be identified and described for guidance to prospective bidders and for reference by library and purchasing department staff. Several topics might be included in this section.

Inquiries about the RFP. The name, title, mailing address, and telephone number should be listed for the person or persons who can be contacted by vendors for additional information or for clarification of information in the RFP. The library may, for legal or documentation purposes, require that all inquiries be in writing and submitted by a specified date.

> *Example:* After receipt of this RFP, vendors will be given an opportunity to consult with the library staff. Appointments should be made through Shirley Doe, Automation Librarian, Atlantis Library, 1800 Any Drive, Atlantis 99999, Telephone 123-456-7890
>
> *Example:* Any questions requiring responses affecting the bid and related responses that arise during preparation of the vendor's response to the RFP should be directed in writing to the person above. Questions may be submitted up to 14 days prior to bid opening.

RFP Expenses. The preparation of responses to the RFP should be a business expense for vendors and should not be charged to the library. A statement to this effect should be included in this section of the RFP.

> *Example:* Expenses for developing the bids and demonstrations of equipment are entirely the responsibility of the vendor and shall not be chargeable, in any manner, to the library or to the state.

Alternate Bids. If alternate bids can be submitted by vendors in response to the RFP, this should be stipulated and instructions given in this section of the RFP.

> *Example:* A vendor may submit more than one bid, at its option. If a vendor elects to submit more than one bid, it is requested that a bid be identified as either primary or alternate. Only one primary bid will be accepted. Each bid submitted, primary or alternate, should follow the rules and regulations outlined in this RFP.

Delivery of Bids. Instructions concerning the delivery of bids should be stated in the Administrative Rules for the RFP. The number of copies of RFP responses that should be submitted by vendors, the name and address of the department or person to receive the documents, and the date and time of day before which responses must be delivered should be included in the administrative rules for the RFP.

Example: Four copies of a bid should be delivered to the Purchasing Department, Atlantis Library, 1800 Any Drive, Atlantis 99999, before 5:00 p.m. CDT, August 12, 198x.

Modification of Bids. If the library will accept modifications to bids after submission by vendors, this should be indicated and the conditions under which changes will be accepted and the procedures for submitting modifications should be given.

Example: Any bidder may modify his bid at any time prior to the scheduled closing time for the receipt of bids. Only telegrams, letters, and other written requests for the modification or correction of a previously submitted bid will be accepted. Requests for the modification or correction of bids cannot be submitted after the scheduled closing time for the receipt of bids.

Withdrawal of Bids. The library may allow the withdrawal of a bid submitted by a vendor. If so, this should be indicated in the RFP and the conditions under which a bid may be withdrawn should be described.

Example: Any bidder may withdraw a bid at any time prior to the scheduled closing time for the receipt of bids, but no bidder may withdraw a bid for a period of 120 days after the scheduled closing time for the receipt of bids.

The Bid Opening. Some vendors prefer to have representatives present for bid openings. If this is permitted, this should be so stated in the administrative rules and the time and place of the opening indicated.

Example: Bids will be opened at 3:00 p.m. Wednesday, October 15, 19xx, in the Administrative Conference Room of the Atlantis Library. Vendor representatives are welcome to attend the opening. All bids and supporting documentation submitted become public property at the time of bid opening.

Evaluation of Bids. How and by whom bids or proposals will be evaluated should be briefly outlined. Criteria for the evaluation process also can be delineated.

Example: Bid responses will be evaluated by a Bid Evaluation Team, consisting of key members of the library staff, assisted by other knowledgeable resource people. The Team plans to select the system that meets all or most of the system requirements outlined in the RFP, will have the least installation or start-up costs, and will cost the least to maintain on an annual basis after system installation. In addition, the Team may contact other users of a vendor's system and utilize any other means of obtaining information regarding the hardware, software, or vendor that is deemed appropriate and would assist in the evaluation.

Disputes. The library should include a statement as to how any dispute concerning the evaluation of bids or award of contract will be settled to the satisfaction of all parties concerned.

Example: In case of any doubt or difference of opinion as to any aspect of a vendor's bid response or of the RFP, the decision of the Director of Purchasing of the Atlantis Library shall be final and binding upon both parties.

Award of Contract. How the contract will be awarded should be detailed. How the library will communicate results of the bid award to other bidders also can be stipulated.

Example: A contract purchase order, with terms acceptable to both the Atlantis Library and the successful bidder, will be sent to the vendor receiving the award. All other bidders will be able to review the bid file to determine bid award.

Calendar of Events. Finally, a timetable of dates and times pertinent to the RFP can be specified.

Example: August 1, 198x—RFP mailed to vendors
September 30, 198x—Responses to RFP due in library
November 15, 198x—Vendor selected
December 15, 198x—Contract signed.

General Requirements

Some general requirements concerning the purchase, installation, acceptance, and payment procedures for the automated system selected should be addressed in this section of the RFP.

Firm Bids. A statement indicating the date until which the costs proposed or quoted by vendors in their bids must be guaranteed without change should be included in this section of the RFP.

Example: All prices bid by a vendor shall be firm for 120 days from the date of the bid opening.

Demonstration of Systems. If the library may require a demonstration of all or some systems bid, the library should have this as a general requirement of the vendor. The purpose of a system demonstration is to determine the ability of the vendor's hardware and software to perform as specified. Usually, dates and details for demonstrations are negotiated with vendors during the evaluation of the responses to the RFP, discussed in Chapter 7.

Example: At the option of the library, a vendor may be required to demonstrate the operation of equipment and/or software during the bid evaluation process. The location of this demonstration will be at a site mutually agreeable to the library and the vendor.

Contract Expectations. Information about the contract expected to be drawn between the library and the successful bidder for purchase of the automated system should be specified in this section.

> *Example:* A copy of the contract for this procurement is available from the library. Each vendor interested in bidding is requested to obtain a copy or request that one be mailed to them. A vendor may agree to this contract as written, take exception to any paragraph and suggest substitute wording, or suggest additional clauses.

RFP Responses as Part of Contract. The responses by a vendor to the library's RFP should be made a part of the contract for the purchase of an automated system to ensure that the library will receive those functions, features, and services that the vendor has stated it will supply. Otherwise, the library would not have a legally binding means of requiring that the vendor fulfill its obligations. This general requirement can be included in this section of the RFP.

> *Example:* The terms and requirements contained in this RFP and a bidder's response to this document shall be considered as a part of the contract between the library and the vendor for purchase of its automated system.

Performance Bond. A statement as to whether a performance bond is to be paid by the vendor supplying an automated system to the library and the amount of the bond should be included as a general requirement. This can be included in this section of the RFP.

> *Example:* A performance bond of 10 percent (or 50 percent or 100 percent) of the total bid, in a form acceptable to the library, will be required for the full term of the purchase order for the automated system.

Delivery of System. The library should specify in this section of the RFP the delivery schedule expected for the automated system it selects.

> *Example:* All hardware and system software items shall be delivered within 120 days after receipt of a purchase order from the library. The application software for the circulation system shall be delivered no later than 90 calendar days after delivery of the hardware and system software (early delivery will be accepted).

Installation of System. The library also should specify in this section of the RFP any general requirements of the vendor regarding installation of the automated system.

> *Example:* Unless indicated to the contrary, items of equipment shall be delivered, uncrated, checked, assembled, set in proper place, and installed ready for use and free from breakage, blemishes, or other defects.

Example: Installation shall include distribution and installation of the terminals in all specified locations.

Example: The library and vendor shall agree beforehand on the location of each piece of equipment, and detailed layouts shall be prepared.

<u>Liquidated Damages</u>. The library should protect itself as much as possible should the vendor fail to install the automated system as scheduled or if the installation is unsatisfactory. A statement outlining how such a situation will be handled should be included in this section of the RFP.

Example: From the compensation otherwise to be paid, the library may retain the sum of $200 each calendar day thereafter that the work of the vendor remains incomplete and unacceptable to the library. This sum is agreed upon as the proper measure of liquidated damages which the library will sustain each day by failure of the vendor to complete the work by the time stipulated, and this sum shall not be construed in any sense as a penalty.

<u>Guarantees/Warranties</u>. The library should require a guarantee or warranty on each piece of hardware for a specified period of time after its installation. A statement of the warranty expected should be included in this section of the RFP.

Example: Each item of hardware that is a part of the automated system shall have a vendor-provided warranty which is effective for a period of 90 calendar days after its installation. The vendor shall replace or repair any defective item free of charge to the library within this time period.

<u>Payment</u>. The library should stipulate how it expects to pay for the automated system it will be purchasing. While the number of payments to be paid and the amount of each payment can be negotiated once the best system has been chosen, this statement in this general requirements section of the RFP will at least provide a bargaining point during the later negotiations.

Example: The library plans to pay for the system in three installments: (a) approximately 50 percent of the total system cost shall be paid upon the signing of a contract or agreement with the vendor, as a down payment; (b) approximately 25 percent of the total system cost shall be paid upon successful passing of the system acceptance test; and (c) the balance shall be paid upon determination that the system meets or exceeds all requirements stated in this RFP or as agreed upon by the vendor and the library.

<u>Title to Hardware and Software</u>. The library should indicate its expectations for ownership title to the hardware and software after all payments have been made to the vendor.

Example: Upon installation, acceptance, and final payment, the library shall receive clear title to all hardware and all software not covered under a licensing agreement.

Acceptance Tests. The library may specify that the automated system it acquires pass one or more acceptance tests before payment is made to the vendor. Details of the test and conditions under which it will be conducted should be included in this section of the RFP.

Example: A full-load response time acceptance test shall be conducted on site after the vendor has installed the system and has certified in writing that the system, as specified in this RFP, is operational, after all software has been installed and tested, and after the initial bibliographic data file has been loaded.

Example: The acceptance test shall provide unequivocal evidence that the system meets response time performance requirements under a peak load condition.

Acceptance tests are discussed further in Chapter 11.

Vendor Response Requirements

The content of vendors' responses to the RFP should be specified by the library. Responses can include a vendor profile, a proposal summary, responses to the system requirements, a list of system components and their costs, environmental and physical specifications, special conditions and terms, and a vendor user list. Additionally, vendors can be asked or encouraged to submit other relevant information, such as technical manuals, brochures, photographs, and schematics, with their responses.

The Vendor Profile. The vendor can be asked to provide any facts it wishes about its organization. The library might require information about the financial stability of the company, the current number of employees, and the names and backgrounds of the staff who will be working with the library in installing and maintaining the automated system to be acquired. Copies of the firm's latest annual report, independent audit, or Dun and Bradstreet rating can be requested.

A Proposal Summary. The vendor can be asked to include a brief summary of its response. The summary can serve as an overview or introduction to the document being submitted to the library in response to the RFP.

Responses to the System Requirements. Instructions for responding to the system requirements detailed in the RFP should be given to vendors in this section.

Example: The vendor must respond to each requirement indicated on the System Requirements Response Forms provided at the end of this RFP. The forms may be removed and reproduced if desired. Either "Yes" or "No" must be used in responding to each requirement. If a vendor can demonstrate that a function or feature can be provided in some other way than that specified in the requirements, that might be acceptable; but the burden of demonstrating the fact is on the bidder.

A List of System Components and their Costs. Each vendor can be asked to submit itemized cost data in a specified format as a part of its response to the RFP.

Example: The vendor must complete each of the Cost Response Forms provided at the end of this RFP. The forms may be removed and reproduced if desired. If any item is omitted, it will be added at no extra cost to the library. Additional narrative information, materials, and documents may be submitted to support cost figures.

Environmental and Physical Specifications. The library can ask the vendor in this section to supply details for any space, air conditioning, electrical power, security, environmental impact, or other conditions which will be required to support or house the proposed hardware or software.

Special Conditions and Terms. The vendor can be asked to identify any special conditions or terms that will apply to its response or to the purchase of its automated system by the library.

A Vendor User List. The library can require that each vendor responding to the RFP submit a list of users of the proposed hardware or software. The library may wish to request the names of nearby users only or limit the list to large public library users or small academic library users, as appropriate.

Example: The vendor must list contact information for at least five users of equipment and software similar to that being bid. List college and university libraries if possible. Equipment should have been in operation for at least six months at the time of the bid opening. Information needed on each user includes the name and address of the library, the date the system was installed, and the name, title, and telephone number of the person in the library who can be contacted for information about the vendor's system.

System Requirements

The main part of the RFP will be the library's requirements for the automated system to be acquired. The system requirements should have been developed by the library in an activity preceding preparation of the RFP, discussed in Chapter 5. These requirements can be transferred into this section of the RFP with little or no change. A set of system requirements for automated library systems is illustrated in the sample RFP in Appendix D.

Vendor Response Forms

An efficient means of ensuring that vendors submit bid information in an orderly manner is to have them prepare their responses to the RFP on predesigned forms included with the document when it is mailed to vendors. Having bid information from vendors organized uniformly will assist the library in its review and evaluation of responses and selection of the best system. Forms should be included in the RFP for vendor responses to the system requirements, the list of system components and their costs, and the vendor user list.

Chapter 7
Bid Solicitation, Evaluation, and Award

Copies of the RFP must be sent to prospective bidders; responses from vendors must be validated, the best system selected, and contracts signed. It is likely that several vendors will submit bids or quotations to the library in response to the RFP for an automated system. This chapter includes various topics related to bid solicitation, evaluation, and award:

- Bid solicitation
- Decision rules for selecting the best system
- The bid evaluation team
- Bid review and evaluation
- Selection of the best system
- Contracts for the system selected
- The bid evaluation report

BID SOLICITATION

After the RFP has been developed and approved, the library or its purchasing agent must distribute copies of the document to appropriate vendors, with the purpose of soliciting bids or quotations for the automated library system. There are several methods of identifying potential respondents to whom the RFP can be sent:

1. Ask the library's automation consultant, if one is used, to suggest names of vendors of automated library systems.
2. Ask colleagues and friends for the names of vendors.
3. Visit the exhibits of vendors at professional conferences and meetings.
4. Examine the literature of library and information science for advertisements and articles about vendors of automated library systems.

5. Place advertisements or notices in library journals indicating that the library is soliciting responses to its RFP.

A combination of approaches may be necessary to compile a good mailing list for the RFP. Often, representatives of vendors of automated systems know which libraries are preparing RFPs and will ask for copies of the document when it is distributed.

Rarely is a RFP so complete and clear that potential respondents will not need additional or clarifying information. The library should insist for documentation purposes that all inquiries about the RFP or the bidding process be in writing. Some vendor representatives may wish to visit the library upon receipt of the RFP, to make presentations of their products. These requests should be welcomed and honored by the library as a supplement to—not as a substitute for—a formal response to the RFP.

DECISION RULES FOR SELECTING THE BEST SYSTEM

The automated system to be acquired by the library should be the one that most closely matches a set of decision rules established before the evaluation of responses or bids from vendors is begun. A decision rule is a criterion or policy by which to judge the automated systems being considered or a standard against which the systems are evaluated. A set of decision rules provides an objective basis from which to select one automated system over another.

Example: Choose the system that meets all or most of the set of mandatory requirements established by the library.

Example: Choose the system that meets all or most of the set of desirable but not mandatory requirements established by the library.

Example: Choose the system that will have the least installation or start-up costs.

Example: Choose the system that will, after installation, cost the least to maintain over its lifetime.

When a library acquires an automated system, it is also entering a relationship with the vendor of that system for the lifetime of the system. The library will be relying on the vendor for installation and operational guidance, training, documentation, enhancements to the system, and probably maintenance of the hardware and software supporting the system throughout its lifetime. If the vendor should become bankrupt or otherwise go out of business during the system's lifetime, the library then would have a system that might not be maintainable. Therefore, it behooves the library to evaluate the vendor of each automated system as well as the system itself. Decision rules for evaluating vendors should be established.

Example: Choose the bid of the vendor who has at least 10 of the same automated systems already installed and operating in other libraries of comparable size.

Example: Choose the vendor who has sold and installed at least three other systems to libraries during the past year.

Example: Choose the vendor who had at least one million dollars of sales during the past year (or during each of the past three years).

Example: Choose the vendor whose representatives seem most professional, straightforward, and responsive to the library's needs.

A draft set of decision rules for selecting the best system should be prepared, then circulated widely among the staff and others for their comments and suggestions. Ideas and advice received should be incorporated into a revised draft for the project steering committee to discuss and refine. The final set of decision rules should have the approval of the project manager, the project steering committee, the library director, and the library's purchasing agent before the bid evaluation process begins.

THE BID EVALUATION TEAM

A team should be established to review and evaluate bids received from vendors in response to the library's RFP and to select the best system for acquisition. The team can consist of the project manager and some or all members of the project steering committee. The project manager can serve as chair of the group. Assistance from the staff of a computing center serving the library and other resource people can be secured, particularly for the evaluation of computer hardware. If an automation consultant is used, this person can assist in the evaluation process by providing general guidance and assistance as needed during the activity, as well as reviewing the bids and the recommendation of the best system to be acquired to ascertain that the evaluation process was thorough, accurate, and complete.

A less desirable alternative to establishing a bid evaluation team is to have an automation consultant review and evaluate the bids and recommend the best system to be acquired. In this case, the project manager and the project steering committee should be briefed thoroughly by the consultant as to the evaluation process to be used and on the choice of the system recommended for acquisition. The library should have the option of either accepting or rejecting the recommendation of the consultant.

BID REVIEW AND EVALUATION

The evaluation of responses to the library's RFP will have a minimum of eight steps, including evaluation of responses to system requirements, evaluation of hardware, evaluation of initial costs, evaluation of annual maintenance costs, evaluation of vendors, system demonstrations, interviews with vendor clients, and site visits.

Evaluation of Responses to System Requirements

The first step of the bid review and evaluation process is to examine responses of vendors to the system requirements included in the RFP, with the purpose of determining which of the library's requirements the vendors feel their systems meet.

Figure 7-1. A Sample Work Chart for Vendor Responses to the Library's System Requirements.

System Requirements*	System 1	System 2	System 3	System 4
1. All software necessary to operate the Online Public Catalog (OPC) shall be supplied.	Y	Y	Y	Y
2. Future enhancements to the software will be made available to the user libraries.	Y	Y	Y	Y
3. Can access OPC through cables, modems, and dial-in arrangements.	Y	N	Y	Y
4. Can retrieve only records from the OPC at terminals.	Y	Y	N	N
5. Will accommodate files and workloads in Appendix A.	Y	Y	Y	Y

System Requirements*	System 1	System 2	System 3	System 4
6. Can differentiate between all types of bibliographic records.	Y	Y	N	Y
7. All field tags and subfield codes shall be accepted and stored.	Y	Y	N	Y
8. Can strip library-specified fields as records are loaded.	Y	Y	Y	N
9. Local data shall be preserved.	Y	Y	N	N
10. Records for titles under consideration, on order, and in process will display in OPC.	Y	Y	N	Y
11. Both full and partial bibliographic records can be accepted and stored.	Y	Y	Y	Y

*Sample—Not all requirements are shown.

A work chart (see Figure 7-1) will facilitate the collection of data during this activity. Separate charts can be constructed for mandatory and optional or desirable requirements; both mandatory and optional requirements can be intermixed in the same chart; or optional requirements can be listed at the end of the set of mandatory requirements in the same chart. The library's system requirements from the RFP are listed briefly along the left side of the chart, and the names of the systems to be evaluated are listed along the top. Each vendor's response to the system requirements in the RFP are entered in the chart. A "Yes" or "Y" is entered in the chart under the system's name and opposite a requirement, if a vendor states that its system does meet the specification, and "No" or "N" if it does not. If a requirement is not applicable to a vendor's system, "N/A" for "not applicable" should be entered. If a vendor does not respond to a requirement, the response should be considered a "No."

When the evaluation team is uncertain whether a vendor has responded correctly or adequately, requirements can be marked for later investigation during interviews with current users of the automated system and during system demonstrations and site visits. In some cases, a vendor may clarify its response to one or more of the library's requirements by appending notes or explanatory material to the bid document. This information should be read carefully to determine if the explanations are acceptable. After studying the appended material, the evaluation team should either accept or reject the vendor's response to a requirement and enter either "Y" or "N" in the work chart. Brief explanatory notes can be added as footnotes to the work chart when necessary.

Evaluation of Hardware

The second step of the bid review and evaluation process is to assess the hardware proposed by each vendor responding to the library's RFP. The evaluation team should validate whether each vendor:

1. Has bid the correct hardware items.
2. Has bid the correct number of hardware items.
3. Has bid hardware which will adequately support an automated system for the library's particular work loads, file capacities, and other needs.
4. Has bid hardware which have the characteristics and features desired by the library.

A work chart (see Figure 7-2) can be prepared to summarize the hardware proposed by each vendor. The chart will provide a checklist to ascertain that all essential pieces of hardware have been included in each bid and that the hardware has been evaluated and will provide a way to compare the hardware bid by one vendor against that of the others.

The hardware items considered essential for the automated system are listed along the left side of the chart, and the names of the systems to be evaluated are listed along the top. The amount, size, capacity, or other information describing the hardware bid by each vendor are entered in the chart under the system's name and opposite the items.

Data for the evaluation can be obtained from the response forms required as part of responses to the RFP; notes, descriptive brochures, and manuals supplied by vendors as part of their bids; interviews with current users of an automated system being bid; system demonstrations; and site visits to libraries already having the automated system installed and operational. In some cases, the evaluation team may have to contact a vendor representative for clarifying or additional information about items of hardware. Brief explanatory notes can be added as footnotes to the work chart when necessary.

Figure 7-2. A Sample Work Chart for the Hardware Bid by Vendors.

Component	System 1	System 2	System 3	System 4
Internal Storage Bid	512KB	256KB	384KB	512KB
Internal Storage Expandable To	1,024KB	512KB	768KB	1,024KB
Operator Console Type	CRT	CRT	Typewriter	CRT
Disk Storage Bid	1,350MB	640MB	960MB	2,025MB
Disk Storage Expandable To	2,700MB	1,280MB	Not Expandable	Not Expandable
Magnetic Tape Density	1600BPI	1600BPI	1600BPI	1600BPI
Magnetic Tape Speed	20 IPS	15 IPS	25 IPS	15 IPS
Line Printer Speed	300 LPM	200 CPS	200 LPM	60 CPS
Modem Speed Bid (Baud)	9600	4800	9600	1200

Evaluation of Initial Costs

The third step of bid review and evaluation is to assess the initial costs of each system bid by vendors in response to the library's RFP. The evaluation team should validate, for each system bid, the total cost to the library for:

1. All hardware items.
2. All software items.
3. Staff training.
4. System documentation.
5. Delivery and installation.
6. Other miscellaneous costs.

A work chart (see Figure 7-3) can be prepared to collect and record the initial costs for each system being considered. The cost elements are listed along the left side of the chart, and the names of the systems to be evaluated are listed along the top. The price quoted for each element by a vendor in its response to the library's RFP is entered in the chart under the system's name and opposite the cost element. Care should be taken that vendors have bid all items of equipment and the correct quantities specified in the RFP. In some cases, the evaluation team may have to contact a vendor representative for clarifying or additional information about prices in a bid response. If necessary, explanatory footnotes can be added to the work chart. All initial costs for each system should be included at the bottom of its column.

Figure 7-3. A Sample Work Chart for the Initial Costs of Automated Systems Bid.

Cost Element	System 1	System 2	System 3	System 4
Hardware	$498,127	$455,125	$420,580	$487,123
Software	$100,000	$95,000	$ 50,000	$ 75,000
Staff Training	*	$ 10,000	*	$ 5,000
Documentation	$ 1,000	*	*	*
Delivery and Installation	$ 5,480	$ 1,500	$ 2,940	$ 4,000
Other	$ 0	$ 500	$ 0	$ 1,000
Totals	$604,607	$562,125	$473,520	$572,123

*Included in software or hardware costs.

Evaluation of Annual Maintenance Costs

The fourth step of bid review and evaluation is to assess the annual maintenance costs during the lifetime of each system bid by vendors in response to the library's RFP. The team should validate, for each system bid, the total cost to the library for:

1. Remedial hardware maintenance for its lifespan.
2. Preventive hardware maintenance for its lifespan.
3. Software maintenance for its lifespan.

A work chart (see Figure 7-4) can be used to collect and record the maintenance costs for each automated system bid by vendors. Separate charts can be made for hardware and software maintenance, or both can be combined into the same chart. Remedial and preventive hardware maintenance often are not quoted separately. The

individual years of the lifespan considered reasonable for an automated system are listed along the left side of the chart. The lifespan
of a system usually is considered to be 5, 7, or 10 years, but any
number can be selected as long as it is the same for all systems. A
minimum lifespan would seem to be five years. The names of the
systems being evaluated are listed along the top of the chart. The
price quoted by a vendor for annual maintenance is entered in the
chart under the system's name and opposite the year of maintenance.

**Figure 7-4. A Sample Work Chart for the Annual Maintenance
Costs of Automated Systems Bid.**

Cost Element	System 1	System 2	System 3	System 4
Hardware Maintenance				
Year 1	$59,775	$59,166	$49,469	$48,712
Year 2	$64,557	$63,899	$53,427	$52,609
Year 3	$69,722	$69,011	$57,701	$56,818
Year 4	$75,299	$74,532	$62,317	$61,363
Year 5	$81,323	$80,495	$67,302	$66,272
Total Hardware Maintenance	$350,676	$347,103	$290,216	$285,774
Software Maintenance				
Year 1	$10,000	$4,000	$8,000	$3,500
Year 2	$10,800	$4,320	$8,640	$3,780
Year 3	$11,664	$4,666	$9,331	$4,082
Year 4	$12,597	$5,039	$10,078	$4,409
Year 5	$13,605	$5,442	$10,884	$4,762
Total Software Maintenance	$58,666	$23,467	$46,933	$20,533
Total Hardware and Software Maintenance	$409,342	$370,570	$337, 149	$306,307

All inflation rates estimated to be 8% a year.

The maintenance costs for the first year after installation of a
system should be quoted by each vendor in its response to the
library's RFP. If equipment is under warranty for a period of time
(for example, 30, 60, or 90 days after installation), the maintenance
costs to the library for the first year should be adjusted accordingly.

Example: A vendor bids hardware maintenance costs of $24,000
per year or $2,000 per month for its system. All equipment is
under warranty for 90 days after installation. Therefore, the cost to

the library for maintenance of the system for the first year would be $18,000 (nine months to pay after the warranty expires times $2,000 per month).

The maintenance costs for each succeeding year of a system's lifespan should be computed next and entered in the work chart. If a vendor specifies a guaranteed maximum rate increase for a number of years, the next year's maintenance costs can be computed by multiplying the previous year's total maintenance cost by the cost rate increase.

Example: A vendor bids maintenance costs of $24,000 per year for its system, with a guarantee that this cost will rise no more than 10 percent a year for the next five years.

The maintenance costs for the five years then would be:

Year 1: $24,000
Year 2: $26,400 ($24,000 plus 10 percent)
Year 3: $29,040 ($26,400 plus 10 percent)
Year 4: $31,944 ($29,040 plus 10 percent)
Year 5: $35,138 ($31,944 plus 10 percent)

If vendors do not specify a guaranteed maximum rate increase for the years of a system's lifespan, the annual rate of inflation can be estimated and included in the cost of each year's maintenance after the first year. The same rate should be used for each alternative system being considered to avoid biasing some systems. If some vendors have a guaranteed maximum rate increase and others do not, the guaranteed rate increase can be used for those systems having it, and a standard inflation rate can be used for the remaining systems.

Footnotes can be added to the work chart if necessary. The maintenance costs for the lifespan of each system should be included at the bottom of its column.

Evaluation of Vendors

The fourth step of bid review and evaluation is to evaluate the vendors responding to the library's RFP. Again, a work chart (see Figure 7-5) will facilitate the collection and recording of the results of the vendor evaluation. The criteria or decision rules to be used are listed along the left side of the chart, and the names of the vendors being evaluated are listed along the top. The results of the evaluation team's assessment of each vendor is entered in the chart under the vendor's name and opposite the criterion or decision rule. Data for the evaluation can be obtained from vendors' responses to the RFP and descriptive brochures and manuals appended to bids. The evaluation team may have to contact vendor representatives or other clients of vendors for some information.

While the evaluation team may be able to assess easily the number of vendor installations and sales, other attributes of a vendor will be more difficult to judge. For example, a well-informed, pleasant, and professional vendor representative is not necessarily indicative of the characteristics of the other staff of the vendor with whom the library will have to work later during system installation and operation. The future relationship with the vendor of the automated system the library chooses can only be guessed. However, the relationship of a vendor with its other library clients, discussed further in this chapter, can be assessed during interviews with those staff and the results used in this step.

Figure 7-5. A Sample Work Chart for Vendor Evaluation.

Criteria	System 1	System 2	System 3	System 4
Has at least 10 systems installed.	Y	Y	N	Y
Has sold at least three systems in last year.	Y	N	Y	Y
Had at least $1 million in sales last year.	Y	N	Y	Y

System Demonstrations

The evaluation team should not rely soley upon vendors' written responses to the library's RFP when selecting the best system for acquisition. Some vendors may misinterpret requirements of the library and respond incorrectly or may claim that their systems will meet the library's requirements when in actuality they cannot. As a fifth step of the bid review and evaluation, the library should request demonstrations of some or all the systems to prove that they can in fact perform as the vendors claim and have the features wanted by the library.

The team can either seek demonstrations of a select few of the total number of systems bid or of all the systems bid. Further evaluation of some systems bid may be considered pointless because it is clear they cannot or will not be chosen for one reason or another. System demonstrations can be time consuming and expensive for both the library and others involved, and the team may not want to continue evaluating those systems it probably will not consider further. If the team does wish to eliminate some systems from further consideration, it should rank the systems according to the process of selecting the best system discussed further in this chapter. Those systems at the top of the ranking can be evaluated further. A short list of three or four systems would be acceptable for demonstrations. Those systems eliminated during this step can, of course, be reconsidered later should the need arise. If the evaluation team does not wish to eliminate any system from being considered further at this time, it can continue the evaluation process on all bids received, rather than only on those at the top of the rankings. An argument for this decision would be that factors may emerge during system demonstrations, site visits, or interviews with staff of other libraries that might make a system ranked low initially a more attractive choice than might otherwise have been expected.

System demonstrations should be conducted in the library that is to be automated or, preferably, in another library of similar size currently using the system. Demonstrations of this nature should not be held in a vendor's plant, office, or exhibit booth at a conference. The hardware and software demonstrated should be the same as that already installed in other libraries and the same as that bid in the vendor's response to the library's RFP and not experimental or prototype. The databases demonstrated should be of a size and nature comparable to that which the evaluating library will have.

The evaluation team should have copies of the RFP and the vendors' responses to the library's system requirements in hand during the demonstrations. An efficient method of conducting the demonstration is to work through each of the library's requirements, one after the other, and have the vendor representative show that his or her system can perform as bid or that the features bid do exist. If several vendor representatives are present, the requirements can be divided among the members of the evaluation team for simultaneous demonstrations to speed up the process. An alternative to this time-consuming process might be to have demonstrations of only those functions or features that were in question during earlier evaluations.

Differences which are detected between the responses made by the vendors to the system requirements in the RFP and the demonstrations should be noted for later consideration during the final selection of the best system.

Interviews with Vendor Clients

The evaluation team, as a seventh step of the bid review and evaluation process, can conduct telephone interviews of staff at sites where the same automated systems being offered to the library have already been installed. The purpose of this step is to verify that other customers having the automated system being offered to the library are pleased with the product and the services of the vendor and to clarify any points noted during the other steps of the evaluation. The team can either interview staff in a select few of the total number of systems bid or conduct interviews for all the systems bid. The process of eliminating some systems was discussed in the previous section.

The names of contact persons in other libraries with the operational systems should have been included in each vendor's response to the RFP. Some questions the team should ask the contact person in a library might include:

1. Is the automated system operating as contracted or as promised by the vendor?
2. Does the system currently have the features contracted for or promised by the vendor?
3. What do you like best and what do you like least about the system?
4. What problems did you have during system installation?
5. What problems do you have when operating the system?
6. How well does the vendor respond to hardware and software maintenance problems?
7. Is the library satisfied with the system and the services of the vendor?
8. Would the library purchase the same system again from the vendor, knowing what it does now about the system?

Also, if the evaluation team has questions about a vendor's ability to meet specific system requirements, the contact person should be asked to comment on these points. All information gathered during the interviews should be noted for later consideration during the final selection of the best system.

Site Visits

Visits by one or more members of the evaluation team to libraries with vendors' systems already installed and operational can be the eighth and last step of the bid review and evaluation process. No vendor representatives should be present during these visits to guarantee frank interchanges of information about the system being considered. Site visits can provide first-hand information about the systems and can enable the evaluation team to see them in operation and talk to people who have installed and now operate them.

Each trip should be well planned. The libraries to be visited should be contacted in advance for permission for the evaluation team to visit. The date and time of the visit, the number of people who will be included in the visit, and the nature of the information to be obtained should be proposed and agreed to by the host library. Courtesy would dictate that the stay be as short as possible. An agenda for a site visit might include interviews with the host library's key staff who were instrumental in installing the system and who now operate it and a brief demonstration of the system being considered. The questions the evaluation team should ask might be similar to those asked during telephone interviews with vendor clients (discussed in the previous section).

SELECTION OF THE BEST SYSTEM

Once evaluations of all systems for which bids were received have been made, the results can be analyzed and summarized and the best system selected, using the decision rules for selecting the best system established at the beginning of this activity.

The results of all evaluations completed in this activity can be transferred into a chart (see Figure 7-6) to facilitate and document the decision-making process used to select the best system. Headings such as mandatory and optional requirements met and unmet, initial costs, annual hardware and software maintenance costs, number of systems operational and annual sales of the vendor, are placed along the left side of the chart. These headings should correspond to the decision rules established for selecting the best system. The names of the systems evaluated are listed at the top of the chart. Summary information from the work charts (see Figures 7-1 through 7-5) prepared during the evaluation process should be transferred to the decision chart.

Figure 7-6. A Sample Work Chart Summarizing the Evaluation Process for All Automated Systems Bid.

Element	System 1	System 2	System 3	System 4
Meets all mandatory requirements	Y	Y	N	N
Meets all option requirements.	N	N	N	N
Total initial costs	$604,607	$562,125	$473,520	$572,123
Maintenance costs for five years.	$409,342	$370,570	$337,149	$306,307
Total initial costs and maintenance for five years.	$1,013,949	$932,695	$810,669	$878,430
Number of systems operational.	55	20	5	43

A study of the evaluation charts and results of system demonstrations, interviews with staff in other libraries, and site visits should indicate which automated system the library should acquire. The system chosen should be the one that best matches all selection criteria established in the decision rules.

SYSTEM CONTRACTS

After responses to the RFP have been reviewed and evaluated and the best automated system selected, the library must negotiate, as a minimum, a purchase contract and a maintenance contract with the successful bidder.

The Purchase Contract

A contract for purchase of the automated system by the library must be prepared, negotiated, and signed. The purpose of this contract is to state the obligations and rights of both the supplier of the system and the library. It is in the best interests of the library not to sign the standard contract offered by the vendor without careful review and study, because this contract will most likely be overly biased toward the vendor. The library should consider the standard contract of the vendor as a document from which changes are to be negotiated until the needs of the library, as well as those of the vendor, are reflected. Modifications to the standard contract can be made by attaching additional clauses called riders which will change wording in the body of the document. Minor changes can be made by striking words or sentences. The library might consider offering a standard contract to the vendor, rather than the reverse, and let the vendor negotiate with the library for changes. In this case, a lawyer knowledgeable in the area of computers should be retained to draft the contract. Regardless of the method of contract preparation and negotiation, it will be in the best interests of the library to have an attorney review the purchase contract for the library before it is signed.

The purchase contract might include a large number of topics, even though some items may have already been included in the RFP as a means for prospective bidders to understand some of the library's contractual requirements.

The Parties to the Contract. A simple statement identifying the vendor and the library as the responsible parties in the acquisition of the automated system is necessary for the purchase contract.

Example: This agreement is made this 21st day of June, 198x, by and between Anyvendor Computers, Inc., of the first part, and Anytown Library, of the second part.

The List and Cost of Items Supplied. A complete and detailed list of all hardware items, software, and other services to be provided by the vendor should be included in the purchase contract.

Where Items Are to be Installed. The locations in the library where items of hardware are to be installed should be detailed as a part of the purchase contract.

Movement of Equipment. The vendor might want the purchase contract to contain a statement requiring the library to notify him when equipment is to be moved from one location to another.

> *Example:* The library shall give the vendor at least 30 days written notice of its desire to move equipment covered by this agreement, with the exception of terminals. Any relocation of such equipment shall be subject to prior approval by the vendor.

Attachment of Foreign Devices. The library will want a clause in the contract stating that devices not supplied by the vendor can be attached to the system. The vendor may agree to this but might want his permission obtained before a device is attached.

> *Example:* The library shall not attach or cause to be attached to the equipment any additional equipment if the vendor can establish to the satisfaction of the library that the system shall be impaired by such additional equipment.

System Delivery and Installation. A statement as to when hardware and software will be delivered and installed should be a part of the purchase contract.

> *Example:* All hardware and software items shall be delivered and installed within 90 days of the signing of this contract.

> *Example:* Items of equipment shall be delivered, uncrated, checked, assembled, set in proper place, and installed ready for use and free from breakage, blemishes, or other defects.

> *Example:* Installation shall include distribution and installation of the terminals in locations agreed on beforehand. Detailed layouts shall be provided to the vendor by the library.

Modification of Hardware and Software. A statement of the library's right, if any, to modify items of hardware and software should be included in the contract. Also, a clear description of future modifications and enhancements to hardware and software by the vendor should be made.

> *Example:* No modifications of any hardware or software supplied by the vendor can be made without the written permission of the vendor.

> *Example:* Future enhancements to the system and application software shall be made available to the library as long as it uses the system.

Example: All changes required by engineering field change orders, including safety changes determined necessary, shall be promptly installed on the equipment by the vendor at no cost to the library.

Ownership of the Equipment. The library may want a statement in the contract identifying itself as owner of the equipment after the final payment is made to the vendor.

Example: Upon installation, acceptance, and final payment, the library shall receive clear title to all hardware and software not covered under a licensing agreement.

Insurance Coverage. The type and amount of insurance required for the system until final payment has been made to the vendor may be included in the purchase contract.

Example: Liability for insurance for the automated system, until and unless clear title is delivered to the library, remains with Anyvendor Computers, Inc.

The RFP As Part of the Contract.The library should insist that a statement be included in the document indicating that the RFP and the vendor's responses to the RFP are a part of the purchase contract.

Example: The terms and requirements contained in the RFP for this system and the vendor's response to the document are considered to be a part of this purchase contract between the library and the vendor.

Guarantees and Warranties. The extent of guarantees and warranties on the hardware offered by the vendor should be defined in the purchase contract.

Example: All hardware items shall be guaranteed to be free of all defects for a period of 90 calendar days after installation. Anyvendor Computers, Inc., shall repair any defects identified during this time at no cost to the library.

Acceptance Tests. The terms of acceptance of the hardware and software by the library should be included as a part of the purchase contract. Acceptance tests are discussed in Chapter 11.

Calendar of System Installation. A detailed calendar or schedule of times for delivery and installation of all hardware and software should be included in the contract.

Training Schedule. A schedule describing the type and amount of training of library staff by the vendor should be included in the contract. A calendar of times and durations for the training should also be included.

Performance Bond. The amount of any performance bond and how it will be met by the vendor should be defined in the purchase contract.

Example: A performance bond of 10 percent of the total contract, in a form acceptable to the library, will be required for the full term of the purchase order.

Payment Schedule. A detailed description of the method of financing the hardware, software, and other items and a schedule of the payments, and upon what conditions the payments will be made, should be included in the purchase contract.

Example: The library will pay for the system in four payments: (1) as a down payment, 40 percent of the total system cost upon the signing of this agreement by Anyvendor Computers, Inc., and the library; (2) 20 percent upon passing of the system reliability test; (3) 20 percent upon passing the functional requirements test; and (4) 20 percent upon passing the full-load response time test.

Penalty Clauses. If desired, a penalty clause for nondelivery or late delivery or installation of contracted items can be made a part of the purchase contract.

Example: From the compensation otherwise to be paid to Anyvendor Computer, Inc., the library may retain the sum of $200 each calendar day thereafter that work of the vendor remains incomplete and unacceptable to the library. This sum is agreed upon as the proper measure of liquidated damages that the library will sustain each day by failure of the vendor to complete the work within the time stipulated, and this sum shall not be construed in any sense as a penalty.

The Maintenance Contract

A contract for the maintenance of the system by the vendor or another party must be prepared or negotiated and signed. The maintenance contract should include as a minimum a list of the equipment and software covered, the location of the equipment, periods of maintenance, equipment corrective maintenance, equipment preventive maintenance, spare parts, software maintenance, the term of maintenance, and charges for services.

A List of the Equipment and Software Covered. The same complete and detailed list of all hardware and software items that was a part of the purchase contract should be included in the maintenance contract. The list can be an attachment to the maintenance contract.

The Location of the Equipment. The location where equipment will be placed in the library and in other places should be identified so that the vendor will know where maintenance is to be performed. These locations also can be in a list attached to the contract.

Period of Maintenance. The period of time during the day and the days of the week for which hardware and software will be covered for maintenance service should be explained.

Example: The principal period of maintenance for hardware shall be 8:30 a.m. through 4:30 p.m., Mondays through Fridays, excluding library and vendor holidays. The principal period for software maintenance shall be 8:00 a.m. until 12:00 midnight, Mondays through Sundays, excluding library and vendor holidays.

A list of library and vendor holidays should be attached to the contract.

Equipment Corrective Maintenance. The corrective maintenance to be provided for hardware should be described. Corrective maintenance means the provision of services on an on-call, unscheduled basis to correct malfunctions in the equipment and to restore the equipment to good operating condition.

Equipment Preventive Maintenance. The preventive maintenance to be provided for hardware should also be described. Preventive maintenance means the inspection, cleaning, adjustment, and repair of equipment; replacement of defective parts; and making engineering change orders to prevent equipment failures. The schedule for preventive maintenance can be specified.

Example: Preventive maintenance shall be performed on a schedule mutually agreed upon by the library and the vendor. This maintenance shall be performed at intervals not to exceed 60 days.

Spare Parts. A requirement that the vendor have spare parts available locally to repair the library's hardware can be a part of the maintenance contract.

Example: The office that shall provide maintenance for the equipment shall at all times be fully equipped with system spare parts throughout the time the library owns or controls the equipment.

Example: The vendor shall have sufficient spare parts available locally to repair 90 percent of all corrective maintenance problems with the equipment.

Software Maintenance. Corrective maintenance for the software should be described in the maintenance contract.

Example: Corrective maintenance to correct malfunctions in the software and to restore it to good operating condition shall be provided by the vendor on an on-call, unscheduled basis.

The Term of the Contract. The time when the maintenance contract begins and ends should be included in the document.

Example: The term of this agreement shall be for a period of one year, from September 1, 198x, through August 31, 198x.

Charges for Services. The cost to the library for the maintenance services covered by the contract should be included in the document. The schedule of payments by the library to the vendor for maintenance services also should be included.

THE BID EVALUATION REPORT

After the systems have been evaluated and compared and the best selected, a request for approval to acquire and install the recommended automated system must be presented to the library director, city manager, mayor, president, board, council, or other governing or funding authorities. A report documenting the bid evaluation process and the recommendation for a bid award should be prepared. The report might include as a minimum:

1. A description of the evaluation method used.
2. The decision rules established for selecting the best system.
3. A list of the systems evaluated, with a brief description of each.
4. The work charts resulting from the comparison of bid responses to the system requirements established by the library and the evaluations of hardware, initial costs, annual maintenance costs, and vendors.
5. The decision chart upon which the selection of the best system was based.
6. The evaluation team's recommendation for the best system to be acquired by the library and the reasons for the recommendation.

Narrative introductions to each item can be included. Other pertinent information can be included in the text or in appendices to the report. It must be remembered that those who will be giving the final approval of the decision will be more interested in brevity and clarity than in length or thickness of the report.

Part IV
System Installation and Operation

Chapter 8
Site Preparation

Site preparation is a project activity that must be completed before a new automated library system can be installed and operated. The amount of work to be accomplished will depend upon the size, nature, and complexity of the automated system to be implemented and can be as simple as installing cables and electrical outlets or as complex as renovating, refurbishing, or constructing complete rooms. This chapter addresses some of the work involved in site preparation for an automated system. Specifically, it includes:

- The in-house computer room
- Online links to remote sites
- Terminal work stations
- Other system space

THE IN-HOUSE COMPUTER ROOM

While microcomputers can be operated in a normal room environment, most minicomputers and all mainframe computers require quarters where temperature, humidity, dust, and security can be carefully maintained and controlled, otherwise malfunctions of the equipment can result. This section includes a discussion of the design and construction of the special room required for an in-house computer system.

Room Specifications

A first step in the design and construction of a computer room is the identification and definition of specifications for the quarters. Environmental requirements for the computer system should be supplied by the vendor of the automated system chosen by the library. If necessary, the library can contact the manufacturer of the hardware for detailed installation specifications. Of concern are specifications for electrical power, air conditioning and air flow, humidity, safety and fire protection, room monitoring, flooring, ceiling and walls, doors and windows, lighting, and storage facilities.

Electrical Power. Electrical power requirements for the computer room should be carefully specified. The architect, contractor, or other person who will prepare the floor layout and construction drawings will require this information during design of the room.

The AC power specifications for amps, volts, phases, and wattage should be identified for each piece of hardware to be installed in the computer room. The type of socket or receptacle required by each item and any restrictions on the length of the power cord should also be determined. Sample electrical specifications for typical hardware items in a computer room are shown in Figure 8-1. Many of the pieces of equipment may require separate circuits for proper operation and protection of the system. In addition, the circuitry should be separate from other power uses outside the computer room, and the circuits for the computer equipment should be independent of those for the air conditioning and lights. Circuit breakers should be provided to protect the equipment from voltage overloads. The wire size from the power distribution panel should be of sufficient size to meet code requirements and also to avoid excessive line drop.

Figure 8-1. Sample Electrical Specifications for Typical Hardware Items in a Computer Room.

Item	AC Socket	Voltage/Current
Central Processing Unit	208V, 20 Amps, (2 lines of 115V), Hubbell 2410 Socket	2 Phase, Neutral and Separate Ground Wire. 20 Amps (i.e., 2 x 10 Amps).
Disk Drives	Hubbell 2320 Socket	208V/6.7 Amps
Line Printer	115V, 15 Amps, Regular 115V Receptacle	115V/2 Amps
Control Console	115V, Regular Receptacle	115V/1 Amp
CRT Terminals	115V, Regular Receptacle	115V/1 Amp
Modems	115V, Regular Receptacles	115V/1 Amp

Power and receptacles that are expected to be required for future equipment should also be specified and installed in the room. For example, sufficient energy and receptacles for twice the number of disk drives to be installed initially can be included in the plans for the room. It will be less expensive to have receptacles installed during the initial construction of the room than later. A number of other general receptacles should be installed around the computer room walls for test equipment, a vacuum cleaner, and other auxiliary needs.

Since computers are very susceptible to various power fluctuations such as surges and brownouts, data may be lost and equipment may be damaged unless a continuous and even flow of energy is supplied to the system. For this reason, the library may wish to have a power control unit installed in the computer room. Such a device acts like a buffer between power entering the room and the equipment by smoothing out surges, brownouts, and interruptions in the energy flow before power reaches the computer. If the library has frequent power interruptions, a standby power generator, which will automatically begin operation the instant a power loss is sensed, should be purchased for the computer room. This generator could also be invaluable during extended power blackouts and emergencies.

Air Conditioning and Air Flow. Since one of the more troublesome problems with an in-house computer system can be temperature control, sufficient cooling power and air flow must be specified by the designers of the computer room. The tolerable temperature range for, and the heat generated by, each piece of hardware to be installed in the computer room should be identified. The same should be estimated for all equipment planned for future installation in the room. This information should be supplied by the vendor of the automated system or the manufacturer of the equipment.

Ideally, the ambient temperature in the computer room should be held constant in a 70 to 72 degree Fahrenheit range. Lower temperatures do not affect the operation of the system as do higher temperatures. Excessive heat can lead to malfunctions of the hardware and shorten its lifetime or permanently damage the computer system. The heat generated by each piece of equipment should be specified as the number of British Thermal Units (BTUs) of heat output per hour (see Figure 8-2). The aggregate of the heat output for all pieces of equipment, present and future, will guide the architect or construction designer in determining the amount of air conditioning required to handle the heat load. Air flow around pieces of hardware also is important, because heat builds up around the equipment and must be dispersed as rapidly and evenly as possible. If possible, the air in the room should be filtered to remove dust particles. Dust adversely affects the magnetic recording media used by the system.

The air conditioning system for the room should be totally independent of that for other parts of the library in order to provide better control over the temperature in the room and to allow the air conditioning for other parts of the building to be shut down or cycled during certain parts of the day or night. As a minimum, the computer room air conditioner should have its own compressor.

Figure 8-2. Sample British Thermal Units (BTUs) of Heat Output per Hour by Typical Hardware Items in a Computer Room.

Item	BTUs Per Hour
Central Processing Unit	4,000
Control Console	350
Disk Drive (each)	4,760
Line Printer	520
CRT Terminal	350
Modems	Negligible

Because it is usually recommended that a computer system run 24 hours a day, the air conditioning system must also run around the clock, seven days a week, without interruption. While the cooling system installed must be as reliable as possible, it must be expected that it will occasionally fail or require maintenance and therefore be unavailable to cool the room. For this reason, the library may wish to consider installing a secondary or auxiliary air conditioning system which will automatically begin operation when the main unit becomes inoperable.

Humidity. Relative humidity in the in-house computer room should be specified to remain constant within a range of 35 to 60 percent noncondensing. Excessive humidity can cause corrosion of the mechanical parts of most computer hardware. Conversely, when the humidity drops below 35 or 40 percent, static electricity tends to build up around disk drives, tape drives, and other moving parts of the system. Either high or low humidity can change the operating characteristics of the system's magnetic disks and tapes, potentially causing misreads of stored data. Maintenance of a proper humidity level and the use of antistatic mats can eliminate these problems.

Safety and Fire Protection. Adherence to local safety and fire codes should be specified for materials used in the computer room. All materials such as paint, tile, carpeting, and fabrics to be used should be specified as flame or fire retardant. Smoke detectors, with both audible and visual alarms wired into a central fire alarm panel, should be required. Several portable fire extinguishers should be specified for wall hangers in the room. These extinguishers should be of the carbon dioxide or dry chemical type for fires in live electrical equipment (Class C fires).

Room Monitoring. Since the computer system will operate 24 hours a day, seven days a week, a means of monitoring the environmental conditions within the computer room should be specified. In addition to the smoke detectors discussed above, devices are available to sense temperature and humidity changes in the room. When the temperature or humidity reaches critical levels, alarms are activated to summon someone to take corrective action. Such a device can be wired into a central alarm panel in another part of the library or in a fire or police center. Some devices will automatically shut off electrical power to the computer system when the temperature in the room reaches a predefined level. It is possible to purchase a battery pack for the computer so that an orderly process of shutting down the system safely without loss of data can proceed when the power is removed after a heat build-up is detected. Still another device can automatically dial one or more telephone numbers and transmit a recorded message to library or maintenance staff when environmental problems are sensed in the computer room.

Flooring. Specifications for flooring in the computer room should be prepared. There are two basic types of flooring for a computer room. In most circumstances, an existing subfloor will be adequate for the room, but a qualified engineer should check its condition before heavy computer equipment is installed, particularly if the subfloor is not prestressed or reinforced concrete.

The second type of flooring is a raised floor made of squares of prestressed building tiles laid on a frame. The raised floor redistributes the weight of the hardware on the subfloor, conceals the numerous unsightly and hazardous power and data cables necessary to connect the pieces of equipment, and allows air conditioning ducts to be installed at floor level for better distribution of air flow around the equipment. However, the raised floor is expensive to install. In most libraries which will have only a small computer with limited peripheral equipment, a raised floor will not be required and the existing flooring should suffice. Power cords and cables can be placed behind equipment where people will not ordinarily be walking, and cable bridges can be installed to protect the wires and maintain a neat appearance in the room. Power poles that hang from the ceiling can also be used to conceal cabling.

Vinyl or similar tile floor covering is recommended for the computer room to eliminate or minimize the build up of static electricity, but carpeting with a static electricity level below 2,000 static volts is acceptable. Antistatic mats can be placed in front of hardware such as the magnetic disk and tape drives and the CPU, which will be most affected by static electricity. The floor, whether tile or carpeting, must be vacuumed—not swept—regularly to eliminate dust.

Ceiling and Walls. There are no special requirements for constructing or remodelling walls, partitions, and ceilings for a computer room, except that local building codes should be followed. Sound absorption and temperature retention insulation should be used as liberally as possible.

Doors and Windows. If possible, there should be no windows in the computer room. External windows contribute to heat loss or temperature buildups from sunlight entering the room. Interior windows also should be avoided because of the loss of wall space inside the room. The door should be well insulated for air tightness. Double doors should be specified, with no center post, so that bulky equipment can be moved in and out without difficulty. The door lock can be a conventional type or a push-button security lock.

Lighting. Normal room lighting is adequate for a computer room, although light fixtures that generate a lot of heat should be avoided since they will only add to the heat load that the air conditioning will have to handle. The lighting handbook of the Illumination Engineering Society (IES) can be consulted for proper levels of lighting for various tasks within the room.

Storage Facilities. Adequate storage facilities in a computer room are essential for spare and backup disk packs, magnetic tapes, paper and forms, printer ribbons, cleaning supplies, spare equipment and parts, and other supplies and equipment essential to the maintenance and operation of the computer system. A small room adjoining the computer room is ideal for such storage, but shelves or storage cabinets along the computer room walls are also adequate. If magnetic materials are to be stored, the temperature and humidity of the storage area should be maintained at a level similar to that for the computer. Magnetic materials should also be protected from dust and stray magnetic fields. Wood or other nonmagnetizable material should be used for shelves for storage of such materials when possible.

Site Selection

Once specifications for the in-house computer room have been identified and defined, a site for the room must be selected. The site selected in an existing building will depend upon the available space or upon how other staff or functions can be moved to make space for the computer. Within those constraints, some general considerations for selecting a site within the library for a computer room include the following.

1. The room should be readily accessible to staff who must operate and monitor the machines.
2. The room should be in an area of the library where access by unauthorized persons can be controlled by locked doors or staff on duty.

3. The room should be convenient and adequate for delivery of bulky equipment and supplies.
4. The floor should be able to withstand the weight of the computer equipment.
5. The room should be located near an outside wall to minimize the distance between the air conditioning unit in the room and its compressor, which must be located outside the building.

Space Layout

Good layout of floor space in the computer room is critical for the efficient and effective operation and maintenance of the computer system supporting the automated library system. Some general considerations for organizing and arranging hardware and furniture in the room include the following:

1. Specifications of the vendor or manufacturer for placement and spacing of equipment should be followed.
2. The arrangement should provide for efficient use of the space.
3. Sufficient space should remain around equipment for ease of operation and maintenance.
4. The layout should allow for future expansion or modification as new hardware is installed or as conditions change.
5. Recognized safety specifications for entrances and exits and access to them should be followed.

The boundaries of the space for the computer room can be drawn on grid paper or on blank paper, using a scale of one-tenth, one-fourth, or other reasonable length to one foot of floor space. The location of all doors, windows, and columns, if any, should be precisely indicated. Equipment and furniture can be drawn to scale on the chart in the positions where they are to be located, or model cutouts of each piece of hardware and furniture can be prepared to scale and positioned on the chart until a proper and pleasing arrangement meeting all requirements for the room have been met. Once the best arrangement for hardware and furniture has been determined, the cutouts can be glued to the chart. Later modifications to the layout may be necessary as construction specifications are prepared. Layout for a typical computer room is shown in Figure 8-3.

Room Construction

After specifications and engineering drawings have been prepared, the room can be constructed. How this will be accomplished depends upon the library's capabilities and the rules and regulations

Figure 8-3. Layout for a Typical Computer Room.

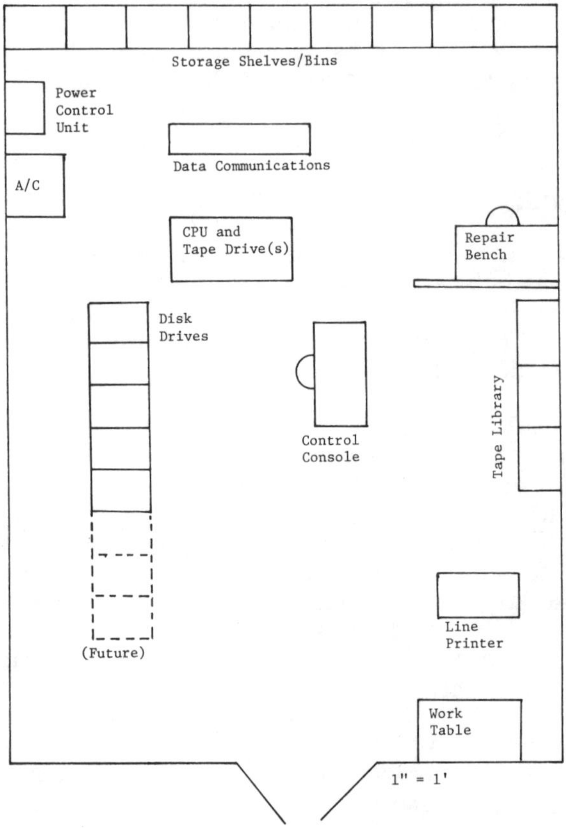

Storage Shelves/Bins

Power Control Unit

Data Communications

A/C

CPU and Tape Drive(s)

Repair Bench

Disk Drives

Control Console

Tape Library

Line Printer

(Future)

Work Table

1" = 1'

governing its powers. Some libraries can initiate such work by simply forwarding a construction request along with the required layout, specifications, and drawings to the appropriate department within the parent organization or institution, while others must go through the process of soliciting, receiving, and evaluating bids for construction before awarding a contract for the work. Some libraries can have some site preparation completed by staff of its parent organization, while other work must be contracted out.

Once site preparation has been initiated, the work should be monitored to ensure adherence to the specifications and timetables established. The project manager should inspect the site at regular and frequent intervals and be available at all times to answer questions from those who are performing the work. After the site has been prepared, the work must be accepted and approved before payment is made and before installation of any hardware and furniture can begin. The work should be checked carefully against the layout chart and the site preparation specifications. Oversights or work improperly performed should be corrected before approval of the site is given.

ONLINE LINKS TO REMOTE SITES

Terminals, printers, and other input-output equipment online to the computer system must be linked to the CPU for proper operation. There are several ways this can be accomplished.

Short Distances

Devices within several hundred feet of the computer room can be connected directly to the CPU by cable. One end of the cable is connected to a port on the computer system and the other end to a connector block on the back of the terminal or other input-output device (see Figure 8-4). Often, other devices such as a printer and even other CRT terminals can be chained to the first, using only the one cable connected to the CPU.

This direct method of attaching terminals to the computer is commonly used when the remote devices are in the same building as the computer room. It must be remembered, however, that the path the cable must take from the CPU to the remote site may not be the most direct or shortest route. The cable may have to be installed inside columns, walls, ceilings, and other conduits in a circuitous route. The cable should be unspliced and fire resistant and should not be laid near electric motors, heat ducts, or other devices that might cause it damage or otherwise interfere with data transmission.

The vendor of the automated system should supply the library with specifictions for the cable type to be used and should provide assistance and instructions for installing and connecting the links. For connection into a Local Area Network (LAN), specifications, installation instructions, and assistance should be sought from the manager of the network.

Medium Distances

While input-output devices can be connected directly to the CPU by cable for short distances, the digital signals sent further than several hundred feet can become so distorted that errors in data transmission can occur. For distances over several hundred feet but under 50 miles, a limited distance modem or line driver can provide an inexpensive method of connecting remote terminals to the computer system. The effective distance will depend upon the modem and the baud rate used for transmission of the data.

Figure 8-4. Typical Connections of Peripheral Devices to a Central Processing Unit.

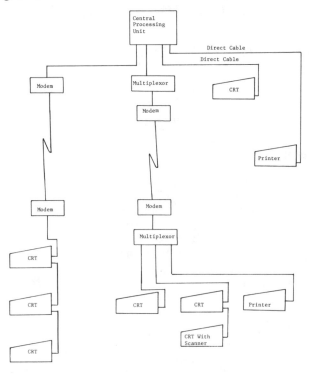

A cable is connected from a port on the computer system to a connector block on the back of the modem. A second connection is made from the modem to a transmission cable or leased line that runs between the computer room and the remote site (see Figure 8-4). A compatible modem is connected between the transmission cable and the input-output device. As with the direct connect method, other devices such as a printer and other CRT terminals can be chained to the first, using only the one link to the computer. The vendor of the automated library system should supply the library with specifications for the limited distance modems, cables, and /or telephone lines that can be used and provide instructions and assistance for installing and connecting the link.

Long Distances

When the distance between the computer and a remote terminal is great, standard modems and other data communications equipment will be required.

A simple data communications system requires a cable from the CPU to a modem, which is then connected to a communications channel to the remote site (see Figure 8-4). A compatible modem at the remote site will be connected to the input-output device, similar to that described for short and medium distances.

A more complex system requires the use of multiplexors. A multiplexor will accept, combine, and transmit signals from several remote terminal devices to the computer over one common communications channel. A compatible multiplexor at the computer will separate the signals before they are input for processing.

A typical multiplexor configuration is shown in Figure 8-4. A cable for each channel of the multiplexor is connected from ports on the computer to connector blocks on the back of the multiplexor. The multiplexor is connected to a modem which in turn is connected to the communications channel linking the computer with the remote terminals. At the terminal site, a comparable modem is connected between the communications link and the multiplexor, which separates the signals of the several chains of input-output devices.

The vendor of the automated system should supply the library with specifications for the communications equipment, which can be used for long distances, and provide instructions and assistance in installing and connecting the links.

TERMINAL WORK STATIONS

Attention should be paid to the design and preparation of the physical environment for the remote terminals and other input-output devices. The physical welfare of the staff can be improved if their work space is arranged properly in a way that enhances rather than prohibits good performance and comfort. Typically, the components of a terminal work station include a CRT terminal, a CRT table, seating, lighting, and other environmental factors such as temperature and noise.

The CRT Terminal

The CRT terminal consists of a monitor or visual display screen and a keyboard. Ideally, the keyboard should be detachable for flexibility and easy arrangement for operator use. The visual display should be positioned so that the operator's head can remain level and the display can be viewed at approximately 15 degrees below eye level. The screen should be able to be adjusted by the operator up and down and to the left and right to suit personal preferance angles. The keyboard should be at a height that enables the operator's elbows to remain at a 90 degree angle and the wrists straight rather than angled downward or upward. For the average operator, this will mean a keyboard height from the floor of approximately 26 inches.

The CRT Table

The desk or table for the CRT should reflect the needs of the operator, allowing him or her to use the device with minimum fatigue and discomfort. Ideally, the part of the table holding the keyboard should be adjustable in a range of approximately 24 to 28 inches from the floor, and the remainder should be stationary for proper viewing of the visual display screen. In this way, the work station can be used comfortably by a number of operators through adjustment of the seating, keyboard height, and the angle of the visual display screen. Space for work forms or other documents should be provided at each side of the terminal thereby supporting both right- and left-handed operators. Most operators prefer to have work copy in front of them, positioned directly below the screen and above the keyboard. This configuration allows easy eye movement from the copy to the screen without the strain of turning the head to the right or left to view the documents.

Seating

Proper seating is probably one of the most important components of the terminal work station. The chair must adjust not only to the height of the keyboard, visual display screen, and work documents but also to the weight distribution and posture requirements of the operator. The seat height should be adjustable so that the thighs of the operator remain at a 90-degree angle to the floor with the feet flat on the floor. The depth of the seat should not exceed 17 inches and the width not less than 16 inches. The back edge of the seat should be approximately three degrees lower than the front edge. In addition, in order to provide firm support for the lower back of the operator, the seat back should be adjustable up and down and should tilt back and forth.

Lighting

Lighting level and glare are two important aspects of illumination for a terminal work station. The proper level of illumination for work at CRT terminals is controversial, with various experts recommending differing values. However, it is agreed that a "reasonable" level of general illumination is necessary for the work area. The IES Lighting Handbook should be consulted for specific standards of lighting.

Glare from windows and ceiling lights on the visual display screen and work documents should be minimized as much as possible. The work space should be located away from windows, or if this is not possible or desirable, the windows should be shaded. The visual display screen can be tilted to reduce glare from overhead lighting. Shields and mesh covering the screen can reduce glare further.

Other Environmental Factors

Other environmental factors such as temperature and noise should be controlled for optimum working comfort. While these too can be controversial, good design and location of the work space can minimize problems. Three sample layouts that could be used to support a multiple CRT operation are shown in Figure 8-5.

Figure 8-5. Three Sample Layouts for a Multiple CRT Work Station Operation.

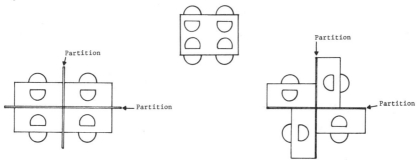

OTHER SYSTEM SPACE

Good layout of space for areas other than the computer room and terminal work stations is also critical to the efficient and effective operation of the automated library system. Charts should be prepared depicting the physical arrangement of equipment and furniture in the space alloted to the system. Flexibility and the ease of work flow and communications through the physical space should be emphasized. A layout flowchart can assist in identifying traffic patterns and reducing traffic congestion and movement of work through the system. Lines showing anticipated movement of people, information, and materials can be superimposed on a space layout chart, with arrows indicating the direction of the flow of work. If separate flows for different people, information, or materials are necessary, different colors can be used for each. The separate work flows from work station to work station can be identified by numbers keyed to a chart legend.

Chapter 9
Database Conversion

Machine-readable information is an indispensable element of any automated library system. Some of that information, such as circulation, acquisitions, and management information, will be routinely generated as the system is operated on a day-to-day basis. Other information, such as bibliographic and copy information, must be created in advance and stored for retrieval and use by the computer as it performs its required tasks. This chapter discusses the building of five typical files required by automated library systems before they can operate properly. Specifically, the topics include:

- Bibliographic files
- Copy files
- Borrower files
- Vendor files
- Fund accounting files

BIBLIOGRAPHIC FILES

A bibliographic file containing records describing materials in the library's collections for cataloging, indexing, and accountability purposes will be required by automated acquisitions and circulation systems and online catalogs. This section discusses the MARC (Machine-Readable Cataloging) format, methods of bibliographic record conversion, choosing a method of record conversion, loading bibliographic records, checking and editing bibliographic records, authority control, and indexes to the bibliographic file.

The MARC Format

Except for indentions, spacings, and the order of data, there is nothing in a traditional catalog record that explicitly identifies the main entry, the imprint, the notes, and other parts of the record. The length of data varies considerably, and specific types of data may or may not be present in particular records. For example, the main entry may or may not include an author's birth and death dates, a title of nobility; or other explanatory matter; or the title statement may or may not include a subtitle. Also, there are subtle differences between many pieces of data. For example, a main entry may be for either a personal, a corporate, or a conference author.

While the librarian and other users have been trained or have learned to distinguish between an author and a title or to identify omissions, the computer cannot do so. The computer must be told exactly and specifically what each piece of data is before it can identify and manipulate or process bibliographic records satisfactorily. The standardized format, MARC, developed by the Library of Congress and the library community for the transfer or communication of bibliographic information in machine-readable form between libraries, has been adopted by many libraries as the format for computer processing and storage of bibliographic records in their local machine files. Other libraries receive or transmit records in the MARC format but translate them to their own internal computer format developed by the vendor of their automated systems for local record retention and manipulation.

Using a standard format such as MARC has the advantage of enabling the library to exchange and receive bibliographic records from other libraries and information centers and commercial vendors easily with bibliographic utilities such as OCLC (Online Computer Library Center), Inc. This is important particularly when the library is building its bibliographic file and must rely on others as a source of machine-readable records. This compatibility will also be important should the library wish to join in cooperative programs with other libraries involving the exchange of bibliographic information. A disadvantage of using the MARC format for storage of bibliographic records locally is that its tags, subfield codes, and other special features require extra storage space.

Separate MARC formats, using the same basic structure, have been developed for monographs, serials, maps, films, music, electronic data files, and manuscripts. In each format, data fields such as main entry, title, notes, imprint, and added entries have been assigned unique three-character numeric tags. For example:

Tag 100 Main entry (personal name)
Tag 110 Main entry (corporate name)
Tag 240 Title
Tag 261 Place of publication
Tag 300 Collation
Tag 651 Geographic subject heading
Tag 700 Personal name added entry
Tag 810 Series added entry (corporate name)

Many of the data fields are divided into subfields, each designated for computer identification by a lower-case alphabetic letter preceded by a special symbol. For example, some subfields of a personal author (Tag 100) are as follows.

$a Name
$b Lineage number (for kings, etc.)
$c Title of nobility
$d Birth and death dates

Subfield codes not needed for a particular author may be omitted. The subfield code, "$a," is often omitted as long as the data are recorded first in the field. Thus, some tagged main entry fields for a personal name may appear as follows.

100 $a Mason, George Ford $c Lord $d 1742 -1805
100 James, William John $d 1935-
100 Tiberius $c Emperor of Rome $d 42 B.C. -37
100 Louis $b IX $c King of France

Other codes and symbols associated with variable-length data fields have been developed. Special fixed fields are designated to provide record attributes such as the language of the work represented, the date the record was last edited, and the type of work such as a monograph or serial. Additional tags are designated for data such as Library of Congress Card Number (LCCN), International Standard Book Number (ISBN), International Standard Serial Number (ISSN), and call number.

Methods of Bibliographic Record Conversion

Conversion of the library's bibliographic records from catalog cards, which a computer cannot accept, to machine-readable form for use in an online catalog or an automated acquisitions or circulation system can be accomplished by several different methods.

Method 1. One of the most common ways of converting the library's bibliographic records to a machine-readable form is through the use of a bibliographic utility such as OCLC. The following steps describe this method.

1. The library staff searches the files of the bibliographic utility for records that match materials being cataloged.
2. The staff edits located records to match the material in hand. If records for items in hand are not located, the material is held for searching again at a later time, or the records may be entered manually into the utility's files.
3. Machine-readable records are produced on the edited or newly entered records.
4. Periodically, the library purchases from the utility or from its regional network—such as AMIGOS Bibliographic Council, Southeastern Library Network (SOLINET), or the Indiana Cooperative Library Services Authority

(INCOLSA)—machine-readable copies of the records it has produced during the past week, month, quarter, or year.

5. The bibliographic utility or network office sends to the library a batch of records on one or more reels of magnetic tape.

6. The library batch loads the machine-readable records into its local bibliographic file using the magnetic tape drive on its computer system and the appropriate software provided by the vendor of its automated system.

The library usually pays a charge for each record produced in machine-readable form in addition to the record use charges of the bibliographic utility. Additional fees may be charged by the utility or network for the service or for processing the magnetic tapes. The number of records that can be obtained in machine-readable form depends upon the length of time the library has been using the bibliographic utility before its automated system was acquired.

The main advantage of this method of converting records to a machine-readable form is that the process will be a by-product of the library's day-to-day cataloging activities. Also, the machine-readable records will be relatively error free when received on magnetic tape, because the library's staff will have edited and performed quality checks on each record as it was processed. The disadvantage of the method is the delay between the time the records are edited via the utility and when they are received on magnetic tape for loading into the library's local bibliographic file.

Method 2. A second method of converting bibliographic records to a machine-readable form is to use a bibliographic utility, as in Method 1, but to transfer records individually into the local bibliographic file as materials are cataloged. The following steps describe this method.

1. The library staff searches the files of the bibliographic utility for matches to material being cataloged.

2. The staff edits located records to match the material in hand. If records for items in hand are not located, the material is held for searching again at a later time, or the records may be entered manually into the utility's files.

3. The staff produces a machine-readable record on the edited or newly entered records.

4. The staff commands the system to transmit a copy of each machine-readable record into the library's in-house bibliographic file, using a cable or communications link connecting the two systems. The vendor of the library's automated system must supply the software necessary to accept and process bibliographic records transferred in this manner.

In most cases, after the library pays for the use of the record for cataloging purposes, no additional costs are incurred since the copy of the record is transferred directly into its local bibliographic file.

The advantages of this method are that the process will be a by-product of the library's day-to-day cataloging activities, and records should be relatively error-free after their transfer into the local file, because the library's staff will have edited and performed quality checks on each record as it was processed. Additionally, the individual records transferred by cable directly from the bibliographic utility into the library's file will be available immediately, or at least overnight, for timely use in the library's online catalog or automated acquisitions or circulation systems.

Method 3. A third method of record conversion is to contract with a vendor who maintains an in-house file of bibliographic records for the purposes of record conversion. The following steps describe this method:

1. The library sends to the vendor a magnetic tape or diskette containing the LC card numbers or ISBN/ISSN for the bibliographic records it wishes to receive in machine-readable form. If the library cannot send magnetic tape or diskette, some vendors will accept, for an extra charge, LC card numbers or ISBN/ISSNs typed on forms.
2. The vendor compares the library's requests against its in-house file of bibliographic records.
3. Records that match the library's requests are copied to magnetic tape and returned to the library.
4. The library batch loads the records into its local bibliographic file using the magnetic tape drive on its computer system and the appropriate software provided by the vendor of its automated system.

The library pays a charge for each machine-readable record received on magnetic tape. Some vendors may have an additional per-record processing fee added to the cost of the records found in its files.

The primary advantages of this method of conversion are its low cost in comparison with other conversion methods and the speed by which the library can convert its records to a machine-readable form. The vendor usually can match requests against its in-house files and return machine-readable records faster than the library can submit its requests. Disadvantages of this arrangement are that the records purchased from the vendor may require additional editing after they are loaded into the local bibliographic file, and some records may not be in the vendor's files and therefore must be obtained or converted by other methods.

Method 4. A fourth method of converting records is to contract with a vendor who has access to a bibliographic utility and provides database conversion services to the library for a fee. The following steps describe this method:

1. The library sends its shelf list, several trays at a time, to the vendor.
2. The vendor's staff searches the files of a bibliographic utility such as OCLC, RLIN, or WLN for records that match those in the library's shelf list.
3. The vendor's staff edits located records to match the shelf list cards in hand. If the records for cards in hand are not located, the staff enters them manually into the utility's files.
4. When the shelf list has been completed, the vendor sends the machine-readable copy of the records on magnetic tape to the library.
5. The library batch loads the machine-readable records into its local bibliographic file using the magnetic tape drive on its computer system and the appropriate software provided by the vendor of its automated system.

The library pays a per-record cost for the conversion. Some contractors may charge a higher fee for records that were not found in the utility's files.

The advantages of this method of converting bibliographic records to a machine-readable form are that the library can let the contractor perform the work instead of requiring its own staff to be available for this purpose and the speed by which the library can complete the conversion of all its bibliographic records. The disadvantages are that some records may still require some editing after loading into the local bibliographic file and that the cost may be prohibitive to the library.

Method 5. A fifth method of record conversion to a machine-readable form is to contract with a vendor who manually keys the information for each bibliographic record into an online computer file using a CRT terminal or other input device. The machine-readable records are then sent to the library on magnetic tape for loading into the local bibliographic file. This method of converting records may be too expensive for the library, unless only brief records are wanted. Also, data entry errors may be numerous and therefore unacceptable to the library.

Method 6. The last method for converting bibliographic records to a machine-readable form is for the library staff to key each record manually into an online computer file using a CRT terminal. Due to the time required to enter each record and the possibility of keyboarding errors, this method should be used only during rush situations when a few records must be entered into the file rapidly. Many libraries will enter brief records manually, then later overlay or "bump" the abbreviated information with full information when a complete record can be loaded.

Choosing a Method of Record Conversion

The library can use one of several methods to convert its bibliographic records to machine-readable form, depending upon its needs and the funds it has available. A careful comparison should be made before one method is chosen over another. Consideration should be given by the library to the following:

1. The direct cost per record converted through each method.
2. The cost per copy of each machine-readable record received on magnetic tape, if not included in 1 above.
3. Library staff costs of preparing requests for submission to a vendor for searching its in-house bibliographic files.
4. Library staff costs of editing records after they have been loaded inito the local bibliographic file. Records edited intially by the library staff before loading may require little or no additional work, whereas those received from contractors may require minimum or substantial editing before they are acceptable.

Loading Bibliographic Records

The library should load all machine-readable bibliographic records it has on hand into the auxiliary storage of its new computer system at the time the automated system is installed. These records will comprise the library's base or initial load, which will be supplemented later as new materials are acquired and cataloged, or as records not in machine-readable form are converted and merged with the initial load.

Records may be stored temporarily in a magnetic disk work file after loading, then later sorted and merged into a master bibliographic file, or records may be merged immediately into a master file, depending upon the design of the software and the file structure of the automated system.

Checking and Editing Bibliographic Records

As records are loaded into the library's in-house bibliographic file, either in batches or individually, some checking and editing must take place. The computer can perform most of this work, but humans must perform some.

Matching Records against the Library's Format. The library must establish a profile of what it considers to be a good bibliographic record. The profile will contain a list of all tags, subfield codes, and other field codes and symbols that constitute a record in the library's internal format. If specific tags or data must be present for a record to be accepted, this must be stipulated. In many cases, the library must specify what constitutes valid data in some specific fields of a record.

Each bibliographic record loaded into the computer system via magnetic tape or transferred from a bibliographic utility must be matched by the computer against the profile to determine that all required tags, codes, and data are present and correct. Records with all required elements and correct data can be loaded into the library's master bibliographic file, but those with requisite parts missing or incorrect or those containing tags or codes not specified in the profile may be held in a work file or tagged until corrections can be made by the library staff.

Correcting Detected Errors. The computer should report problems encountered during loading machine-readable records into the library's bibliographic file to the staff for review and correction, if necessary. Problems can be reported to the staff through a printout or an online display or a combination of both printed and online reports. The operator then adds missing data, tags, codes, and delimeters, corrects errors as appropriate, or approves data that the software thought questionable. The corrected records may be matched once again against the library's bibliographic record profile to detect further anomalies. If additional errors are detected, the records appear on another problem report, but if no errors are detected, the records may be loaded into the master bibliographic file.

The computer can detect errors in tags, codes, and data in fixed fields, but errors in bibliographic information itself cannot be identified by the computer. Records must be proofread by humans before they are loaded into the bibliographic file. If errors are detected after records have been loaded, copies of the records are displayed on a CRT screen for correction by an operator. The updated information then replaces the incorrect information.

Authority Control

A means of maintaining consistency in the library's local machine-stored bibliographic file is desirable. The forms of names, subjects, series, and uniform titles, and cross-references between these terms, require particular attention. While the library may perform the steps of providing consistency of headings in its bibliographic file if it has the software, sufficient hardware, and an authority file in machine-readable form, it is assumed that a contract vendor will perform this service, at least initially. Several steps are necessary in providing authority control for a local file of bibliographic records.

Selecting a Vendor. Several commercial firms will take the library's machine-readable bibliographic file, match designated headings against a recognized authority file, and supply corrected or verified headings and cross references. When selecting such a vendor, the library should consider:

1. The origin and nature of the authority file against which a vendor will match the library's bibliographic file headings. While the Library of Congress authority file is considered the best, it is limited to names and subject headings. No series authorities are available from the Library of Congress at the time of this writing. Some vendors may have added names, subjects, and even series headings to the Library of Congress authority file. The library should evaluate carefully, but not necessarily reject, all headings not supplied by the Library of Congress.
2. Whether the vendor can add appropriate "see" and "see also" references to the library's authority control system.
3. The supplemental services, such as editing partial matches and providing the library with reports of partial and no-matches, which a vendor can offer.
4. The costs of the services to the library. Vendors usually charge a per-record cost for each record submitted for authority file processing. Some may have additional charges such as tape processing, editorial, and report fees.

Defining Headings to Be under Authority Control. The library must decide specifically which fields or subfields of records are to be under authority control. Usually, the library will want authors (MARC tags 100, 110, 111, 400, 410, 700, 710, 711, 800, 810, and 811), titles (MARC tags 240 and 243), subjects (MARC tags 600, 610, 611, 630, 650, and 651), and series (MARC tags 400, 410, 411, 800, 810, and 811) matched against a recognized authority file such as that from the Library of Congress or a commercial firm such as Blackwell North America.

Submitting the Bibliographic File to the Vendor. After a vendor has been selected and the headings to be under authority control have been identified, the library must submit a copy of its bibliographic file on magnetic tape to the contractor. If the MARC format is not used for records on the tape, the format should be defined for the vendor. Some vendors will accept records only in the MARC format or, for an extra fee, a format that can be converted easily to MARC.

Normalizing Headings to Be Matched against the Authority File. The first step for the vendor is to prepare the library's bibliographic file for matching against the authority file. After checking that records are readable, the vendor "normalizes" each heading to be matched against the authority file. This usually entails converting all characters to upper case, removing all punctuation, creating a standard number of blanks between words, and performing other similar steps to maximize the number of matches.

Matching the Normalized Headings against the Authority File. The next step is to match the library's normalized headings against headings in the authority file. If there are complete matches, the headings are accepted as authoritative. Punctuation, hyphens, blanks, and diacritical marks in the library's headings are corrected, if necessary, to match those in the authority file. If parts of headings in the library's normalized headings do not match those in the authority file, a staff member reviews each for acceptance, rejection, or correction as authoritative headings. The library may wish the vendor to perform some or all of this editorial work, or it may want a printed report returned for review by its own staff. Edited headings must be recycled back through the matching process. Those headings with no matches must be reviewed and rejected or added using the library's own authority control system.

Adding References. The library may want cross-references added to its bibliographic file to guide the user from headings not used to those that are used and to "see also" references that suggest additional headings to the user. The vendor's software usually will perform this step as headings are matched against the authority file.

Processing in the Library. The vendor will send to the library a magnetic tape of authority records for its bibliographic file. The library must load the new authority file into its computer system and link all records in its bibliographic file to the appropriate authority records, using software supplied by the authority file vendor or the vendor of the library's automated system.

Updating the Local Authority File. The library must consider how it will keep headings in its bibliographic file correct after the records have been processed against an external authority file.

One way this can be done is to send batches of new records on a quarterly, annual, or other timely basis to the vendor to have new headings matched against the vendor's authority file. This supplementary authority file is returned to the library and loaded into the library's computer system as was the initial authority file.

Another way is to check manually the headings for new records in an authority such as the supplement to LC Subject Headings and make corrections online, when necessary, in the bibliographic records.

Indexes to the Bibliographic File

Several indexes to the bibliographic file should be built and maintained. Software for generating indexes should be supplied by the vendor of the automated system acquired by the library. Common indexes for bibliographic records used in an online catalog and automated acquisitions and circulation systems include author; title; author-title combination; keywords in authors, titles, and subjects; call number; OCLC number; and ISBN/ISSN.

The library must define which data fields and subfields of the bibliographic records are to be included in each index.

Example: MARC tags 100, 110, and 111 should be included in the author index.

Example: MARC tags 240 and 245 should be included in the title index.

Example: MARC tags 600, 610, 611, 630, 650, 651, 690, 691, 692, 693, 694, and 695 should be included in the subject index.

COPY FILES

An item or copy file, which contains a record of each copy of material owned by the library, will be required for use with automated acquisitions and circulation systems and online catalogs. Copy records are linked to the appropriate records in the bibliographic file. Typically, a copy record might include a copy number, a location within the library, a material type designation, the call number, a barcode or optical character number, and perhaps the cost of the copy and the date it was acquired. Usually, creation of the bibliographic and copy files coincides with the addition of machine-readable barcode or optical character labels to materials in the library's collections. The MARC format does include a specified format for copy records. This section discusses several options for copy record creation, copy linking to bibliographic records, and collection preparation. In actuality, a library may use a combination of these methods when preparing its records and collections for an automated system.

Method 1

One option for preparing copy records is to have the computer generate a copy record for each bibliographic record on file, on the assumption that the library will own at least one copy of each title. The following steps describe this option:

1. The computer generates one default copy record for each bibliographic record on file. A barcode or optical character number is assigned by the computer to each copy.
2. The computer prints labels containing the barcodes or optical characters assigned to the copies of materials. The call number and/or author and title can be printed below the barcode or optical characters for ease of matching labels to materials on the shelves. The labels can be printed in shelf order.
3. The library staff takes the barcode or optical character labels to the shelves, matches the labels to the materials, and places the labels in the appropriate copies of materials.

The advantage of this option is that the computer can simultaneously generate copy records and link these records for a large part of the library's collections, without requiring human effort. An inventory of the collection can be taken as the labels are affixed to materials; copies not found or copies with no labels can be checked and records corrected as appropriate. A disadvantage to the method is that the staff must generate records and labels for all copies other than the first. Also, a contract vendor will most likely have to generate the copy records and labels unless the library has a barcode or optical character printer online to its computer system.

Method 2

Another option for preparing copy records includes the following steps:

1. Shelf list trays and sets of preprinted barcode or optical character labels are taken to the materials.
2. Shelf list cards are matched to the materials.
3. A barcode or optical character label is placed in each copy matched. A duplicate of the label is placed on the shelf list card.
4. Completed trays of cards are taken to a terminal online to the library's computer.
5. The bibliographic file is searched for records in the shelf list with barcode or optical character labels attached.
6. When bibliographic records are located for the shelf list cards, information for each copy record is added to the machine file manually. If the terminal has a barcode or optical character scanner, the labels attached to the shelf list cards can be scanned and added to the file.

An advantage to this method is that an inventory of the library's collection can be taken as the labels are added to materials. The disadvantage is that this approach to creating machine-readable copy records and labels and preparing the collection is time consuming, labor intensive, and therefore costly.

Method 3

A third option is to create copy records at the time materials circulate. The following steps are taken in this case:

1. A borrower brings materials to be charged out to the circulation desk.
2. The circulation staff adds a preprinted barcode or optical character label in the copy to be charged out.
3. The staff searches the bibliographic file for a record to match the copy to be circulated.
4. When a matching bibliographic record is located, information for the copy record is manually keyed into the system and linked to the bibliographic record.

5. The barcode or optical character label on the copy is scanned to add the number to its record.
6. The item is then charged out to the borrower.

The advantage to this option is that an advance project to add barcode or optical character labels to materials need not be completed before the library's automated circulation system can become operational. The disadvantage is that building the copy records while users wait is time consuming, particularly when a borrower has many books to be charged and other users are waiting their turn. Also, some copies may not have bibliographic records on file in the automated system, in which case brief records must be manually keyed into the file before the item can be circulated.

BORROWER FILES

A file of machine-readable records containing borrowers' names, addresses, and other personal information is required by an automated circulation system. Borrower records usually are brief and well structured, but as yet, there is no standard format accepted by the library community. This section describes two common methods of creating the borrower file.

Method 1

Perhaps the most often used method of building a borrower file is to create each record manually. The following steps describe this process:

1. Each borrower completes a registration form, giving pertinent information such as name, address, and telephone number.
2. The borrower gives the registration form to the circulation attendant, who keys the information on the form into a CRT terminal online to the computer.
3. The operator assigns a barcode or optical character number to the borrower. The number is keyed or scanned into the borrower's online record, and a label with the same number is attached to a borrower card.
4. The borrower card is given or mailed later to the user.

The advantage to this approach is that no records need be created and stored unless users wish to borrow materials. The disadvantage is that users charging materials out for the first time will have to wait for their borrower records and cards to be prepared.

Method 2

A second option for preparing the borrower file is to batch load records from another machine-readable file such as a file of students, faculty, and staff records maintained by the registrar or admissions office of a university or college, the tax rolls of a city or county, or other similar records maintained by the library's parent organization. Special software for extracting the data needed for the library's borrower file and for batch loading the records must be written or supplied by the vendor of the automated system.

An advantage of this option is that manual keyboarding of individual borrower records will be eliminated, and the records will be on file and ready to use when borrowers wish to charge out materials. The disadvantage is that records for many people who will never come to the library or wish to check out materials will be added to the library's online files.

VENDOR FILES

A vendor file, which contains the name, address, and other information such as discounts given and names of sales representatives for each vendor to which the library expects to send purchase orders for materials, will be required for use with an automated acquisitions system. Most libraries must build this file by taking an existing manual file of vendors to a CRT terminal and manually keying the required information into the system using software supplied by the vendor of the system. Some libraries may be able to acquire a magnetic tape of vendors which can be batch loaded into the system if the software will support this method of loading vendor information. Some data in the vendor file, such as shortest, longest, and average times of delivery for materials, will be gathered and recorded by the software as the system operates over a period of time.

FUND ACCOUNTING FILES

The library will have to set up a machine-stored fund accounting file for its new automated library system. This file will consist of records of each fund account the library wishes to use, the amount of funds in each account, and the names and passwords of those people who will have access to the accounts. The system vendor will supply the essential software for the fund accounting file and should assist the library in developing an effective and efficient system of accounts.

Chapter 10
Staff and User Education and Training

Installing any new system in the library is disruptive for both staff and users. Introducing a new automated system can be particularly traumatic because it involves change and technology, two societal elements that some people fear and distrust. Since the success of any new system depends to a great extent upon the cooperation and interest of those who will manage, operate, and use it, the library should have a well-planned and well-executed education and training component of its library automation project. This chapter discusses the essential education and training of staff and users needed when an automated system is acquired and installed. Specifically, it includes:

- General education of staff for automation
- System operator training
- Supervisor training
- Basic operator training
- Follow-up training
- User education

GENERAL EDUCATION OF STAFF FOR AUTOMATION

Not everyone on the library staff will require the same level of education and training for automation. For example, staff who will work directly with the automated system will require more knowledge than those who work indirectly or not at all with the system. However, every staff member, regardless of their responsibilities or relationship with the automated system, probably should have a basic understanding of computers and automation if they are to work in a library with substantial automation. Such education could enable staff to gain better insight into their jobs, give better service to the public, and become more valuable employees in general. This section discusses goals, alternatives, and a timetable for a program of general education for automation.

Goals for an Education Program

A goal should be established for the program to educate library staff about computers and automation in general. Such a goal will provide a focal point for designing and administering the program.

Example: The goal of the program is to provide each staff member with a basic understanding of the general principles of computers and automation.

Example: The goal of the program is to prepare each staff member for productive and harmonious work in a highly automated library environment.

Example: The primary purpose of this educational program is to provide opportunities for the library staff to learn the fundamental concepts and terminology of computers and automation for application in libraries.

The expected outcome of the program should be defined in terms of knowledge or specific competencies which staff should have upon completion of the educational opportunities to be made available. For example, upon completion of the program, each staff member might be expected to be able to:

1. Differentiate between a microcomputer, a minicomputer, and a mainframe computer.
2. Identify the basic components of a computer and define the purpose or function of each.
3. Trace the flow of information into and out of the computer system.
4. Define the structure of library records and their organization in files.
5. Recognize and understand the basic terminology of computers and automation.

An actual list would be much longer and would resemble an outline of topics that staff should be familiar with as a result of the education program.

Theoretically, tests should be conducted to determine if staff indeed do have the prescribed competencies. However, except for most formal courses, testing after an educational program is not often done. Proof of knowledge about automation can be ascertained indirectly through improved performance on the job, greater participation in work requiring knowledge of computers and automation, and a reduction of anxiety about computers and automation.

Alternative Educational Opportunities

There are several alternatives for education of staff for automation, including formal courses, workshops and seminars, self-paced instruction, site visits, conference exhibits, and involvement.

Formal Courses. One way of providing educational opportunities to library staff to enable them to become knowledgeable about computers and automation in general is through formal courses offered by the library's host organization, a nearby college or university, or other educational institutions or groups. For most staff, the course should be on a survey or introductory level. The library should allow staff time with pay to attend such courses and should, if possible, pay tuition and other expenses.

Workshops and Seminars. Another typical method of educating staff for automation is through workshops and seminars sponsored by the library or by others, held in the library or in other locations. Many local, state, regional, and national library organizations sponsor such educational opportunities year round in various parts of the country and at nominal costs. Many are held during library conferences. The library should allow staff time with pay to attend such sessions and should, if possible, pay expenses such as travel, per diem, and registration for attending.

Self-Paced Instruction. Staff can learn much about computers and automation through self-paced instruction. A reading list or text is supplied to the staff member, who reads the material at his or her own pace. If available, Computer Assisted Instruction (CAI) courses can be used effectively for teaching staff about automation. The library should prepare the reading list, provide staff with the material or CAI system, and allow staff time to read the material or use the CAI system.

Site Visits. Tours of other libraries with automated systems is another way of educating library staff about automation. Staff can see and, in some cases, operate computer equipment, examine the system's operation, and talk with staff who manage and operate the automated system. If there are no automated systems in nearby libraries, special trips can be organized, or staff can be encouraged to visit automated libraries when attending conferences in other cities. The library should allow staff time with pay for site visits and pay expenses for the visits when possible.

Conference Exhibits. Quite a bit can be learned about computers and automation by visiting exhibits at library and other conferences and meetings. Staff can usually see and operate equipment, listen to presentations by vendor representatives, see demonstrations of the equipment and systems, and ask questions when information is not clear. The library should allow staff time with pay to attend conferences with exhibits and pay expenses when possible.

Involvement. One of the best methods of educating staff about computers and automation is to involve them extensively in the library automation project. As they serve on advisory committees or assist in preparation of system requirements, staff can be introduced to the new topics by the project manager or automation consultant. Usually, staff are willing and eager to learn when they see an obvious need for new knowledge.

Timetable for an Education Program

Education of staff for automation should begin as far in advance of installation of an automated system as possible. Since this type of orientation will be general in nature, the automated system itself need not be installed and operational at the time staff are learning about computers and automation in general.

SYSTEM OPERATOR TRAINING

Staff must be trained to operate and monitor an automated system's hardware and software. A system operator actually manipulates and monitors the computer's controls and performs such duties as operating peripheral equipment including tape drives and printers, initiating batch programs from the system console, and performing file backups and recoveries. Such training usually will be supplied by the vendor of the system. This section includes discussions relating to who should receive system operator training and information on documentation, content, and the location and timing of system operator training.

Who Should Receive Operator Training

Contractual arrangements with the vendor usually limit system operator training to a small number of staff. Determining who should receive the training will be dependent on the nature of the system and the available staff. A minimum of two to three staff members should be trained to operate and manage the hardware and software. In this way, if one staff member is unavailable or resigns, another would already be trained to assume system operator duties or could train someone else to do the work.

Documentation for System Operator Training

Adequate system documentation is essential for proper training and orientation of staff and to their later effective management and operation of the automated system. The documentation will serve as an instructional tool or training manual that will allow staff to familiarize themselves with the system and to help to ensure that procedures are performed in a standardized manner. In addition, the documentation will serve as a historical reference that will indicate how the system was initially configured prior to any subsequent modifications and improvements.

Prior to system operator training, the vendor of the automated system should supply the library with the following documentation, as a minimum:

1. A general overview description of the system and its functions and features.
2. A manual for each separate equipment model supporting the system. The manuals should contain diagrams of each device with a legend describing the parts and their purposes or functions, brief yet clear instructions for operating each device, and instructions for checking the equipment and correcting problems when malfunctions occur.
3. A manual which describes how to start up, shut down, monitor, operate, and troubleshoot problems with the system.
4. A procedures manual for preparing file backups and recoveries, reports, notices, and other batch operations.
5. Manuals for the operating system, system utilities, database management system, and programming languages for the system.

The staff training manual giving step-by-step procedures showing how to use the system itself can also be helpful in system operator training.

Content of System Operator Training

The competencies expected of staff upon completion of system operator training should be established. The competencies may have been specified in the library's RFP or in the purchase contract between the library and the vendor of the automated system. As a minimum, system operators should be able to:

1. Start up, shut down, monitor, and operate the CPU, disk drives, tape drives, printers, terminals, data communications equipment, and other hardware of the automated system.
2. Start up, shut down, and monitor the software for the system.
3. Load and install software enhancements received from the vendor.
4. Load records from external storage such as magnetic tape and handle associated problems.
5. Run file backups and restore operations.
6. Operate the system printer and handle print jobs generated by the system.
7. Handle the system's software utilities.

8. Schedule and initiate required batch jobs for effective utilization of the system.
9. Maintain and use logs of operations.
10. Set up and maintain a tape library.
11. Monitor the environment of the computer room.
12. Keep the equipment clean.
13. Troubleshoot and solve simple problems in lieu of calling vendor maintenance staff.
14. Handle emergency situations with the computer system.

Each trainee should be given an opportunity for hands-on experience with the equipment, following step-by-step instructions and using test data records. The trainer should provide encouragement, correct mistakes, and coach the learner in the individual tasks to be performed.

Location and Timing of System Operator Training

Some vendors offer system operator training periodically during the year at strategic locations around the country. This training usually is at nominal or no cost to the library except for staff transportation, lodging, and meals. Other vendors may train the staff in the library, depending upon contractual arrangements made during system acquisition. The library should receive system operator training in the library on its own equipment, if at all possible.

The training should not be held until the vendor has installed and tested the hardware and software and the library has accepted delivery of the system. Information learned during training held before installation may be forgotten by the time the system is installed and the knowledge needed. Training held at a date much later could delay further implementation of the system. Ideally, system operator training should be held within a week or so of hardware and software installation, testing, and delivery acceptance.

SUPERVISOR TRAINING

Supervisors must be trained in advance to operate and manage the hardware and software in order to direct the staff who will use the new automated system on a day-to-day basis. As in system operator training, supervisor training will usually be supplied by the vendor of the system. This section includes discussions relating to who should receive supervisor training as well as documentation, content, and the location and timing of supervisor training.

Who Should Receive Supervisor Training

Selecting the staff who should receive supervisor training on the new automated system depends upon the system and the organization of the library. The department head and other key staff who will be responsible for supervising and training other staff to use the system in their day-to-day work should receive this level of training. The library director and other key management staff may also wish to receive this same training in order to understand the functional capabilities and limitations of the system and to explain and demonstrate it to other administrators, officials, or guests of the library.

Documentation for Supervisor Training

Prior to supervisor training, the vendor of the automated system should supply, as a minimum, the following documentation to the library:

1. A general overview describing the system and its functions and features.
2. A descriptive and operations manual for each separate equipment model of hardware for general staff use.
3. A staff training manual giving step-by-step procedures showing how to operate the system.

Content of Supervisor Training

The competencies expected of staff upon completion of supervisor training should be established. The competencies may have been specified in the library's RFP or in the contract between the library and the vendor of the automated system. As a minimum, supervisors should be able to:

1. Understand the overall capabilities and limitations of the system.
2. Use each functional component of the automated system.
3. Start up, shut down, monitor, and operate the equipment, such as terminals, printers, and modems supporting the various functions of the system.
4. Train other staff members in daily use of the system.
5. Handle emergencies which might arise until computer room supervisors or vendor maintenance staff can arrive.
6. Troubleshoot and solve simple problems in lieu of calling computer room supervisory personnel or vendor maintenance staff.

Location and Timing of Supervisor Training

Supervisor training should be conducted in the library on its own equipment if at all possible. It will be helpful if the training is conducted away from functional departments or work areas, in order to minimize interruptions of other staff, the public, and their activities and needs. This level of training should be conducted after all equipment has been installed and tested and the library has accepted delivery of the system, and after the software the supervisors will be using on a daily basis has been installed and tested and is operating satisfactorily.

BASIC OPERATOR TRAINING

Staff who will use the automated system on a daily basis while performing their assigned responsibilities also must receive proper training. Depending upon the contractual arrangements between the library and the vendor, this training may be supplied by the vendor of the automated system or may be supplied by those who received supervisor training.

This section includes discussions relating to who should receive basic operator training and the documentation, content, and location and timing of basic operator training.

Who Should Receive Basic Operator Training

All staff who must use the automated system to perform their assigned tasks should receive basic operator training. Others can be trained as the need arises.

Documentation for Basic Operator Training

Prior to basic operator training, the vendor of the automated system should supply, as a minimum, the following documentation to the library:

1. A general overview description of the system and its functions and features.
2. A staff training manual giving step-by-step procedures showing how to operate the system.

Content of Basic Operator Training

The competencies expected of staff upon completion of basic operator training should be established. Usually, the hardware included in basic operator training will be limited to the CRT terminal and perhaps a scanning wand or a slave printer. As a minimum, basic operators should be able to:

1. Identify the parts of the equipment to be used on a daily basis and their functions.
2. Turn on, turn off, adjust, check, and clean the equipment to be used on a daily basis.
3. Perform the step-by-step operations essential for proper use of the system during assigned responsibilities.
4. Identify problems with the system and take necessary action to protect it from undue harm until supervisory staff arrive.

Location and Timing of Basic Operator Training

Basic operator training should be received in the library at a work station identical to that on which the staff will perform their assigned tasks. The training should be conducted after all equipment has been installed and tested and the library has accepted delivery of the system, after the software has been installed, tested, and is fully operational, and after supervisor training has been completed.

FOLLOW-UP TRAINING

Follow-up sessions should be conducted as necessary to reinforce training, allow identification and correction of problems encountered during the first sessions, and enable the staff to ask additional questions after they have more confidence and have overcome the initial trauma of learning something new. As enhancements to the automated system are added, additional training should be conducted for all levels of staff affected.

USER EDUCATION

The library's users are the ultimate benefactors of a new automated system, either directly or indirectly. Invariably, there will be conversion and installation problems which might adversely affect services to users on a temporary basis and other problems which could affect their utilization of the system. Inconveniences to users can be minimized by a good user education program. Then, when problems do arise, users can better understand that the inconveniences are temporary and that the new system, once installed and operating successfully, will provide them with better and faster services.

This section includes discussions of some methods of user education, including general publicity, user education classes, individual tutorials, and "how to use" brochures.

General Publicity

A well-planned general public relations or publicity program should be initiated well in advance of the installation of the automated system. Some techniques for general publicity might include news releases, staff interviews by the media, posters and handouts, and announcements in public meetings.

News Releases. One or more news releases about the new system can be written and distributed to local newspapers, radio and television stations, and others. Copies can be sent as well to state, regional, and national library periodicals. Most editors are pleased to use the information in their publications or programs when they can. New releases should be prepared and distributed during the various phases of library automation project to retain and refresh the public's awareness and interest about the new system.

Staff Interviews by Media. The library can ask local newspapers and radio and television stations to send reporters to interview the library director, the project manager, and other staff about the new automated system. Try to have photographs or films of staff or patrons using the new equipment when possible. Repeat interviews should be sought as the project progresses.

Posters and Handouts. Posters advertising the impending installation of the automated system can be prepared and placed in strategic locations in the library, particularly where the public will be in direct contact with the new system. Brochures, bookmarks, and other handouts describing the new system can be prepared and distributed at service desks and other places in the library.

Announcements in Discussions and Meetings. Another effective means of general publicity is through announcements about the automated system in public meetings attended by library staff and by having staff mention the progress on the system in discussions with administrators, officials, and others outside the library organization. The staff may be asked to give presentations on the automated system to local clubs, associations, societies, and other groups of interested people.

User Education Classes

Many academic libraries now have user education classes to assist students and faculty in learning how to use the library. Information about the new automated system can be incorporated into the class content. If slides or films are used by the instructor, pictures of the computer, the terminals, and staff and students using the system can be shown. If library tours are included in the class, users can see first hand how the new system operates.

Individual Tutorials

In some cases, a library may individually tutor users in response to questions or interest shown in the automated system. This situation arises quite often when the new system is an online catalog. Also, most online catalogs have information to assist users built into the system, activated by pressing a special function key or entering a command such as "help."

"How to Use" Brochures

Finally, a very efficient means of training users to operate a new automated system is to prepare clear, brief brochures for their self-instruction. The brochures can be placed at service desks, near online catalog terminals, and in racks containing library publications.

Chapter 11
System Installation, Acceptance, and Operation

System installation, acceptance, and operation is the culmination of a long series of difficult and time-consuming activities in a library automation project. While much work has preceded this phase of the project, even more difficult work is yet to come. This chapter discusses the activities and tasks of system installation, acceptance, and operation. Specifically, it includes:

- Acquisition of supplies, forms, and equipment
- Hardware and software installation
- File loading
- Workflow and space alignment
- Realignment of staff
- System activation
- System acceptance
- Computer room management

ACQUISITION OF SUPPLIES, FORMS, AND EQUIPMENT

An automated system will require some special supplies, forms, and equipment not ordinarily needed by manual systems. Acquisition of most special equipment will be a one-time expense to the library, while stocks of most special supplies and forms must be replenished periodically. This section identifies supplies, forms, and equipment to support automated library systems and discusses their acquisition.

Special Supplies for an Automated System

The special supplies needed for an automated system will depend upon the type, nature, and size of the system to be installed and whether or not an in-house computer will be used. The vendor of the automated system should assist the library in determining which supplies should be acquired. A checklist of special supplies for typical automated library systems is shown in Appendix C. General office supplies, such as pencils, pens, paper clips, and the like are not included in the list.

Custom Forms for an Automated System

While many reports generated by an automated library system can be printed on blank paper, some custom forms may be necessary. A custom form has preprinted information, such as the name and address of the library, column heading designations, and instructions, designed specifically to fit the needs of the library for its automated system. Variable information which changes from record to record will be printed by the computer as notices and reports are prepared. Custom forms are more expensive than stock forms maintained by a forms supplier for use by a variety of customers. A checklist of typical custom-designed forms required by automated library systems can be found in Appendix C.

Special Equipment for an Automated System

Some special equipment such as desks, chairs, and cabinets designed specifically for use with computer hardware may be needed for an automated library system. The type and quantity of equipment needed will depend upon the automated system. A checklist of special equipment for typical automated library systems can be found in Appendix C.

Ordering Supplies, Forms, and Equipment

How and from whom supplies, forms, and equipment are ordered will depend upon the rules and regulations governing the purchasing powers and the policies and procedures of the library. Some libraries may order from any vendor they choose, while others must order from specific firms using prenegotiated purchasing contracts. Still others must go through a process of advertising and soliciting bids for all purchases. The library's purchasing agent should be able to assist in identifying vendors and prices and placing the necessary orders. A number of nationally recognized firms specialize in handling supplies, forms, and equipment designed for use with automated systems. Local data processing and computer supply businesses can also assist the library in their purchases.

The amount of supplies and forms to be acquired also will depend upon the type, nature, and size of the automated system being installed and the amount of funds available to the library. Sufficient quantities to operate the new system for at least a year should be ordered initially if possible. Stocks of many of the supplies and forms must be replenished from time to time and thus will be an annual expense to the library.

Supplies, forms, and equipment for an automated system should be ordered in advance of hardware and software delivery and installation to ensure receipt prior to system activation. Some of the necessary equipment, such as desks or tables, also should be ordered in sufficient time for delivery prior to hardware installation.

HARDWARE AND SOFTWARE INSTALLATION

Once the site for the automated system has been prepared and accepted, the hardware and software for the new system can be delivered and installed. This activity usually consists of hardware and software delivery, installation, testing, and acceptance.

Hardware and Software Delivery

The computer system and other hardware should be delivered to the location or locations specified by the library in its purchase order, contract, or letter of agreement with the vendor. Usually, the various pieces of hardware will be in separate crates for later assembly by an employee of the vendor. The software may be delivered at the same time or separately, or the vendor's field engineer may bring it with him or her, on magnetic tape, when he or she comes to install the hardware.

If possible, hardware should not be delivered until the library's site is ready, although the timetables of system manufacturers and vendors often cannot be controlled or predicted in advance. Prematurely delivered equipment should be left unopened in its crates in a secure area until the arrival of those who will install the hardware or until the project manager authorizes installation by others. If there is no space to store the hardware until the site is ready, the library should make it clear to the vendor that it cannot accept early delivery of equipment. The timetable for delivery of the system should have been agreed upon in advance by both the library and the vendor.

Hardware Installation and Testing

The library should have identified the location of each piece of hardware prior to delivery of the system, but nothing should be installed until the site has been prepared and accepted. The project manager should supervise or at least closely monitor the installation of all hardware to make certain that nothing is damaged and that items are placed in their predetermined locations. During this activity, the installer should:

1. Unpack, assemble, and clean the equipment.
2. Identify, report, obtain, and install any missing pieces.

3. Place the equipment in designated locations and make certain that it is stable and level, if this is critical.
4. Connect all essential cables and power cords and install cable bridges if necessary to secure cables in place.

The hardware installer should conduct general tests to make certain that each piece of hardware is operating normally and properly. The installer should:

1. Energize the equipment.
2. Ascertain that all motors and heat dispersion fans are operating normally.
3. Test the hardware in an operational mode. For the computer itself, this step cannot be completed until the software has been installed.
4. Check that all status lights illuminate properly and under the appropriate conditions.
5. Check that all audible and visual alarms are in good working condition.

Software Installation and Testing

Once hardware has been installed and checked generally, the software can be installed and tested. The installer will load the operating system and diagnostic routines first to ensure that the CPU, disk drives, and other hardware are performing satisfactorily. Results of these tests may be used to adjust the hardware or replace defective parts identified by the diagnostics.

Next, the application software is loaded and tested to make certain that it is operating as expected. Each function of the system should be checked using test data, and any errors or malfunctions should be reported and corrected before staff training is begun and before the new system is activated.

Hardware and Software Acceptance

A final step of this activity is to accept delivery of hardware and software. This is not to be confused with final acceptance of the system, discussed later in this chapter, which usually is done after extensive evaluation of both hardware and software. Initial acceptance of the hardware and software simply acknowledges that the proper pieces and amounts of hardware and software have been delivered, installed, and tested and are functioning properly.

FILE LOADING

Some machine-readable data files must be loaded into the online auxiliary storage prior to activation of the automated system, while other files will be built after system activation as the system is operated. Data conversion is discussed extensively in Chapter 9.

WORKFLOW AND SPACE ALIGNMENT

Some alignment of workflow and space will be necessary as an automated system is installed. The alignment may be simple or complex, depending upon the automated system being installed. This section discusses two tools which can be used in examining and adjusting workflow and space for an automated system.

Decision Flowcharts

A decision flowchart is a graphic or pictorial representation of the sequence of operations performed on information, materials, and other physical objects moving through a system and specifies all decisions that are to be made in the flow of work and the alternative courses of action to be taken as a result of these decisions. Flowcharts are useful as:

1. An aid in visualizing the workflow as the processing operations are realigned for the automated system.
2. A part of documentation for the new system. The charts provide a snapshot of the system and become the standard for operation of the automated system.
3. A general communications device for teaching and training others how the system will operate. Since flowcharts are widely used and understood, they are a medium of communication between the designer and others who wish to understand the system.

Decision flowcharts are constructed by stringing together symbols or boxes of varying shapes representing operations or processes, decisions, storage, and other activities. Short, concise descriptions and explanations are placed inside the symbols. Standardized symbols have been accepted by both the American National Standards Institute (ANSI) and the International Standards Organization (ISO). Over 30 basic, input/output, equipment, and special process symbols are available. Only a handful of symbols are essential in most cases; these are shown in Figure 11-1.

Flowlines are used to connect the symbols in a chart, with arrowheads indicating the direction of the flow of work. The normal sequence of a flowchart is from the top of a page downward and then

Figure 11-1. Basic Flowcharting Symbols.

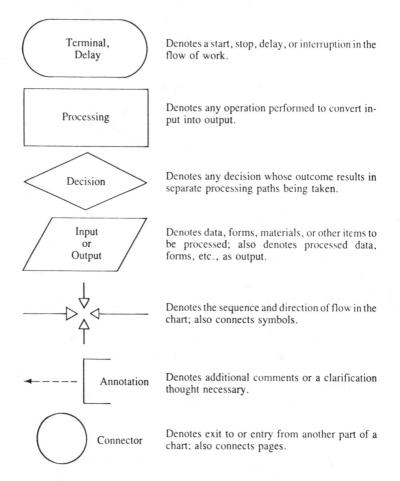

Terminal, Delay — Denotes a start, stop, delay, or interruption in the flow of work.

Processing — Denotes any operation performed to convert input into output.

Decision — Denotes any decision whose outcome results in separate processing paths being taken.

Input or Output — Denotes data, forms, materials, or other items to be processed; also denotes processed data, forms, etc., as output.

Denotes the sequence and direction of flow in the chart; also connects symbols.

Annotation — Denotes additional comments or a clarification thought necessary.

Connector — Denotes exit to or entry from another part of a chart; also connects pages.

from the left to right. However, a flowchart using only a sequence from the left side of the page to the right is not uncommon. Each page of a set of charts should be fully identified and numbered. The connector symbol is used to guide the reader from one page of the set to another. When a decision is necessary during the processing flow, a decision block is inserted, with a "yes" line emerging from one point of the diamond and a "no" line from another; no other choices are usually possible. The processing flow is thus broken into two diverging sequences of steps indicating processing steps resulting if either possible path is taken. A sample decision flowchart for part of an automated circulation system is shown in Figure 11-2.

Figure 11-2. A Sample Decision Flowchart for Part of an Automated Circulation System.

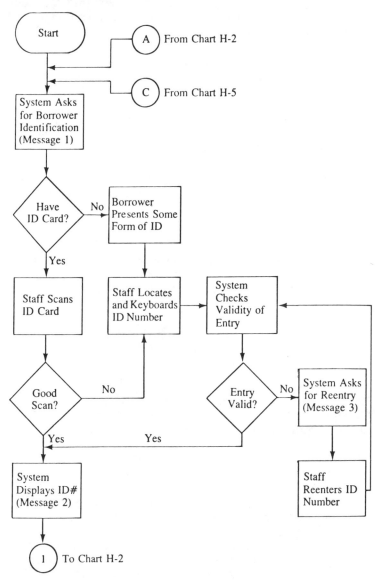

A set of narrative descriptions for each block in a flowchart for a system can be prepared if it is necessary to provide a more detailed description or explanation of the workflow than can be included in the charts themselves. Some designers prefer to begin development of a function's workflow with a narrative description of the processes, then prepare the necessary flowcharts. The narrative descriptions can be placed on the flowcharts on the same pages as their accompanying symbols, or each symbol in the charts can be numbered and the descriptions placed on separate sheets with corresponding numbers linking them to the charts.

Layout Flowcharts

The layout flowchart is also a graphic or pictorial representation of the movement of information, materials, and /or people through the physical space in which a system is operated. Work areas and their furniture and equipment are shown, and lines or arrows are drawn to depict the movement or path of the information, materials, or people from area to area as work flows through the system. Layout flowcharts are useful as:

1. An aid in visualizing the arrangement of equipment and furniture in the space used for an automated system by showing the location and relationship of its work areas.
2. A means of identifying traffic patterns and traffic congestion.
3. A means of spotting excessive travel and backtracking of people, materials, and information in a system.

Figure 11-3 depicts the space for a typical automated circulation system. The outside boundaries of the space in which the automated system will be operated are depicted, as described for an in-house computer room in Chapter 8. The furniture and equipment are sketched on the drawing, also to approximate scale. Small cutouts representing the furniture and equipment can be made and moved around into various configurations to aid in planning the space arrangement before the final drawing is made. Flexibility and ease of workflow and communications through the physical space should be emphasized. Lines showing anticipated movement of people, information, and materials are superimposed on the chart with arrows indicating the direction of the workflow. If separate flows for different people, information, or materials are necessary, different colors can be used for each. The separate work flows from work station to work station can be identified by numbers keyed to a chart legend. Layout flowcharts are not exceptionally useful when only one or two work areas are involved or when most operations are performed at one work station.

Figure 11-3. A Sample Layout Chart Depicting Traffic Flow for an Automated Circulation System.

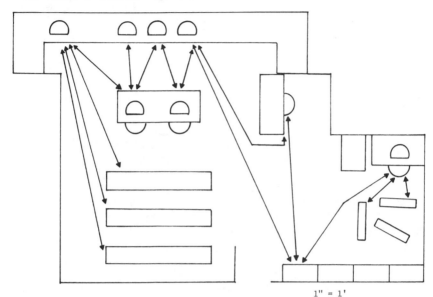

1" = 1'

REALIGNMENT OF STAFF

After installation of the automated system, some realignment of staff will be necessary. This might take the form of either changed duties and responsibilities within the system or possibly staff reductions.

Changed Duties and Responsibilities

An automated system often eliminates or changes many routines and introduces many new ones which do not exist in a manual system, thus requiring a totally new organizational structure or at least new assignments and retraining of some staff. The extent of changes of staff duties and responsibilities to accommodate an automated system will depend upon the nature of the system and the degree of change brought about by its installation. Some staff may have few new or changed responsibilities, while others may have radically different duties.

A suggested method for handling changed duties and responsibilities might be as follows:

1. Prepare new job descriptions for each staff member whose duties and responsibilities will change once the automated system is installed.

2. Discuss the new duties and responsibilities with the staff, stressing their continued importance to the library and the system.
3. Orient each staff member in general to automation and the automated system (see Chapter 10).
4. Train each staff member for his or her specific new duties and responsibilities.

Staff Reductions

It may be necessary to eliminate some staff positions entirely when an automated system is installed. This situation can be handled through transfers to other departments, attrition, or, as a last resort, terminations.

Transfer of Staff to Other Departments. Most libraries simply transfer surplus staff from an automated system to other departments within the library or possibly outside the library in other departments of the university, city, or company of which the library is a part. Thus, while there will be a reduction of staff within the system upon its automation, the number of staff in the library overall might remain the same. Selection of the staff to be transferred might depend upon the individual's skills and seniority and his or her desire for a transfer.

Staff Attrition. In some cases, the library can reduce staff of an automated system through attrition. That is, when a staff member resigns or retires, the person is not replaced and the position is dissolved or transferred to another area of the library. This option is always preferred to staff terminations.

Termination of Staff. As a last resort, the library may have to terminate some staff not needed in an automated system. This step should be taken only if excess staff cannot be transferred to other departments or if positions cannot be eliminated through attrition and when other duties and responsibilities for some staff cannot be identified within the new automated system.

SYSTEM ACTIVATION

Once hardware and software have been installed and tested, supplies, forms, and equipment have been ordered and received, staff have been trained, and essential files have been created and loaded, the automated system can be activated. This process often is referred to as "bringing up the system" or "going live with the system."

There are several approaches to activation of a new automated system, each with its own particular advantages and disadvantages for a specific project. Sometimes a combination of approaches to activating the system may be necessary. Typical approaches are the total, pilot, phased, and parallel approaches.

Total Approach

In the total or all-at-once approach to new system activation, the old system is abandoned completely on a given date and time, and the automated system takes its place. This approach is by far the most demanding of the four methods and requires careful planning and coordination. Hardware and software must be thoroughly tested and checked and staff must be well oriented and trained in advance to operate and manage the new system. This approach probably should not be used when the automated system involves widely separated elements in the operation, such as branch libraries.

Pilot Approach

When the library has several relatively self-contained and geographically separate branches, it may be better to implement a new system first in only one of the units on a pilot project basis. This approach permits the selection of the particular organizational unit in which the staff are most ready to accept the new system, while installation in other units of the library need not begin until everyone is satisfied that the pilot installation is running smoothly. The successful operation of the new system in one branch can strongly motivate hesitant staff in other units. The activation of the system on a small scale can usually be accomplished more quickly than for the all-at-once approach and also permits the overall installation to progress at a more relaxed pace.

Phased Approach

In the phased approach to system activation, the automated system is separated into a number of modules or subsystems that are installed one at a time. Although this approach takes longer, there is more time to work with the problems that arise in the individual parts. Unfortunately, not every system can be installed in this manner because it may not be possible to separate a system into significant, relatively independent subsystems.

Parallel Approach

The parallel approach to automated system activation requires that the old and the new systems operate side by side for a period of time. The old system is gradually or suddenly phased out as soon as the automated system is performing satisfactorily. This approach is best when the consequences of failing to produce satisfactory results with the new system would be disastrous. It is the most conservative and costliest of approaches, because two systems must be operated simultaneously to perform the same functions. On the other hand, this approach does permit the staff to solve problems encountered with the new system before abandoning the old.

SYSTEM ACCEPTANCE

The automated system must be evaluated to determine if it meets the requirements for acceptance before final payment is made to the vendor. Acceptance requirements must be developed in advance and agreed upon by the library and the vendor of the automated system. The requirements can be identified in detail in either the RFP or in the contract negotiated between the library and the vendor upon selection of the system for acquisition. Several acceptance tests are commonly used by automated library systems, among them being the system reliability, functional, and response time tests. Most libraries require that a system pass all three of these tests before acceptance is given and before final payment is made to the vendor. Partial payment can be given to the vendor upon passing each of these tests.

System Reliability Test

A reliability test is conducted to determine if the automated system can operate at a defined level of effectiveness for a stated period of time.

> *Example:* The system is expected to operate reliably for a period of 45 (or 60 or 90) consecutive days at an uptime level of 95% (or 96% or 97%).

The meaning of the term "uptime" must be agreed upon by the library and the vendor before the test is begun.

> *Example:* Uptime shall mean the operational use time (the amount of time the system should be available for use by the library), minus downtime (the amount of time the system is not available for use by the library due to hardware or software malfunctions), divided by the operational use time:
>
> Uptime = (Operational Use Time) minus
> (Downtime) / Operational Use Time

Thus, the uptime for a system whose operational use time is 24 hours a day, but which was down 2 hours, will be:

> Uptime = (24-2) / 24 or 91.7%

A common problem which the library might encounter is that a part of the automated system will be down for a period of time, but other parts will be operating satisfactorily. For example, a light pen will cease functioning, but the remainder of the system is performing well. While this will be of a noncritical nature, other system parts such as a disk drive or the charging function software are critical and would seriously affect use of the system. For these reasons, some libraries define a level of reliability based upon downtime of various components of the system.

Example: The downtime factor shall be calculated by multiplying the downtime hours (those daily operational hours between the time the vendor has been notified of a system failure and the time the system is fully operating again) by a downtime coefficient. Total system downtime shall equal the sum of the downtime factors divided by the sum of daily library operation hours.

The coefficients then must be defined for both critical and noncritical operations failures.

Example: The coefficients for critical operations failures shall be defined as follows:
Catalog record creation = 1.0
Online catalog searches = 1.0
Charge and discharge = 1.0
Holds and renewals = 1.0
Borrower record creation = 1.0
Requisition order preparation = 1.0
Receiving materials = 1.0

Example: The coefficients for noncritical operations failures, such as report printing, shall be 0.25 after a 24-hour grace period.

Example: Other software failures not significantly affecting system operation shall have a coefficient of 0.1 beginning five days after a call to the vendor for service.

Coefficients for hardware failures should also be defined. For example:

Central processing unit = 1.0
Disk drive = 1.0
Tape drive = 1.0
Line printer = 1.0
CRT terminal = 0.1 per terminal
Optical scanner = 0.1 per scanner
Communications equipment = 0.1 per piece

Thus, if during a 45-day test period (or 450 hours at 10 hours operational use time daily) the charge system was down for 4 hours, a disk drive for 2 hours, and a terminal for 20 hours, the calculations for downtime would be as follows:

Charge system   1.0 x 4 hours = 4
Disk drive   1.0 x 2 hours = 2

Terminal   0.1 x 20 hours = 2
Total   8

The downtime for the 45-day period will be 8/450 or 1.7%. Conversely, the uptime will be 98.3%, or the downtime subtracted from 100%.

The library should notify the vendor of the automated system when the reliability test will begin. If desired, the vendor can be reminded of the terms of the test. Logs of downtime should be maintained by the library during the test, with times recorded to the nearest one-tenth hour when a component of the system becomes inoperable and again when the item is made operational.

The library should state in writing what will happen should the system not pass the reliability test.

> *Example:* In the event of a failure on the part of the system to meet the 95% (or 96% or 97%) uptime minimum, the 45 (or 60 or 90) consecutive day acceptance test shall begin anew.

A part of the library's payment to the vendor can be predicated upon the passing of the reliability test by the automated system.

Functional Test

A functional test is conducted to determine if the automated system meets all requirements as specified in the library's RFP and modified by the vendor's response or as stated by the vendor in advertisements, promotional literature, or in other written documentation. Representatives of the library and the vendor should check the availability and performance of each function or feature. Each feature or function should be checked in turn, and the system should be expected to perform as specified in the RFP or as stated in the vendor's literature. The entire system may be evaluated during one session, or the process can be segmented into several sessions during which only one or a few functions or features are evaluated at a time. The hardware and/or software should not be accepted until all requirements have been met.

Response Time Test

A response time test is conducted to determine if the system can perform operations and tasks at the rates or levels specified by the library and advertised by the vendor, with an acceptable response time.

> *Example:* A full-load response time acceptance test shall be conducted on-site after the vendor has installed the system and has certified in writing that the system as specified in the RFP is operational, after all software has been installed and passed the

functional acceptance test and after the initial bibliographic data file has been loaded.

Example: The response time test shall provide unequivocal evidence (i.e., the results may be entered into a written log) that the system meets response time performance requirements under the peak load condition.

In short, this test measures the time required for the system to complete typical transactions. The time required for the system to complete a transaction must be carefully defined.

Example: Response time means the elapsed time between the submission of a query or command (the pressing of the "return" or "send" key) and the return of the complete response to the operator (the screen is filled).

Example: Response time means the time between the pressing of the return or send key after entry of queries or commands and the time the first character of the system's response is displayed on the screen.

The load on the system during the test should be specified by the library.

Example: A library-specified mix of terminal dedications; e.g., 50% of the terminals dedicated to the searches/inquiries in the Online Public Catalog; 20% to data input-edit; 15% to circulation; and 15% to acquisitions.

Example: A library-specified "peak load" or "worst case" job mix; e.g., 1,000 charge and renewal transactions; 200 discharges; 200 file inquiries (100 of which are subject inquiries); 100 data input-edits; and two batch jobs, in a single hour.

In addition, the acceptable response times for various functions or activities should be specified by the library.

Example: The system shall, operating in the worst case test, exhibit average response times not exceeding:
Six seconds for data input-edit
Six seconds for file inquiries (nonsubject)
Eight seconds for file inquiries (subject)
Two seconds for charge, renewal, discharge, and other circulation and acquisitions functions.

Example: Average system response times are the totals of all the transaction times in a category (e.g., charges) divided by the total number of transactions in those categories.

The response time test should be carefully planned in advance. The library's automation consultant, if one is used, can assist in designing and setting up the test. The library should provide operators, test log keepers, and data recorders for each terminal during the test. Stop watches may be used to measure response times.

Vendor representatives should be present during the test, if possible. Should the system not pass the response time test, additional tests can be conducted after the vendor has had time to make adjustments to the software or hardware. The library may withhold payment or partial payment until the response time test has been passed.

COMPUTER ROOM MANAGEMENT

A large part of the success of an automated system will depend upon how effectively and efficiently the computer itself is operated. This section discusses the day-to-day efforts necessary to manage activities in the area where the computer supporting the automated system is housed and operated.

Computer Room Activities

The activities in the computer room will depend upon the nature, size, and complexity of the automated system. Typical activities in a library computer room include operating and monitoring the computer, maintaining the tape or disk library, troubleshooting problems, maintaining a supply and forms inventory, and monitoring security and safety.

Operating and Monitoring the Computer. Most operations performed by modern computers are completely automatic and do not require staff intervention. However, there are some operations that the computer cannot perform itself. Library staff must:

1. Start or "boot" and shut down the computer as necessary. Most library computers operate 24 hours a day, seven days a week but will occasionally be shut down for maintenance and repair or when problems such as air conditioning failure arise.
2. Start or "bring up" and stop or "bring down" software as necessary. For example, the circulation system may be brought up at 7:00 a.m. and brought down at 11:45 p.m. daily. While many computers now can start and stop software automatically at preset times, staff often must know how to perform this procedure at nonscheduled times when software problems arise or during other emergencies.
3. Start and monitor batch jobs. There are many batch jobs, such as building indexes, compiling and preparing reports, updating and checking files, and compiling and recompiling programs which must be started and monitored until their completion. While most of these jobs too are completed automatically after their initiation, software malfunctions can arise. An operator must then correct the problem, call

vendor support staff to correct the problem, restart the job, or take other appropriate action.

4. Operate and monitor peripheral equipment. Staff must mount correct tapes on the magnetic tape drive, remove reports from the line printer, clear paper jams, change forms, and replenish the paper supply in the printer as necessary.

5. Schedule jobs. Staff must organize and schedule, in conjunction with the system users, batch jobs that are to be performed by the computer.

6. Maintain logs of activities. Staff must record in a log events such as the initiation and completion of jobs, problems encountered, actions taken to correct problems, malfunctions of equipment, and other similar activities.

7. Perform system back-ups. Staff must perform software backups on a scheduled basis. This might include mounting and changing tapes or disk packs, starting and monitoring the backup software, solving problems encountered during the process, and recording the activities in a log.

8. Restore files. When software fails and other problems are encountered, staff may be required to restore files and other software, using backup tapes or disk files.

9. Monitor the system in general. Staff must monitor the console for programmed messages from the system and check that all systems and jobs are functioning properly.

Maintaining the Tape or Disk Library. An automated library system will have backup or duplicate copies of data files and software on tape or disk maintained offline from the computer. These tapes or disks are maintained in a "library" in the computer room or an adjacent area, with additional copies kept away from the computer area in a vault or other secure area. The tapes or disks must be carefully labelled and stored in racks or other storage cabinets. The vendor of the automated system should assist the library staff in organizing the tape or disk library and in labelling and rotating the reels or disks.

Troubleshooting Problems. In modern automated library systems, search requests, data, and commands are entered into the computer system from remote terminals and the results transmitted back to the same distant locations away from the computer room. Users of the system may be scattered throughout the library building and in branch libraries miles from the computer itself. Many problems with equipment and software can be solved by staff at the remote sites, but other problems must be handled centrally. For example, staff in the computer room, in response to a problem reported by a remote user, may have to start up, stop, or reset software or hardware, call vendor maintenance personnel, or provide instructions for handling a situation at the distant location.

Maintaining a Supply and Forms Inventory. A variety of supplies and custom forms may be used by the automated system, most of which will be used in the computer room. An inventory of these supplies and forms must be carefully maintained to make certain that stocks are adequate at all times. As supplies and forms are used, orders must be placed to replenish stock as needed.

Monitoring Safety and Security. A last important activity in the computer room is the monitoring of safety and security. While security devices such as smoke, heat, and humidity detectors will perform most of the work, staff must check that security to the room is maintained and that the sensing devices are in proper repair. Tests of the sensing devices and fire extinguishers should be conducted periodically and any necessary maintenance should be conducted promptly.

Computer Room Staffing

The level of staffing of a computer room will also depend upon the nature, size, and complexity of the library system. For a small automated system, computer room duties may simply be added to the responsibilities of staff in a circulation, acquisitions, or cataloging department. For larger systems, a cadre of staff may be necessary. Typical staff for a computer room include a computer room manager and one or more computer operators.

The Computer Operations Manager. The primary responsibility of a computer operations manager is the efficient operation of the computer system while providing quality services to all its users. The manager may be full-time or part-time, depending upon the size and complexity of the automated system and upon the ability of the library to hire staff. Computer operations management may be assigned to a staff member with other responsibilities. For example, the head of the circulation department may also be responsible for managing the computer operations. For large computer systems, a full-time manager will be needed. Qualifications of a computer operations manager might include:

1. Good management abilities.
2. A firm understanding of the computer equipment and its detailed operation.
3. A willingness to be concerned with detail.
4. An ability to communicate effectively with users of the system, with management, and with others.
5. An ability to work in a constantly changing environment.

Responsibilities of the computer operations manager are similar to those of other department heads within the library. The computer operations manager might be required to:

1. Formulate policies and procedures regarding the computer system and its users within the framework of the library organization.
2. Recruit, hire, train, and schedule staff to operate the computer.
3. Establish job schedules for the computer, in conjuction with users of the automated system.
4. Establish and maintain good working relations with vendor support and maintenance staff.
5. Keep library management and system users informed about problems and activities in the computer room.

A sample job description for a computer operations manager is shown in Appendix B.

Computer Operator. One or several full- or part-time computer operators may be necessary for the computer room, depending upon the size and nature of the automated system. Qualifications of a computer operator may include:

1. A firm understanding of the computer equipment and its detailed operation.
2. An ability to follow instructions and procedures carefully and completely.
3. An ability to handle calmly and effectively problems which will occur.

Responsibilities of a computer operator may be confined to activities involving the computer or may include other duties in the computer room. The computer operator may be required to:

1. Start and monitor batch jobs and other programs.
2. Bring up and bring down software at scheduled times.
3. Mount tapes and disk packs on the proper devices when needed by the system.
4. Operate and monitor other peripheral equipment.
5. Perform system backups on a scheduled basis.
6. Maintain logs of activities.

Since the operator may be the only person in the computer room for long periods of time, he or she may also be required to monitor security and safety in the room, take inventory of supplies and forms, and troubleshoot problems reported from remote users. A sample job description for a computer operator is shown in Appendix B.

Appendices

Appendix A
Sample Phases, Activities, and Tasks of a Library Automation Project

I. Project Organization and Staffing
   A. Establish an organization for the project
      1. Identify the options for organizing the project
      2. Examine the advantages and disadvantages of each option
      3. Select the method of project organization to be used
   B. Select and appoint a project manager
      1. Define the qualifications desired of the project manager
      2. Define the responsibilities of the project manager
      3. Select and appoint the project manager
   C. Select and appoint other project staff, if any
      1. Identify other project staff which will be required
      2. Define the qualifications of the other staff
      3. Define the responsibilities of the other staff
      4. Select and appoint the other staff
   D. Establish a project steering committee
      1. Define the responsibilities of the project steering committee
      2. Select and appoint the members of the project steering committee
   E. Locate and hire an automation consultant, if one is to be used
      1. Define the responsibilities of the automation consultant
      2. Prepare a Request For Proposal (RFP) for the consultant
      3. Solicit automation proposals or applications from consultants, using the RFP
      4. Evaluate the proposals received from prospective consultants

   5. Select and hire the best consultant submitting a proposal

  F. Identify other project resource people

 II. Project Planning and Control

  A. Develop a long-range automation plan
   1. Define the library mission statement
   2. Identify general automation goals
   3. Identify specific automation goals
   4. Develop a long-range strategy for automation
   5. Circulate drafts of the plan for discussion and comments
   6. Incorporate comments received into the plan
   7. Obtain approval of the plan

  B. Prepare a justification for the library automation project
   1. Identify the problem or problems facing the library
   2. Prepare a problem statement

  C. Define the goal of the project

  D. Identify any constraints on the project

  E. Prepare an outline of the project phases, activities, and steps

  F. Prepare a schedule and calendar of the project's phases, activities, and steps

  G. Establish how the automated system will be funded
   1. Estimate the start-up or developmental costs for the automated system
   2. Describe how the developmental costs will be funded
   3. Estimate the annual operating costs for the automated system
   4. Describe how the annual operating costs for the automated system will be funded

  H. Obtain project approval
   1. Incorporate the project justification, goal, constraints, outline, schedule, calendar, and funding strategy into a draft report
   2. Circulate the draft for suggestions and comments
   3. Incorporate comments and suggestions into the draft
   4. Submit the draft for approval

III. Requirements for an Automated System

  A. Define a focal point for developing the requirements
   1. Identify the goal of the library automation project
   2. Identify the goal of the system to be automated, or:
   3. Identify the general automation goals established by the library

  B. Gather sample requirements from other libraries

  C. Establish a task force to develop the requirements

      1. Define the responsibilities of the task force
      2. Select and appoint the task force members
  D. Subdivide the requirements among the task force members
      1. Identify the categories of requirements needed
      2. Assign each category to one or more task force members for development
  E. Prepare, study, and approve a set of requirements
      1. Prepare a draft of each category of requirements
      2. Consolidate the drafts into a single document
      3. Circulate the draft requirements for study, suggestions, and comments
      4. Revise the draft to incorporate comments and suggestions received
      5. Submit the draft set of requirements for approval

IV. The Request For Proposal
  A. Assign the writing of a draft RFP to a person or committee
  B. Prepare, study, and approve the RFP
      1. Identify requirements of the library's purchasing department for the RFP
      2. Prepare an outline for the RFP
      3. Gather information for the RFP
      4. Prepare a draft RFP for discussion and study
      5. Circulate copies of the draft widely
      6. Study and discuss the draft RFP
      7. Revise the draft to incorporate comments and suggestions received
      8. Obtain approval of the draft RFP prior to submission to vendors

V. Bid Solicitation, Evaluation, and Award
  A. Solicit responses to the RFP
      1. Identify vendors to whom copies of the RFP will be sent
      2. Mail copies of the RFP to vendors
  B. Respond to questions about the RFP or the library automation project
  C. Establish rules for selecting the best response to the RFP
      1. Prepare a draft set of decision rules
      2. Circulate the draft for comments and suggestions
      3. Obtain approval of the decision rules
  D. Establish a bid evaluation team
      1. Define the responsibilities of the bid evaluation team
      2. Select and appoint the bid evaluation team members
  E. Review and evaluate bids from vendors

1. Evaluate responses to the library's system requirements
2. Evaluate the hardware bid by each vendor
3. Evaluate the initial costs for each system bid
4. Evaluate the annual maintenance costs for each system bid
5. Evaluate the vendors
6. Conduct system demonstrations
7. Conduct interviews with vendor clients
8. Conduct site visits to other libraries with the systems bid

F. Select the best system
  1. Summarize the results of bid evaluation and review
  2. Study the results of bid evaluation
  3. Select the system which meets most or all of the library's decision criteria or rules
  4. Prepare an evaluation report

G. Negotiate contracts for the system selected
  1. Negotiate and sign a purchase contract for the system selected
  2. Negotiate and sign a maintenance contract for the system selected

VI. Site Preparation
  A. Develop specifications for the in-house computer room
    1. Develop electrical power specifications for the room
    2. Develop air conditioning and air flow specifications for the room
    3. Develop humidity specifications for the room
    4. Develop safety and fire protection specifications for the room
    5. Develop monitoring specifications for the room
    6. Develop flooring specifications for the room
    7. Develop ceiling and wall specifications for the room
    8. Develop door and window specifications for the room
    9. Develop lighting specifications for the room
    10. Develop storage facility specifications for the room
  B. Select a site for the in-house computer room
  C. Design the layout of the computer room
  D. Construct the computer room
    1. Initiate the work
    2. Monitor the work
    3. Approve the site
  E. Prepare the sites of remote terminal work stations
    1. Identify the location of each remote terminal
    2. Identify the equipment to be at each location
    3. Develop specifications for each site

4. Design the space layout for each terminal work station
5. Install cables from the CPU to each remote site or initiate telephone line installation for modems
6. Install any necessary electrical outlets
7. Initiate other site construction or renovation

F. Prepare other system space if necessary
1. Develop specifications for the system space
2. Design the space layout
3. Initiate work for any necessary construction, renovation, or movement of equipment and furniture

VII. Database Conversion
A. Identify the files to be created or converted
B. Determine how each file will be created or converted
C. Establish schedules for each creation and conversion
D. Prepare existing records for conversion, if necessary
E. Convert or create the records
F. Check the accuracy of the conversion or creation

VIII. Staff and User Education and Training
A. Orient and train the staff
1. Develop a plan for staff orientation and training
2. Prepare a calendar for staff orientation and training
3. Obtain training documentation from the vendor and others
4. Conduct system operator training
5. Conduct supervisor training
6. Conduct basic operator training

B. Provide follow-up training as necessary
C. Educate users about the automated system
1. Develop a general publicity program
2. Develop and implement user education classes
3. Develop and implement tutorials for individual users
4. Design, prepare, and distribute "how to use" brochures for the automated system

IX. System Installation, Acceptance, and Operation
A. Acquire supplies, forms, and equipment for the automated system
1. Identify the supplies, forms, and equipment for the automated system
2. Prepare specifications for the supplies, forms, and equipment
3. Order and receive the supplies, forms, and equipment

B. Install, test, and accept the hardware and software
1. Install and test the hardware

    2. Install and test the software
    3. Accept the hardware and software
C. Load necessary files into computer storage
D. Align workflow and space to the automated system
    1. Prepare design flowcharts for the new automated procedures
    2. Prepare layout flowcharts for the space to be occupied by the automated system
    3. Rearrange furniture and equipment, if necessary, to accomodate the new system
    4. Prepare new policy and procedure manuals for the new system
E. Realign staff
    1. Determine staffing requirements for the automated system
    2. Develop new or revise old job descriptions for staff
    3. Counsel staff about new or revised duties
    4. Implement training or retraining program for staff
F. Activate the automated system
    1. Determine the method of system activation to be used
    2. Prepare a calendar for the activiation
    3. Begin operation of the new system
G. Conduct system acceptance test
    1. Review the system acceptance test specifications
    2. Prepare detailed plans for system test execution
    3. Prepare a calendar for the acceptance tests
    4. Conduct the system reliability test
    5. Conduct the functional test
    6. Conduct the full-load response time test
    7. Repeat tests if necessary
    8. Accept the system
H. Provide computer operations management
    1. Identify activities in the computer room
    2. Define the responsibilities of the computer operations manager and computer operators
    3. Develop job descriptions for the computer operations manager and computer operators
    4. Hire and train staff to fill the positions

Appendix B
Sample Job Descriptions

JOB 1
AUTOMATION LIBRARIAN

General Function

Under direction of the University Librarian, responsible for the successful planning, development, acquisition, implementation, evaluation, and maintenance of automated systems and new technologies in the library.

Specific Duties/Responsibilities

1. Prepares system proposals and requirements, in consultation with library staff and others, for automated and new systems in the library.
2. Serves as manager of automation and systems projects within the library.
3. Coordinates automated systems in the library with other local, state, regional, and national systems and programs.
4. Coordinates and directs the work of committees and task forces involving systems projects.
5. Develops and maintains liaisons with campus and state computing personnel and with vendors of automated systems.
6. Prepares both short- and long-range plans for library automation and new technologies.
7. Hires, trains, and supervises other project and computer operations staff.
8. Conducts or coordinates training for library staff in regard to library automation.
9. Maintains an awareness of developments in library automation.

10. Attends and participates in meetings and discussions relating to library automation.
11. Serves as a resource person for library staff and others regarding library automation.
12. Prepares grant proposals and pursues other sources of funding for support of the library's automated systems.
13. Performs other related duties as required.

Supervision

Works under the general administrative direction of the University Librarian. Supervises project and computer operations staff.

Minimum Qualifications

Master's degree in library science, information science, or computer science and a minimum of three years related experience with automated library systems. Knowledge of current library and automation practices. Strong organizational, management, and interpersonal skills are essential. Good verbal and written communication skills are important. Ability to work efficiently and independently is important.

JOB 2
LIBRARY SYSTEMS ANALYST

General Function

Under direction of the Automation Librarian, responsible for analyzing, designing, and evaluating automated and other systems in the library.

Specific Duties/Responsibilities

1. Prepares analytical studies and critiques of existing and new manual and automated systems in the library.
2. Designs new workflows for existing and new systems.
3. Prepares narrative specifications and flowcharts for activities and routines within existing and proposed systems in the library.
4. Studies and keeps abreast of trends and developments in library automation, systems, and related technologies to advise the Automation Librarian and others.
5. Performs other related duties as required.

Supervision

Works under the general direction of the Automation Librarian. No supervisory responsibilities.

Minimum Qualifications

Master's degree in library science, information science, or computer science, and a minimum of three years related experience with automated library systems or systems analysis. Strong interpersonal skills and verbal and written communication skills are essential. Ability to work efficiently and independently is important.

JOB 3
COMPUTER PROGRAMMER

General Function

Under direction of the Automation Librarian, responsible for designing, writing, testing, and maintaining software for automated systems in the library.

Specific Duties/Responsibilities

1. Designs, codes, and tests new software for the library's automated systems.
2. Maintains the software for operational automated systems in the library.
3. Identifies and evaluates software from other organizations and libraries for possible acquisition and use.
4. Studies and keeps abreast of trends and developments in computer programming to advise the Automation Librarian and others.
5. Performs other related duties as required.

Supervision

Works under the general direction of the Automation Librarian. No supervisory responsibilities.

Minimum Qualifications

Bachelor's degree in computer science, with a minimum of two years experience as a computer programmer. Experience with automated library systems desirable. Knowledge of programming principles and ability to write complex programs in at least one high-level language (preferably COBOL) essential. Ability to work efficiently and independently is important.

JOB 4
COMPUTER OPERATIONS MANAGER

General Function

Under direction of the Automation Librarian, responsible for computer operations for the library.

Specific Duties/Responsibilities

1. Responsible for the daily operation and monitoring of the library's computer system.
2. Responsible for organizing, initiating, monitoring, and completing all batch processing programs on the computer.
3. Hires, trains, and supervises the computer operators and other operations staff.
4. Maintains the inventory of special supplies for the computer room and requests new stock as necessary.
5. Coordinates the maintenance of hardware and software for the automated systems of the library.
6. Performs other related duties as required.

Supervision

Works under the general direction of the Automation Librarian. Supervises computer operators and other operations support staff.

Minimum Qualifications

High school graduation or equivalent, with high school or college level courses in data processing preferred. At least one year of computer experience, with operation of a computer preferred. Good organizational, management, and interpersonal skills are essential. Ability to work efficiently and independently is important.

JOB 5
COMPUTER OPERATOR

General Function

Under direction of the Computer Operations Manager, responsible for assisting in operations related to the maintenance of online systems in the library.

Specific Duties/Responsibilities

1. Operates and monitors the library's computer system.
2. Prints reports generated from overnight processing.
3. Initiates, monitors, and completes batch processing programs.
4. Prepares routine copies of database files as necessary.
5. Inspects and cleans the tape drives and printer daily.
6. Maintains logs of backups and batches completed.
7. Maintains logs of system problems.
8. Performs other related duties as required.

Supervision

Works under the direction of the Computer Operations Manager. No supervisory responsibilities.

Minimum Qualifications

High school graduation or equivalent, with high school or college level courses in data processing preferred. At least one year of computer or data processing experience, with operation of a computer preferred. Ability to work efficiently and independently is important.

Other

Must be able to work nights.

Appendix C
A List of Typical Hardware,
Equipment, and Supplies for
Automated Library Systems

HARDWARE, EQUIPMENT, AND SUPPLIES FOR AN IN-HOUSE COMPUTER ROOM

Computer Hardware

Central Processing Unit (CPU)
Control or Operator Console
Magnetic Tape Drives
Magnetic Disk Drives
Line printers

Software

Operating System
System Utilities
Programming Languages
Application Software
(Acquisitions, Serials Control,
Online Public Catalog,
Circulation, etc.)

Other Equipment

Modems
Multiplexors
Magnetic Disk Packs
Power Control Unit

Desk or Table for Control
Console
Operator Chair
Forms Racks for Line Printer
Table for Handling Forms
Magnetic Tape Storage Cabinets
or Shelves
Magnetic Disk Storage Cabinets
or Shelves
Magnetic Tape Storage Racks
Wall Clock
Portable Vacuum Cleaner
Bulletin or Message Board
Fire Extinguishers
Air Conditioners
Smoke Detectors
Shelving/Cabinets for Supplies,
Spare Parts, Forms, etc.
Forms Burster
Forms Decollator
Hygrometer
Thermometer
Antistatic Mats
Racks for Operator/Procedure
Manuals
Screwdrivers (Regular and
Phillips)

Special Consumable Supplies

Magnetic Tape on Reels or in Cassettes
Ribbons for Line Printer
Magnetic Disk Labels
Magnetic Tape Reel Labels
Fan-Fold Blank Paper (Various Sizes)
Notebooks for Logs
Isopropyl Alcohol or Cleaning Pads for Cleaning Equipment
Vacuum Cleaner Filter Bags
Disposable Gloves for Changing Printer Ribbons
Extra Fuses
Printout Binders
Spare Cable
Connector Pin Crimper
Spare Cable Connectors
Spare Connector Pins

Custom Forms

Order Request Cards or Forms (Acquisitions)
Purchase Order Forms (Acquisitions)
Claims Forms (Acquisitions)
Cancellation Forms (Acquisitions)
Vouchers (Acquisitions)
Checks (Acquisitions)
Borrower Registration Cards/Forms (Circulation)
Borrower Identification Cards (Circulation)
Overdue Notices (Circulation)
Recall Notices (Circulation)
Hold Availability Notices (Circulation)

HARDWARE, EQUIPMENT, AND OTHER SUPPLIES FOR REMOTE SITES

Computer Hardware

CRT Terminals
Screen/Video Printers
Date-Due/Receipt Printers
Barcode/OCR Scanners
Portable Scanners/Terminals
Microcomputers for Backup Systems

Other Equipment

Desks or Tables for Terminals
Operator Chairs
Printer Stands
Modems
Multiplexors
CRT Turntables
Printer Acoustic Enclosures
Printer Forms Shelves/Buckets
Copy Holders
Footrests
CRT Screen Filters
Extension Cords
Screwdrivers (Regular and Phillips)

Special Consumable Supplies

OCR or Barcode Labels
Fuses for OCR/Barcode Scanners and CRTs
Bulbs for Scanning Wands
Ribbons for Printers
Blank Paper for Printers
Screen Cleaning Cloths
CRT Dust Covers
Printwheels

Appendix D
A Sample RFP for an
Integrated Library System

INTRODUCTION

Purpose of the RFP

The purpose of this Request for Proposal (RFP) is to define the specifications and requirements for, and solicit quotations or bids from, prospective vendors for acquisition, delivery, installation, and maintenance of an automated, turnkey Integrated Library System for the University of Anytown Libraries. Each acceptable response shall include quotations or bids for the application software for an online public catalog, a circulation system, and an acquisitions system; and the computer system to support the software, including system software, documentation, training, and hardware and software maintenance.

Description of the Library

The University of Anytown was founded 55 years ago as Anytown Normal School, and today is an institution comprised of nine colleges with an enrollment of 22,000 students. Colleges include Business Administration, Education, Liberal Arts, Science, Engineering, Nursing, Law, Computer Science, Music, and Library Science.

The Libraries consist of more than 800,000 volumes, 6,500 periodical subscriptions, and sizeable collections of microforms, maps, and audiovisual materials. About 300,000 of these titles have been cataloged through OCLC since 1977. The libraries on campus include the main library and law, music, science, and library science branches.

Overview of the Existing System

The Libraries have had an automated circulation system since 1974. This system has served the Libraries well, but its short titles and limited capabilities restrict its expansion unless a complete replacement of hardware, software, and database is undertaken. An in-house key-to-disk computer has supported a batch process acquisitions system. While the circulation system can at least interface with OCLC, the acquisitions system cannot interface with any existing system; due to their design, the two highly interrelated systems must be operated independently. In short, several separate computer systems are used in an inefficient and ineffective manner.

Overview of the Planned System

The Libraries intend to build a online public catalog for holdings of its main and branch libraries, with access terminals located in those libraries and in offices and laboratories throughout the campus. The catalog will equalize bibliographic access to the libraries by enabling centralized, online identification of materials. In addition, users may determine the availability of materials (on the shelf, in circulation, in process, on order, at bindery, missing, etc.). Functions to be performed by the new automated system include database creation and maintenance; authority control for names, subjects, and titles; searching by author, title, subject, call number, etc.; search results printing; and statistical report display and printing.

The circulation system will provide online borrower file creation and maintenance; charging, discharging, and renewal of loans; hold and recall entry and maintenance; fine and fee entry and maintenance; overdue, recall, and fee notice production; delinquency list production; reserve room maintenance; and statistical report display and printing.

The acquisitions system will provide online selection entry and review, requisition preparation, receiving, fund accounting, claiming and cancelling, supplier file creation and maintenance, and statistical report display and printing.

ADMINISTRATIVE RULES FOR THE RFP

Inquiries about the RFP

After receipt of this RFP, vendors will be given an opportunity to consult with the Libraries' staff, upon request. Appointments should be made through:

James Doe, Systems Librarian
University Libraries

University of Anytown
123 Broad Avenue
Anytown 12345
Telephone 123-456-7890

The individual listed above may be telephoned or visited for clarification of the specifications only. No authority is intended or implied that specifications may be amended or alternates accepted prior to bid opening.

Any questions requiring responses affecting the bid and related responses that arise during the preparation of the vendor's response to this RFP should be directed in writing to the person above, with copies to:

Jack Jones, Purchasing Agent
Purchasing Department
University of Anytown
123 Broad Avenue
Anytown 12345

Responses that are of a general nature will be prepared and distributed to all bidders. Responses of a specific nature will be provided to the requesting vendor only. The Libraries shall be the sole judge of whether a request is general or specific. Questions may be submitted up to 14 days prior to bid opening.

RFP Expenses

Expenses for developing the bids and demonstrations of equipment and systems are entirely the responsibility of the vendor and shall not be chargeable, in any manner, to the Libraries or to the University.

Alternate Bids

A vendor may submit more than one bid, at his or her option. If a vendor elects to submit more than one bid, it is requested that each bid be identified as either primary or alternate. Only one primary bid will be accepted. Each bid submitted, primary or alternate, should follow the vendor response specifications described in this document.

For alternate bids, a vendor may refer by name and number to specific sections or paragraphs in the primary bid, rather than reproduce information that has not changed. Information in the primary bid that is referenced in the alternate bid will be considered as an integral part of the alternate bid for evaluation and contractual purposes.

Delivery of Bids

Three (3) copies of bids should be delivered no later than 5:00 p.m., CDT, March 29, 198x, to:

Jack Jones, Purchasing Agent
Purchasing Department
University of Anytown
123 Broad Avenue
Anytown 12345

Proposals should be delivered in a sealed envelope plainly marked "Library System Proposal."

Modification or Withdrawal of Bids

Any bidder may withdraw his or her bid at any time prior to the scheduled closing time for the receipt of bids, but no bidder may withdraw his or her bid for a period of 120 days after the scheduled closing time for the receipt of bids. Only telegrams, letters, and other written requests for the modification or correction of a previously submitted bid that are addressed in the same manner as bids and are received by the University prior to the scheduled closing time for the receipt of bids will be accepted. The bid will be corrected in accordance with such written requests, provided that any such written request is in a sealed envelope that is plainly marked "Modification of Bid on (item described)." Oral or telephoned modifications or corrections will not be recognized or considered.

Bid Opening

Bids will be opened on March 30, 198x, at 9:00 a.m., CDT, in Room 123 of the Administration Building. Vendors are invited to attend. All bids and supporting documentation submitted become public property at the time of bid opening.

Evaluation of Bids

All proposals will be evaluated by a team consisting of representatives from the Libraries, the University Administration, and other such representatives and/or consultants as the University deems appropriate.

The Libraries reserve the right to contact a bidder for clarification of information submitted, to contact current users of equipment or software bid, and to use other sources of obtaining information regarding the hardware, software, or vendor that is deemed appropriate and would assist in the evaluation.

In evaluating the bids, the Libraries reserve the right to accept or reject all or any part of any bid, waive minor technicalities, and award the bid to the vendor deemed to best serve the interests of the University; use any or all of the ideas from bids submitted without limitations; and adopt any part or all of a bid in selecting the optimum system if it is judged in the best interests of the Libraries, such selection to include the privileges of substituting specific hardware items including, but not limited to, tape devices, direct access storage devices, memory, terminals, and other peripheral devices.

The Libraries reserve the right to increase or decrease the number of articles called for in any item of the specifications by as much as 20 percent, if the change is made at the time of the order for items herein, or to eliminate items entirely. The seller's proposal may be adjusted in accordance with the unit prices quoted herein. Total reduction shall not exceed 15 percent of the dollar amount of the proposal.

Disputes

In case of any doubt or difference of opinion as to the items to be furnished hereunder, the decision of the Director of Purchasing of the University shall be final and binding upon both parties.

Award of Contract

A contract purchase order, with terms acceptable to both the University and the successful bidder, will be sent to the vendor receiving the award. All other bidders will be able to review the bid file to determine bid award for all items.

Calendar of Events

RFP sent to vendors...January 31, 198x
Vendors' bid meeting...February 20, 198x
Written inquiries from vendors must be received...February 25, 198x
Written responses to vendors' questions returned...March 1, 198x
Proposals received from vendors...March 29, 198x
Evaluation of vendors' proposals completed...May 10, 198x
Vendor selection...May 17, 198x
Contract signing...July 15, 198x

GENERAL REQUIREMENTS

Firm Bids

All prices bid must be firm for 120 calendar days from due-date of the bid.

Demonstration of Systems

At the option of the Libraries, a vendor may be required to demonstrate the operation of equipment and/or software during the bid evaluation process. The location of this demonstration will be at a site mutually agreeable to the Libraries and the vendor. The specific requirements and location would be detailed in a separate letter. The vendor must demonstrate his or her proposed equipment and software within 15 days of receipt of this written notice.

Contractual Expectations

The terms and specifications contained in this RFP and a bidder's response to this invitation shall be considered as a part of the contract. In submitting a proposal, a bidder agrees to accept a contract or purchase order accompanied by a memorandum of agreement incorporating all additional points mutually agreed upon. A vendor may elect to charge an additional amount in consideration for the acceptance of any paragraph or section of the proposed contract. If the vendor wishes to specify a charge for any item, it should identify the item and specify the amount of the charge.

Performance and Bid Bonds

A performance bond of 100 percent of the total bid, in a form acceptable to the University, will be required for the full term of the purchase order. A 5 percent bid bond is required with each bid.

Delivery of the System

All hardware items shall be delivered within 120 days after receipt of the order. The system software (the operating system, the database management system, if used, system utilities, etc.) and the online public catalog software shall be delivered within 120 days after receipt of order. The circulation system software shall be delivered no later than 90 calendar days after delivery of the hardware and system software (early delivery will be accepted). The acquisitions system software shall be delivered no later than 30 calendar days after delivery of the circulation system software (early delivery will be accepted).

Installation of the System

Unless indicated to the contrary, items of equipment shall be delivered, uncrated, checked, assembled, set in proper place, and installed ready for use, and free from breakage, blemishes, or other defects. Installation shall include distribution of the terminals in all specified locations. The online public catalog CRT terminals shall not be installed until after the initial load has been completed and the Libraries are ready to offer the catalog to the public.

The installation shall be under the general direction of the Libraries, in accordance with the applicable specifications. The Libraries and the vendor shall agree beforehand on the location of each piece of equipment, and detailed layouts shall be prepared. The vendor shall repair, refinish, and make good any damage to the building resulting from any of his or her operations. This shall include any damage to plaster, tile work, wall coverings, paint, ceilings, floors, or any other finished work. All minor adjustments, relocations of individual pieces of equipment, and similar final corrections shall be executed by the vendor as directed by the Libraries as part of the work under this contract.

The vendor shall have free access to the premises for the purpose of acquainting himself or herself with the conditions, delivering equipment, and performing the work necessary to fulfill the contract. The vendor shall sweep, dust, and clean up all trash, rubbish, and other waste scattered throughout the buildings caused by the installation of equipment under this contract. Any containers or other trash that constitute a fire hazard or an obstacle to the work of others shall be removed daily. The extent of the final cleaning up shall be determined by the Libraries after a final inspection at the completion of the installation of all items covered by the purchase order.

A temporary installation of substitute hardware, software, or other items pending delivery of items bid for permanent installation shall not be allowed.

Liquidated Damages

From the compensation otherwise to be paid, the Libraries may retain the sum of $200 each calendar day thereafter that the work of the vendor remains incomplete and unacceptable to the Libraries, which sum is agreed upon as the proper measure of liquidated damages which the Libraries will sustain per diem by failure of the vendor to complete the work by the time stipulated, and this sum shall not be construed in any sense as a penalty.

Vendor Warranties

The vendor shall warrant that the system shall operate in conformance with the specifications contained in this RFP and the vendor's written response. The vendor warrants that the system shall be merchantable and fit for the purposes for which it is intended. The vendor shall warrant that the equipment as installed shall have adequate capacity to handle the Libraries' existing and expected future workloads specified in this RFP. The vendor warrants that all hardware will be free of any defects in workmanship or materials for a period of ninety (90) days after installation and installation acceptance by the Libraries.

Payment

The Libraries plan to pay for the system in four (4) payments:

1. 40 percent of the total system cost shall be paid upon the signing of a purchase contract between the Libraries and the vendor.
2. 20 percent to be paid upon satisfactory completion and demonstration of a Functional Acceptance Test.
3. 20 percent to be paid upon satisfactory completion of demonstration of a System Reliability Test.
4. 20 percent to be paid upon satisfactory completion and demonstration of a Full-Load Response Time Test.

Title to Hardware and Software

Upon installation, acceptance, and final payment, the Libraries shall receive clear title to all hardware and software not under a licensing arrangement.

Acceptance Tests

Three acceptance tests shall be required of the vendor: System Reliability, Functional, and Full-Load Response Time Tests.

System Reliability Test. A System Reliability Test shall be conducted on-site after the vendor has installed the system and has certified in writing that the system as specified in this RFP is operational. The system shall operate at an average level of reliability of no less than 97 percent for a period of 45 consecutive days. The average level of reliability shall be determined as follows:

The downtime factor shall be calculated by multiplying the downtime hours (those daily operational hours between the time the vendor has been notified of a system failure and the time the system is fully operational again) by a downtime coefficient, as defined in a Downtime Coefficient Table. For example, critical operations failures (online catalog record creation and maintenance, online catalog searches, charges and discharges, holds and renewals, borrower record creation and maintenace, requisition order preparation, and receiving) shall have a coefficient of 1.0; noncritical operations failures (report printing, for example) shall have a coefficient of 0.25 after a 24-hour grace period; and other software failures not significantly affecting system operation will have a coefficient of 0.1 beginning five days after service call. CPU, disk drives, tape drives, and line printers shall have a coefficient of 1.0; each CRT terminal shall have a coefficient of

0.1; and communications equipment shall have a coefficient of 0.1 per piece.

Total system downtime shall equal the sum of the downtime factors divided by the sum of daily library operation hours. Maintenance logs shall be kept by the Libraries in order to facilitate the measurement of system reliability. Downtime shall be calculated to the nearest one-tenth hour and calculated as a percentage of the library total operating hours during the period. In the event of a failure to meet the 3 percent downtime maximum, the 45 days acceptance test shall begin again when the problem is resolved.

Functional Acceptance Test. A Functional Acceptance Test shall be conducted on-site after the vendor has installed the system and has certified in writing that the system as specified in this RFP is operational. Representatives of the Libraries and the vendor shall check the availability and performance of each feature or function. Each function or feature shall be tested in turn, and the system must perform as specified in the RFP and as stated in the vendor's literature.

Full-Load Response Time Test. A Full-Load Response Time Test shall be conducted on-site after the vendor has installed the system and has certified in writing that the system as specified in this RFP is operational after all software has been installed and passed the Functional Acceptance Test and after the initial bibliographic data file has been loaded.

The Libraries shall provide operators, test log keepers, and data recorders for each terminal during the tests. The test shall evaluate the system within the following constraints:

1. A library-specified mix of terminal dedications, e.g., 50 percent of the terminals dedicated to searches in the online catalog; 20 percent of data input and edit; 15 percent to circulation; and 15 percent to acquisitions.
2. A library-specified "peak load" or "worst case" job mix, e.g., 1,000 charge and renewal transactions; 200 discharges; 200 file inquiries (100 of which are subject inquiries); 100 data input and edits; and two batch-mode jobs, in a single hour.

The test shall provide unequivocal evidence that the system meets response time performance requirements under the "peak load" condition. The test results may be inspected and evaluated by a consultant or other library- or vendor-specified party.

The system shall, operating in the worst case test, exhibit average response times not exceeding:

1. Six seconds for data input and edit.
2. Six seconds for file inquiries by nonsubject indexes.
3. Eight seconds for file inquiries by subject index.
4. Two seconds for charge, renewal, discharge, and other circulation and acquisitions functions.

Average system response times are the totals of all the transaction times in a category (e.g., charges) divided by the total number of transactions in those categories.

VENDOR RESPONSE REQUIREMENTS

There is no intent to limit the contents of proposals. Bidders may include any information deemed pertinent in addition to that outlined below. It is requested that the following section headings be used in vendor responses to this RFP and that these headings be arranged in the order listed below. Bidders should provide a table of contents and should include labelled divider tabs between the sections.

Vendor Profile

Include brief facts you wish to present about your company. A copy of your company's latest annual report and/or Dun and Bradstreet's rating must be included in this section as part of your response, or other sources of financial information must be provided to permit the Libraries to be satisfied with your financial stability.

Proposal Summary

Provide a brief narrative in which you present an overview of the system you are bidding in compliance with the specifications outlined in this RFP. Please present a summary of the complete hardware configuration being bid and each software package you are recommending.

Responses to the System Requirements

The vendor must respond to each requirement indicated on the System Requirements Response Forms provided at the end of this RFP. The forms may be removed and reproduced if desired.

Part of the requirements are mandatory and the remainder are optional or desirable; each item is considered mandatory unless otherwise specified. The mandatory requirements specify the minimum capabilities required of the system or required as minimum services to be provided by the successful vendor. If a bidder can demonstrate that a function or feature can be provided in some other way, that is acceptable, but the burden of demonstrating the fact is on the bidder.

Only information supplied by the Libraries in writing or in this RFP should be used in preparing vendor responses. All contacts that a vendor may have had before or after receipt of this RFP with any individuals, employees, or representatives of the Libraries and any information that may have been read in any news media or seen or heard on any communication facility regarding the acquisition of a computer system by the Libraries should be disregarded in preparing responses.

Cost Response Forms

The vendor must complete each of the Cost Response Forms provided at the end of this RFP. The forms may be removed and reproduced if desired. It is the Libraries' intent that each vendor disclose the total cost of the hardware and software bid. Bids should be provided on each item where applicable. If any item is omitted, it will be added at no extra cost to the Libraries. Additional narrative information, materials, and documents may be submitted to support a bid.

List of Operational Installations

The vendor must complete the List of Operational Installations forms found at the end of this document, providing contact information for at least three users of the system similar to that being bid. The forms may be removed and reproduced if desired. List college and university libraries if possible. Systems listed should have been in operation for at least three months at the time of the bid opening. Representatives of the Libraries, at their discretion, may call any of the libraries listed, or any others known, to verify the performance of identical systems bids, quality of maintenance, vendor responsiveness, etc. This information may be used in the bid evaluation.

SYSTEM REQUIREMENTS

1. Online Public Catalog

1.1 General

1.1.1 All software necessary to operate the online public catalog as specified in this section and as amended in the contract between the Libraries and the vendor shall be supplied by the vendor.

1.1.2 Future enhancements to the online public catalog software bid shall be made available to the Libraries as long as it uses the system bid.

1.1.3 The online public catalog shall interface with the circulation and acquisitions systems.

1.1.4 The online public catalog shall provide access to its database through direct-connect cables, through modems dedicated to specific terminals, and through the use of dial-in ports.

1.1.5 Public access terminals shall be available only to retrieve records from the online public catalog database.

1.2 Bibliographic Records

1.2.1 The system shall accommodate the file sizes and workloads described in Appendix A to this RFP, without additional disk storage or processing capabilities beyond the initial installation.

1.2.2 The system shall accept and differentiate between all bibliographic formats (monographs, serials, audiovisual media, sound recordings, electronic data files, scores, maps, and manuscripts).

1.2.3 All field tags and subfield codes shall be accepted and stored so that records in the MARC II (OCLC/MARC) format can be reconstructed without additional manual editing or input.

1.2.4 The system shall be able to strip library-specified fields of data not required to construct indexes automatically as records are loaded.

1.2.5 Local bibliographic data, such as local subject headings, notes, call numbers, etc., shall be preserved if entered in bibliographic records through OCLC terminals.

1.2.6 Records for titles under consideration, titles on order, and titles in process, in addition to records for titles already in the collections, shall be stored and this status information displayed when the records are retrieved.

1.2.7 Both full and partial bibliographic records shall be accepted and stored by the system.

1.2.8 All Roman alphabet characters and all non-Roman alphabet languages if transliterated shall be accepted.

1.2.9 (Optional) The system shall accept, store, retrieve, print, and display all diacritical marks in MARC/OCLC records.

1.3 Copy Records

1.3.1 The system shall accommodate the file sizes indicated in Appendix A of this RFP, without additional disk storage or processing capabilities beyond the initial installation.

1.3.2 The system shall accommodate and differentiate between the copy holdings of a minimum of 10 branches or agencies.

1.3.3 The system shall accommodate and differentiate between the copy holdings of a minimum of 20 separate collections within each branch library.

1.3.4 Circulating copies shall be distinguishable from noncirculating items.

1.3.5 Up to 1,000 copies shall be linkable to a single master bibliographic record.

1.3.6 The system shall automatically link copy records to bibliographic records as they are loaded if appropriate copy information is placed in specified MARC fields.

1.3.7 (Optional) The system shall print spine labels for items.

1.3.8 (Optional) Multiple bibliographic records shall be accommodated on one physical item (music material, collected works, bound-withs, etc.).

1.4 Indexes

1.4.1 An index containing personal names, corporate names, and conference names, including names that are part of series, shall be provided for the file of bibliographic records.

1.4.2 An index containing titles, parallel titles, uniform titles, variant titles, and series titles shall be provided for the file of records.

1.4.3 An index containing subject headings (main headings and subdivisions), including cross references, shall be provided.

1.4.4 An index containing OCLC numbers assigned to titles shall be provided.

1.4.5 An index containing copy numbers (OCR or barcode numbers) of physical items in the database shall be provided.

1.4.6 An index or a method of retrieving keywords from titles and subjects shall be provided.

1.4.7 An index containing ISBN/ISSN numbers for titles shall be provided.

1.4.8 An index of LC card numbers assigned to titles shall be provided.

1.4.9 (Optional) An index of Monthly Catalog item numbers shall be provided for government documents in the database.

1.5 Authority Control

1.5.1 The system shall include an online, interactive authority control system to establish a single, authoritative form for headings.

1.5.2 The authority control system shall include control for personal names, corporate names, meeting/conference names, uniform titles, series (both traced and untraced), geographic subject headings, and topical subject headings.

1.5.3 The system shall use MARC tags designed for authority records.

1.5.4 The system shall record who established the form of names and sources used.

1.5.5 Each official heading in the authority control system shall be linked automatically to each occurrence of those headings in the database.

1.5.6 The system shall make, when commanded, global changes with a single command.

1.5.7 The system shall not allow bibliographic records to be attached to invalid headings.

1.5.8 The system shall relink bibliographic records automatically to authority records when authorities are merged or changed.

1.5.9 The system shall include "see" references which direct users from unauthorized headings to authorized headings.

1.5.10 The system shall include "see also" references which direct users from authorized headings to other authorized headings for similar topics.

1.5.11 The system shall not allow cross-references to unused headings (blind references).

1.5.12 The system shall allow online, manual maintenance of all fields of individual authority records.

1.5.13 The system shall display problems with matches of headings against authority records and shall allow online resolution of problems by an operator.

1.5.14 (Optional) Multiple authorities for headings shall be accommodated by the system.

1.5.15 (Optional) The system shall accommodate the batch loading of authority control records from the Library of Congress magnetic tapes.

1.5.16 (Optional) The system shall include "earlier/former name" and "later name" references which indicate relationships between two authorized corporate or meeting conference and series headings.

1.5.17 (Optional) The system shall accommodate the electronic transfer of individual authority control records from an OCLC terminal into the database.

1.6 Database Creation and Maintenance

1.6.1 The system shall accommodate the electronic transfer of individual bibliographic records from an OCLC terminal into the database.

1.6.2 The system shall accommodate the batch loading of bibliographic records from OCLC archival tapes into the database.

1.6.3 The system shall enable the batch loading of bibliographic records from other tapes in the MARC format, such as those from BroDart, Blackwell North America, etc., into the database.

1.6.4 The system shall enable the manual keyboarding of individual bibliographic, copy, authority, and cross-reference records into the database.

1.6.5 All records with lower MARC encoding levels shall be replaced automatically as new records are loaded into the database.

1.6.6 An online display or printout of encoding level match problems shall be generated to allow staff to make record replacement decisions.

1.6.7 The system shall allow the staff manually to load or delete records with encoding level problems.

1.6.8 The system shall generate and file all appropriate index entries for each record as it is filed into the database.

1.6.9 Online modification (addition or deletion of data elements or fields, changes to data within fields, etc.) of all fields in individual bibliographic and copy records in the database shall be possible.

1.6.10 Modifications or corrections in data fields of records shall be possible without retyping the entire line or data field.

1.6.11 Online, manual deletion of individual bibliographic records and copy records from the database shall be possible.

1.6.12 Deletion of bibliographic records shall not be allowed if any copies remain attached to a record.

1.6.13 The system shall automatically correct or delete all appropriate index entries as changes are made in bibliographic and copy records or as these records are deleted from the database.

1.6.14 The system shall accommodate the updating or deletion of all occurrences of a name or subject heading in the database from one transaction.

1.6.15 The system shall accommodate the manual addition of tagged data to individual records.

1.6.16 The system shall be able to generate a magnetic tape in MARC/OCLC format of all records in the database.

1.6.17 The system shall provide a printout of call numbers for inventory purposes arranged in the order materials stand on the shelves.

1.7 Searches/Inquiries

1.7.1 The system shall enable users to search the holdings of all libraries in the database and of collections within branches.

1.7.2 The system shall allow simple, character-by-character author, title, and subject searches with no requirement that users enter a full heading or term or derived search keys.

1.7.3 The system shall allow implicit Boolean searching. That is, the system shall allow users to enter keywords with Boolean connectors and process a search as if "and" connectors were used.

1.7.4 The system shall allow explicit Boolean searching. That is, the system shall allow users to use "and," "or," "and not" operators both inside the same index or across indexes.

1.7.5 It shall be possible to qualify searches by date of publication or range of dates, language, and type of material, both before a search is begun and after the system determines that more than one record matches a search argument.

1.7.6 The system shall permit browsing through the catalog by allowing users to enter the best available form of search arguments and then display index entries in the alphabetic neighborhood of the terms entered (for example, 5 entries preceding and 10 entries following), using brief headings from the appropriate files.

1.7.7 The system shall ignore or forgive variations in punctuation, spacing, and use of upper and lower case letters and special characters such as diacritics.

1.7.8 The system shall defend itself from unnecessary searches by stopping a search and informing the user that the search is too long, as determined by a library-specified parameter.

1.7.9 The system shall provide the user, when long searches are identified, the option of continuing the search, previewing some of the hits, narrowing the search process, or terminating the search.

1.7.10 The system shall support a break key or similar feature which will allow users to interrupt long searches.

1.7.11 The system shall retain on the screen the term or terms used as a search argument for an inquiry against the database until the user goes to another search to allow checking for errors in input if no matches are found.

1.7.12 The system shall enhance searches by suggesting related headings or terms to users.

1.7.13 The system shall guide the user in continuing a search if no match is found.

1.7.14 The system shall provide a means by which users can ask for help from the system at any time during a search.

1.7.15 The system shall have easy-to-follow prompts throughout the inquiry process.

1.7.16 The system shall return promptly and directly to the beginning of the search process when requested or upon completion of a search.

1.7.17 The system shall allow paging both forward and backward from a specific point in all searches.

1.7.18 The system shall have an online, general tutorial on using the catalog and conducting searches.

1.7.19 The system shall display the options for the next stage of a search process as each preceding stage is finished.

1.7.20 The system shall provide different levels of instructions and prompts for beginners and for experienced users of the catalog.

1.7.21 (Optional) The system shall allow the use of library-specified stop words to be instituted when desired.

1.7.22 (Optional) The system shall recognize a defined, right-hand truncation symbol such as the " $" on keyword searching.

1.8 Search Results

1.8.1 The system shall display a brief record, with locations of holdings shown, if more than one library holds a particular title.

1.8.2 The system shall include on order and in process records when results of searches are displayed.

1.8.3 The system shall return a summary screen whenever a search yields more than one hit, where each matching record is numbered and takes up no more than one or two lines, and allow the user to continue searching by referring to the line number of a desired record or records.

1.8.4 The system shall display matches in alphabetic order.

1.8.5 The system shall inform the user how many records will be retrieved by a search term.

1.8.6 The system shall indicate the status of items displayed as a result of a search (on order, in process, in circulation, on shelf, lost, missing, pending order, etc.).

1.8.7 The system shall indicate location (branch and location in branch) for each item displayed.

1.8.8 The system shall support at least three levels of fullness of bibliographic displays: (a) minimum, in which one or two lines of information for each title, containing author, title, edition statement, and date, are displayed; (b) descriptive, in which the descriptive cataloging portion of a bibliographic record plus call number and location are shown; and (c) full, in which all fields that would be on a full catalog record are displayed.

1.8.9 The system shall supply more level of detail as the user narrows a search to fewer records.

1.8.10 The system shall vary the fullness of display detail according to a parameter which can be set for each terminal when a search has been narrowed to a single title.

1.8.11 The system shall provide for printouts of search results, either on a printer attached to the CRT terminal or on the line printer at the CPU site.

1.8.12 The system shall enable the library to specify the limit to the number of citations that can be printed for a user.

1.8.13 (Optional) The system shall enable the user to specify the sort order of a listing by either author, title, or class number.

1.9 Public Online Catalog Statistical Reports

1.9.1 The system shall provide online statistical reports, with an option to print the reports.

1.9.2 Each statistical report shall include statistics for both month-to-date and year-to-date.

1.9.3 All statistics shall be separated by campus, branch, and location within branch.

1.9.4 Statistics shall be provided for the number of search commands entered, by terminal.

1.9.5 Statistics shall be provided for the total time each terminal is in use during searches, with low, high, and mean response times given.

1.9.6 Statistics shall be provided for the number of times "help" requests are made, by terminal.

1.9.7 Statistics shall be provided for the number of unacceptable commands entered, by terminal.

1.9.8 Statistics shall be provided for the number of citations printed, by terminal or device.

1.9.9 Statistics shall be provided for the number of titles and copy records currently in the database.

1.9.10 Statistics shall be provided for the number of modifications made to bibliographic and copy records.

1.9.11 Statistics shall be provided for the number of bibliographic and copy records deleted.

1.9.12 Statistics shall be provided for the number of authority records currently in the database.

1.9.13 Statistics shall be provided for the number of "see" and "see also" records currently in the database.

1.9.14 Statistics shall be provided for the number of searches through each index (author, title, subject, call number, etc.).

2. Circulation System

2.1 General

2.1.1 All application software necessary to operate the circulation system as specified in this section and as amended in the contract between the Libraries and the vendor shall be supplied by the vendor.

2.1.2 Future enhancements to the circulation system shall be made available to the Libraries as long as it uses the system bid.

2.1.3 The circulation system, as part of an integrated library system, shall interface with the public online catalog and the acquisitions system.

2.1.4 The system shall be usable independently and concurrently by all branches of the Libraries.

2.1.5 The availability (in circulation, on shelf, lost, at bindery, etc.) of materials of each library circulating materials on the system shall be shown in the public online catalog.

2.1.6 The system shall accommodate the current and future files and workload described in Appendix A of this RFP without additional disk storage or processing capabilities beyond the initial installation.

2.2 Borrower Control

2.2.1 The system shall provide for borrower records which include the following data as a minimum: (a) borrower identification number; (b) borrower surname, first name, and middle initial; (c) local street or box address, city, state, and ZIP code; (d) local telephone number; (e) permanent street or box number, city, state, and ZIP code; (f) permanent telephone number, including area code; (g) borrower classification code; (h) expiration date of authorization to borrow; and (i) academic class code.

2.2.2 The system shall enable the retrieval and display of borrower records both by borrower identification number and borrower name.

2.2.3 The system shall utilize variable-length fields in borrower records, except those fields such as identification number, ZIP code, telephone number, and other predefined codes and abbreviations.

2.2.4 An operator shall be able to create borrower records online at a CRT terminal.

2.2.5 An operator shall be able to modify borrower records online at a CRT terminal.

2.2.6 An operator shall be able to delete borrower records online, except when outstanding obligations exist.

2.2.7 (Optional) The system shall accommodate the batch loading of borrower records using data supplied by the University Registrar (documentation of the record formats can be supplied upon request).

2.3 Charge Activities

2.3.1 The system shall notify the terminal operator if a borrower is not registered and shall prompt for further processing.

2.3.2 The system shall check borrower status and shall provide clear visual and auditory signals to the operator of any exception condition, including excessive number of books charges, fines/fees owed, etc., and shall permit supervisory override.

2.3.3 The system shall verify that material is not on hold for another borrower.

2.3.4 The system shall verify that material is allowed to circulate before it is charged to a borrower.

2.3.5 The system shall associate a unique material identifier with a unique borrower identifier and store the record in a circulation file for each loan.

2.3.6 The system shall provide a swift, accurate method of optically scanning unique identifiers affixed to borrower ID cards and books and other materials.

2.3.7 The system shall allow "on-the-fly" circulation of materials.

2.3.8 The system shall permit charges to library units and collections (e.g., ILL, binding, etc.) and subsequent charges from those units and collections to borrowers or other libraries.

2.3.9 The system shall calculate loan periods and due-dates according to the type of borrower, type of material, and library service hours, allowing for holidays.

2.3.10 The system shall allow due-dates to be changed online.

2.3.11 The system shall display due-date on the charge terminal screen.

2.3.12 (Optional) The system shall print at the charging location a due-date slip to be inserted in the charged item.

2.4 Renewal Activities

2.4.1 The system shall calculate and display the new due-date for renewals.

2.4.2 The system shall permit record display and renewal even if the item and/or borrower are remote (e.g., renewal by telephone).

2.4.3 The system shall check the circulation record for a current charge and shall block renewal if one is found, or if the current charge is to another borrower.

2.4.4 The system shall check the circulation file for holds on items to be renewed, shall block renewal if holds are found, and shall prompt hold processing.

2.4.5 The system shall check the borrower record for any exceptions (e.g., unpaid fines) during renewal.

2.4.6 The system shall check for overdue status, shall calculate and display any fine, and shall permit immediate payment or generate a notice or other billing document (see section below regarding fines and fees).

2.4.7 (Optional) The system shall allow a renewal to be made for all items charged to a borrower with a single renewal request.

2.5 Discharge Activities

2.5.1 The system shall disassociate the unique item identifier from the unique borrower identifier and shall remove the record from the circulation file, unless a fine is to be assessed.

2.5.2 The system shall permit discharge by either scanning an item's identifier or keyboarding the identifier.

2.5.3 The system shall permit the setting of a discharge date by the operator.

2.5.4 The system shall signal the operator if an item being discharged is owned by another library or branch and shall prompt for further processing.

2.5.5 The system shall check for holds or blocks, shall signal the operator if holds or blocks are found, and shall prompt for appropriate processing.

2.5.6 The system shall determine if an item being discharged is overdue.

2.5.7 The system shall calculate any fine during discharge and allow immediate payment.

2.5.8 The system shall calculate any fine, display the borrower's account, and automatically increment the account or permit operator incrementation to the account.

2.5.9 The system shall print a fine/fee notice or other billing document either immediately or later via batch mode.

2.5.10 The system shall permit discharge of materials from terminals other than the one originating the charge.

2.5.11 (Optional) The system shall provide a discharge receipt to the borrower, if requested.

2.6 Blocks

2.6.1 The system shall automatically block privileges for borrowers whose registration has expired.

2.6.2 The system shall automatically block privileges for borrowers who have a library-specified number of items overdue.

2.6.3 The system shall automatically block privileges for borrowers who have a library-specified number of items already checked out.

2.6.4 The system shall automatically block privileges for borrowers who have unpaid fines/fees over a library-specified amount.

2.6.5 The system shall allow the addition of manual blocks against borrower records.

2.6.6 The system shall allow manual override by authorized staff of all blocks against borrowers.

2.7 Holds and Recalls

2.7.1 The system shall allow holds to be placed on materials in circulation.

2.7.2 The system shall place individual/agency/system-wide holds at the copy or title level, at the library's specification.

2.7.3 The system shall queue at least 10 hold requests on a single item in the sequence in which they are entered.

2.7.4 The system shall display or print a list of the hold queue for an item upon request.

2.7.5 The system shall notify the operator at the time of discharge of any hold or recall on discharged materials and shall prompt for further processing.

2.7.6 The system shall check the hold queue at the time of charge and shall block charge to a borrower not at the head of the queue.

2.7.7 The system shall allow authorized terminal operators to override the automatic sequence of processing holds.

2.7.8 The system shall prepare and print recall notices to borrowers that items on hold are available.

2.7.9 The system shall prepare and print recall notices for items charged to borrowers.

2.7.10 The system shall prepare and print a report of items/titles which are in heavy demand, such as that the number of holds placed on the same item/title exceeded a library-specified number.

2.7.11 The system shall check the hold shelf inventory and produce a notice to be sent to the next borrower in the queue when items are not claimed within a specified time.

2.7.12 The system shall provide for modification of hold data.

2.7.13 The system shall provide for hold cancellations at the library's discretion and shall produce notices to be sent to borrowers.

2.7.14 The system shall allow recalls to be placed on material in circulation.

2.7.15 The system shall allow modification of recall data.

2.7.16 The system shall permit the deletion of recall data.

2.8 Fines and Fees

2.8.1 The system shall calculate and record fines and fees for overdue and lost items.

2.8.2 The system shall store and display a borrower's current fine and fee records.

2.8.3 The system shall maintain online financial records for overdue and lost items including, as a minimum: (a) borrower identification, including number, name, and address; (b) total amount of fines owed; (c) identification of each item for which a fine was levied, including item identification number, call number, author, and short title; (d) a history of each item for which a fine was levied, including the date the item was checked out, the due-date, the date it was returned, and the date the fine was assessed; (e) the amount of fine levied for each item; and (f) the amount paid and date on which paid.

2.8.4 The system shall retrieve and display on demand the fines and fees owed by a borrower, using either the borrower identification number or name as a search key.

2.8.5 The system shall allow modification of fine records by authorized staff members.

2.8.6 The system shall allow deletion of fines by authorized staff members.

2.8.7 The system shall allow the fine and fee schedules to be changed without modification of the software.

2.8.8 The system shall allow specification of different fines for different classes of borrowers.

2.8.9 The system shall allow the fine schedule to be set so that no fines are levied for a particular type of material and a particular class of borrower.

2.8.10 The system shall produce upon demand a list of borrowers, arranged by borrower name or by borrower identification number, with outstanding fines and fees which occurred within a library-specified time range.

2.8.11 The system shall purge cleared transactions on a regular basis with the retention of historical data for management information only.

2.8.12 The system shall prepare and print fine notices which include the following data as a minimum: (a) borrower identification, including number, name, and address; (b) identification of items for which fines are due, including identification number, call number, author, and short title; (c) amount of fine on each item; (d) total amount of fines; and (e) date the notice was prepared.

2.8.13 The system shall permit an operator to record payment received for fines and fees.

2.8.14 The system shall provide consolidated fine/fee records for all branches.

2.8.15 The system shall calculate fines at the time of discharge or renewal according to loan period, date of discharge, and specified fine for the type of material.

2.8.16 The system shall calculate fines beginning with a specified minimum dollar amount and ending with a specified maximum.

2.8.17 The system shall cumulate fines below a library-specified dollar minimum on a borrower record for assessment at a library-defined threshhold.

2.8.18 The system shall permit input of library-calculated item replacement and processing fees.

2.8.19 The system shall print a list of lost items for staff use in searching shelves and inputting replacement and processing fees.

2.8.20 The system shall permit an operator to tag items as lost at any time.

2.8.21 The system shall permit an operator to tag lost items as replaced following reorder.

2.9 Overdues

2.9.1 The system shall prepare and print first, second, and third overdue notices to borrowers.

2.9.2 The library shall be able to specify the number of days to wait after a due-date before overdue notices are prepared.

2.9.3 The system shall print a list of borrowers, arranged optionally either by borrower name or by borrower identification number, with over a library-specified number of overdue materials.

2.9.4 The library shall be able to specify the number of days to wait between overdue notices.

2.9.5 Overdue notices shall include the following data as a minimum: (a) borrower identification number, name, and address; (b) identification of overdue material by item number, call number, author, and short title; (c) due-dates of overdue materials; and (d) the date the notice was prepared.

2.9.6 The library shall be able to specify whether overdue notices are sent to local or permanent borrower addresses.

2.10 Reserve Component

2.10.1 The system shall have a reserve component which will provide identification and control of loans of materials on reserve for specific courses and for other reasons.

2.10.2 The system shall maintain the following data elements about materials on reserve as a minimum: (a) author, (b) title, (c) call number, (d) course number, (e) name of faculty member or other person placing an item on reserve, and (f) the item identification number.

2.10.3 The system shall enable the entry of item and course data for materials on reserve.

2.10.4 The system shall enable the modification of item and course data for materials on reserve.

2.10.5 The system shall enable the deletion of item and course data for materials on reserve.

2.10.6 The system shall permit independent reserve systems to be operated in each branch library.

2.10.7 The system shall permit different loan, fine, and fee policies by the different branches.

2.10.8 The system shall have both course and professor keys for items placed on reserve, in addition to those of author, title, subject, item number, etc.

2.10.9 The system shall accept the entry of personal copies of materials for the duration of reserve only.

2.10.10 The system shall prepare and print a list, on demand, of materials on reserve, arranged both by course number and by professor.

2.10.11 The system shall provide for hourly loans.

2.10.12 Circulation of reserve materials shall be performed using the regular circulation function described above.

2.10.13 Items placed on reserve shall revert to their original locations when taken off reserve.

2.10.14 Reserve fines and fees shall be entered into the financial files of the general circulation system.

2.10.15 The reserve system shall provide for the assessment and reporting of fines and fees.

2.10.16 (Optional) The system shall print upon demand a list of overdue reserve materials, by branch library.

2.11 Circulation System Statistical Reports

2.11.1 The system shall provide online statistical reports, with an option to print the report.

2.11.2 Each statistical report shall include statistics for both month-to-date and year-to-date activities.

2.11.3 All statistics shall be separated by branch and location within branch.

2.11.4 The system shall provide statistics for daily, monthly, and annual charges, discharges, and renewals.

2.11.5 The system shall provide statistics for the number of charges and renewals made each day, month, or annually by a minimum of 300 classification number groupings.

2.11.6 The system shall provide statistics for the number of holds placed, filled, and cancelled each day, month, and year.

2.11.7 The system shall provide statistics for the number and amount of fines and fees levied and collected daily, monthly, and annually.

2.11.8 The system shall provide statistics for the number of overdue, recall, and fine notices printed each day.

2.11.9 The system shall provide statistics for the number of times a given title has been checked out monthly and annually.

2.11.10 The system shall provide statistics for the number of items annually which are recorded as lost, missing, etc.

2.11.11 The system shall provide statistics for the number of items placed on, and taken off, reserve daily, monthly, and annually.

2.11.12 The system shall compile and print a list of items which have circulated over a library-specified number of times in a past year.

2.11.13 (Optional) The system shall provide statistics for the number of times a given title has been placed on hold monthly and annually.

3. Acquisitions System

3.1 General

3.1.1 All application software necessary to operate the acquisitions system as specified in this section and as amended in the contract between the Libraries and the vendor shall be supplied by the vendor.

3.1.2 Future enhancements to the acquisitions system shall be made available to the Libraries as long as it uses the system bid.

3.1.3 The acquisitions system, as part of an integrated library system, shall interface with the public online catalog and the circulation system.

3.2.4 The system shall accommodate the existing and future file and work loads described in Appendix A of this RFP, without additional disk storage or processing capabilities beyond the initial installation.

3.2 Acquisitions Records

3.2.1 Acquisitions bibliographic records shall be included in, and therefore accessible to all users of, the public online catalog.

3.2.2 The system shall accept and differentiate between the following types of acquisitions records, as a minimum: (a) new orders, (b) gifts, (c) exchange items, (d) approval items, (e) standing orders, (f) deposit account items, (g) depository items, and (h) memberships.

3.2.3 Each record status code shall be provided with a date the status is set.

3.2.4 The system shall allow holds to be placed on items on order and in process.

3.2.5 (Optional) A tracking history shall be provided which summarizes items' progress through the acquisitions process.

3.2.6 (Optional) In addition to the access points provided for other records in the public online catalog, acquisition records shall have the following access points: (a) purchase order number, (b) requestor's name or code, (c) order date, (d) vendor invoice number, (e) fund code, and (f) vendor name and/or code.

3.2.7 (Optional) The system shall allow searches of acquisition records to be limited or qualified by type of record (new orders, gifts, approvals, etc.).

3.3 Vendor Records

3.3.1 A vendor file shall be provided which shall contain a record for each supplier used as a source for acquiring materials.

3.3.2 Vendor records shall have fields for: (a) vendor name; (b) vendor address, city, state, and ZIP code; (c) telephone number; (d) vendor account number for the library; (e) a library-supplied number of days which should lapse before claims are made for orders to the vendor; and (f) a counter containing the average delivery time in days for the vendor.

3.3.3 Vendor records shall be accessible by vendor name and by vendor identification number or code.

3.3.4 An operator shall be able to add, delete, and update vendor records manually.

3.3.5 (Optional) The system shall provide for cross-references from one vendor to another.

3.4 Fund Account Records

3.4.1 A fund accounting system shall be provided which will control the expenditure of funds during the acquisitions process, separated by fiscal year.

3.4.2 A fund accounting file shall be provided which will contain a record for each fund established for the purchase of materials.

3.4.3 Each fund shall provide for a minimum of 100 library-specified subject subcodes.

3.4.4 Each fund account record shall provide fields for: (a) fund identification number or code, (b) fund name, (c) amount budgeted, (d) encumberances, (e) expenditures year-to-date, and (f) free balance.

3.4.5 An operator shall be able to adjust manually the amount budgeted in each fund account record.

3.4.6 The system shall automatically post activities to fund accounts as items are ordered, received, and/or cancelled.

3.4.7 Free balances shall automatically be adjusted by the system as amounts are adjusted manually by an operator.

3.4.8 Fund account records shall be accessible by fund code and by fund identification number or code.

3.4.9 A fund accounting report shall be provided online, with an option to print the report, listing all transactions, in title order, posted to accounts since the beginning of the month and summarizing all accounts into grand totals.

3.5 Selection Entry and Review

3.5.1 The system shall allow acquisition records to be created manually online, both for items to be ordered and for items received and in-hand, pending review for addition to the library's collections.

3.5.2 The system shall provide a check for existing records in the public online catalog prior to creation of provisional acquisition records and shall notify the operator if items are duplicates.

3.5.3 An operator shall be able, if desired, to search the holdings of other branches whose holdings are in the public online catalog, prior to creation of acquisition records.

3.5.4 The operator shall be able to order duplicates of materials already in a library's collection or on order or in process for a library.

3.5.5 The system shall enable records for selections to be moved electronically from OCLC terminals into the acquisitions system.

3.5.6 The system shall create provisional records in the public online catalog as selections are entered and append the entry date.

3.5.7 The system shall allow separate copies of selections to be charged to different fund accounts.

3.5.8 An operator shall be able to review or scan online all titles entered for selection review, with the capability of rejecting or accepting selections during the process.

3.5.9 The system shall automatically check fund account records and report to the operator if insufficient funds are available to purchase items to be ordered as selections are approved.

3.5.10 An operator shall be able to overencumber in all accounts.

3.5.11 The system shall not allow records to be approved unless the minimum required fields for creating purchase orders have been entered.

3.5.12 The system shall automatically tag records approved for purchase as ready to be included on requisition orders.

3.5.13 The system shall automatically change the status of records in hand from "pending review" to "in process" as items are approved for addition to the library's collections.

3.5.14 (Optional) The system shall display, upon command, the final purchase orders as they will be printed, prior to this production.

3.6 Purchase Order Preparation
3.6.1 The system shall batch-produce purchase orders for titles approved for purchase.

3.6.2 (Optional) An option shall be provided allowing purchase orders to be printed, written on magnetic tape, or both.

3.7 Receiving
3.7.1 The system shall automatically change the status of items on order to "received" as the operator enters receiving data and shall append the date of receipt to the record.

3.7.2 The system shall automatically update vendor performance statistics as items are received.

3.7.3 The system shall display a summary of all items received on a particular invoice, with itemized discounted prices and a grand invoice total shown, to be used as a check against invoices.

3.7.4 The system shall allow the receipt of a partial number of the total number of copies ordered of a title.

3.7.5 The system shall disencumber from fund account records the list prices of items received, add the discounted prices to the expended fields, and compute a new free balance for the account.

3.7.6 (Optional) The system shall accept and process invoicing information from vendors on magnetic tape.

3.8 Claiming and Cancelling

3.8.1 The system shall search, locate, and retrieve all records for materials which have been on order with vendors for over a specified amount of time but which have not yet been received.

3.8.2 The system shall provide for a minimum of two claims to be made to suppliers.

3.8.3 The library shall be able to specify the length of time which will lapse before items are eligible for claims.

3.8.4 The library shall be able to specify the length of time before claiming.

3.8.5 The system shall allow manual overriding of the automatic claims date.

3.8.6 The system shall print claims lists or letters to suppliers for materials ordered but not received.

3.8.7 The system shall automatically change the status code of records from "on order" to "on order--claimed" as claims notices are printed.

3.8.8 The library shall be able to specify the length of time which shall lapse after claims are made before items are automatically cancelled.

3.8.9 An operator shall be able to override manually the automatic cancellation date and cancel items at any time.

3.8.10 The system shall provide an online list of all items which are to be claimed and cancelled, with an option to print the list.

3.8.11 The system shall produce notices to users who have placed holds on items which have been cancelled.

3.8.12 The system shall automatically change the status code of records from "on order--claimed" to "cancelled."

3.8.13 The system shall print claims lists or letters to suppliers for materials which have been cancelled.

3.8.14 The system shall disencumber from fund account records the list prices of cancelled items and add the amounts back to free balances.

3.8.15 The system shall allow supplier and status codes to be changed so that items can be recycled back through the selection process if so desired, without having to reenter the selection.

3.8.16 The system shall enable the manual addition of status codes such as "NYP," "OP," etc.

3.8.17 (Optional) The system shall provide an online report, with the option to print the report, of all items that should be claimed and that have been claimed.

3.9 Acquistion System Statistical Reports

3.9.1 The system shall provide online statistical reports, with an option to print the reports.

3.9.2 Each statistical report shall include statistics for both month-to-date and year-to-date.

3.9.3 Statistics shall be provided for the number of acquisitions records on file, divided into new orders, gifts, exchanges, approval items, standing orders, deposit account items, and depository items.

3.9.4 Statistics shall be provided for the number of records ready for purchase, on order, claimed, cancelled, and in process.

3.9.5 Statistics shall be provided for the number of vendors in the supplier file and the number of records added and deleted.

3.9.6 Statistics shall be provided for the number of items ordered, received, claimed, and cancelled, arranged by vendor, with grand totals shown.

3.9.7 Statistics shall be provided for the number of requisition orders, claims notices, and cancellation notices produced.

3.9.8 Statistics shall be provided for vendor performance.

4. Hardware

4.1 General

4.1.1 All hardware shall be unmodified, "off-the-shelf" equipment.

4.1.2 All hardware shall have a 90-day warranty effective from the date of installation.

4.1.3 All hardware shall be new, a part of the vendor's standard product line, and certified as maintainable.

4.1.4 All essential cabinets, controllers, cabling, and other interfaces shall be provided as part of a bid.

4.1.5 All hardware shall be certified to qualify for full-coverage preventive and remedial maintenance.

4.1.6 (Optional) The system shall accept a mixture of different manufacturers' CRT terminals.

4.2 Central Processing Unit

4.2.1 The central processing unit bid for initial installation shall have sufficient input /output paths, main memory, and other features to perform the expected workloads described in Appendix A of this RFP and to allow concurrent operation of the peripherals described below.

4.2.2 The system bid shall be a multiprocessor unit.

4.2.3 Each processor of the CPU shall have its own individual power supply and input /output channels to ensure continuous processing should one processor fail.

4.2.4 Each processor shall work concurrently and share the computing load between them to increase total system capacity.

4.2.5 (Optional) In case of failure of one processor, the system shall automatically shift the system's workload to the remaining processor(s) without human intervention.

4.2.6 The CPU shall be capable of accepting modular additions to memory up to twice the installed main memory through addition of memory in each processor or through the addition of additional processors without reprogramming.

4.2.7 The system bid shall include a console with keyboard and visual display for communication between an operator and the computer and for control of batch programs.

4.2.8 The system shall have power failure protection for the equipment.

4.3 Magnetic Disk Storage

4.3.1 Sufficient disk storage shall be bid to store the initial files, described in Appendix A of this RFP, and to store the additional records expected to be added for five years after installation.

4.3.2 Sufficient additional disk storage shall be bid to store the system software and other software.

4.3.3 The system shall be expandable in the future to at least double the disk storage capacity bid without need for additional disk controllers and without changing the basic hardware or software, except for adding new disk drives.

4.3.4 A disk pack shall be included for each drive bid plus sufficient scratch packs required for system maintenance.

4.3.5 All disk packs shall be error-free and formatted.

4.4 Tape Drive

4.4.1 The tape drive shall include any necessary controller.

4.4.2 The tape drive shall be able to read and write, with read-after-write error check.

4.4.3 The tape drive shall accept half-inch nine-track tape, recorded at 1600 BPI.

4.4.4 The tape drive shall operate at speeds of 20-25 IPS minimum.

4.5 Line Printer

4.5.1 The line printer shall include any necessary controller.

4.5.2 The line printer shall have 132 column capability.

4.5.3 The printer shall have print spacing of 10 characters per inch horizontal and six or eight lines per inch vertical, switch-selectable.

4.5.4 The printer shall be adjustable to accept paper or forms from 4 inches to 14 7 /8 inches in size, horizontal.

4.5.5 The printer shall have top-of-forms sensing.

4.5.6 The printer shall have a manual forms eject.

4.5.7 The printer shall have a pin-feed and continuous forms tractor feed capability.

4.5.8 The printer shall have programmed carriage control.

4.5.9 The printer shall have high-quality print on at least four-part paper.

4.5.10 The printer shall have a rated speed of not less than 300 lines per minute when printing full 132-character lines.

4.5.11 The printer shall have a standard ASCII 64-character set, with an optional 96-character ASCII set.

4.5.12 (Optional) The train or chain shall be removable to change type fonts and character sets.

4.6 CRT Terminals

4.6.1 The CRT terminals shall have a minimum display capacity of 1,920 characters with a screen display image of at least 24 lines vertically and 80 characters horizontally on each line.

4.6.2 The terminal shall have at least a 12-inch diagonal screen.

4.6.3 The terminal shall meet all current and reasonable future OSHA and other pertinent regulatory agency requirements regarding radiation electromagnetic interference (EMI), noise level, user fatigue, etc.

4.6.4 The terminal shall have keys designated for special functions in each system.

4.6.5 The terminal shall be capable of displaying both upper and lower case characters.

4.6.6 The terminal shall use American-English block-style alphabetic and numeric characters with true descenders.

4.6.7 The terminal's display resolution shall equal or exceed that obtainable with a dot matrix five dots wide by seven dots high.

4.6.8 The terminal shall operate properly at standard data transmission rates using standard serial asynchronous communications line protocol.

4.6.9 The terminal shall have an additional input /output port which will enable it to interface with a printer device.

4.6.10 (Optional) The ALA 192-character, extended 8-bit ASCII set shall be available on the terminal, which may be interfaced to the system bid.

4.7 Optical Scanners

4.7.1 Hand-held scanners shall be bid, with flexible cords at least 42 inches in length unflexed or six feet flexed.

4.7.2 The scanner shall be capable of reading standard Optical Character Recognition (OCR) labels, or, industry-compatible barcode labels.

4.7.3 All necessary controllers, cables, and other hardware essential to connect the scanners to the CRT terminals shall be bid.

4.7.4 The scanner shall emit an audible tone when a label is read correctly.

4.7.5 The scanner shall be capable of checking digit read automatically.

4.8 CRT Screen Printers

4.8.1 The CRT screen printer shall be RS-232C connectable to the printer or input /output port of the CRT bid.

4.8.2 The printer shall have 80 column capability.

4.8.3 The printer shall have pin-feed and adjustable, continuous forms tractor feed capability.

4.8.4 The printer shall have a full ASCII character set, with upper and lower case.

4.8.5 The printer shall be capable of printing six lines per inch vertically.

4.8.6 The printer shall have a rated speed of not less than 30 CPS when printing full 80-character lines.

4.8.7 The printer shall have top-of-forms sensing.

4.8.8 All necessary cabling to connect the printer to the CRT terminal shall be included.

4.8.9 (Optional) The printer shall have a buffer for a minimum of 1,920 characters of data.

4.9 Communications

4.9.1 Vendors shall configure and bid communications equipment which will best fit their systems and which will maximize communications efficiency and effectiveness while minimizing costs to the Libraries.

4.9.2 Sufficient rotary line interfaces shall be included to allow access to the public online catalog by a minimum of five simultaneous dial-up users.

5. System Software

5.1 General

5.1.1 All system software necessary to operate the computer system to perform the functions outlined and support the functions specified in this RFP shall be supplied.

5.1.2 Future enhancements to the system software shall be made available to the Libraries as long as it uses the system bid.

5.2 Operating System

5.2.1 The system shall include a real-time, multiuser operating system (OS).

5.2.2 The OS shall provide for the processing of jobs in accordance with established priorities by scheduling jobs, overlapping jobs requiring no external intervention, and issuing messages to the operator as needed.

5.2.3 The OS shall provide for the queing and dispatching of input/output operations in order to provide concurrent multi-task I/O support.

5.2.4 The OS shall provide a means of coordinating transfer of control between programs or tasks after completion of external events, waiting on one program or task, starting another, and later restarting the first program or task without loss of program or task integrity.

5.2.5 The OS shall include error-handling routines which allow one task to recover or abnormally terminate while other processing continues and assures that operator intervention is kept to a minimum.

5.2.6 The OS shall adjust to the addition of future vendor-compatible peripheral equipment with only minor software changes.

5.2.7 The OS shall be adequate to manage efficiently the operation of the multiprogrammcd conditions described in the workloads in Appendix A of this RFP.

5.2.8 The OS shall provide for automatic scheduling and loading of programs into memory.

5.2.9 The OS shall provide a set of diagnostic routines, loadable from more than one type of external storage device, which will test all of the hardware units (including the CPU, main memory, magnetic tape drive, disk devices, and other peripherals) and which isolates faults down to the replaceable plug-in level.

5.2.10 The operating system shall protect data files, or parts of them, through the use of passwords and/or other security measures to prevent injury, update, deletion, and creation without proper authorization.

5.3 Database Integrity

5.3.1 Programs shall be provided which perform backup of all system data files onto some removable magnetic storage medium.

5.3.2 Public online catalog, circulation, and acquisition system transactions which result in new data records or in modification of any existing data records, shall be logged on an external storage medium (tape, disk, etc.) physically distinct from the devices holding the databases being thus backed up.

5.3.3 Procedures and programs shall be provided which enable rapid recovery from hardware or software failure.

5.4 System Security

5.4.1 All application and system files shall be protected from unauthorized access (inquiry, update, deletion, or creation as applicable to each piece of data) through the use of passwords and/or other security mechanisms.

5.4.2 Functions not authorized for use by the public shall not be accessible from terminals assigned to the public online catalog.

5.4.3 Entry into all other functions except inquiry shall be impossible from the public online catalog terminals, even through passwords.

5.4.4 A method of preventing determination of users' passwords shall be provided.

5.4.5 The Libraries shall be able to specify which functions can be performed at individual terminals.

5.4.6 The Libraries shall be able to change or delete passwords and to change functions authorized to passwords at will.

6. Documentation

6.1 Hardware Manuals

6.1.1 Two complete sets of descriptive and operational manuals for each separate equipment model bid shall be provided upon its installation.

6.1.2 Schematic drawings for the CRT terminals and accompanying printers shall be provided upon installation.

6.1.3 Modifications or enhancements to the manuals or completely revised manuals shall be provided to the Libraries on a continuing basis for the duration of its contracts with the successful bidder.

6.2 System Software Manuals

6.2.1 Two complete sets of descriptive and operational manuals for the operating system and related system software shall be provided upon software installation.

6.2.2 Two complete reference and programmer guides to the programming language used shall be provided upon software installation.

6.2.3 Modifications or enhancements to the manuals or completely revised manuals shall be provided to the Libraries on a continuing basis for the duration of its contracts with the vendor.

6.3 Application Software Manuals

6.3.1 A minimum of two complete sets of reference, training, and operational manuals for monitoring and operating the system on a day-to-day basis shall be provided.

6.3.2 A minimum of two complete sets of reference, training, and operations manuals for the public online catalog, circulation, and acquisitions systems shall be provided upon system installation (additional copies may be requested).

6.3.3 Modifications or enhancements to manuals or completely revised manuals shall be provided to the Libraries on a continuing basis for the duration of its contracts with the vendor.

7. Training

7.1 Manager Training

7.1.1 The vendor shall orient the library director and other key management personnel to the general capabilities of the system, with expected competencies to include the ability to: (a) understand the functional capabilities and limitations of the system, (b) determine what types of reports are capable of being produced by the system, and (c) use the system at a level sufficient to explain and demonstrate its capabilities to other administrators or to interested official guests of the Libraries.

7.1.2 The vendor shall provide periodic review sessions and training when system enhancements are installed at sites and times that are agreeable to both vendor and the Libraries.

7.2 Computer Room Staff

7.2.1 The vendor shall train computer room personnel to manage and operate the system on a day-to-day basis, with expected competencies to include the ability to: (a) start up and shut down the system, (b) monitor and operate the system on a day-to-day basis in order to be able to train other staff members and to assist them where necessary in using the system effectively, (c) handle emergencies with the system which might arise before the vendor's maintenance staff can arrive, (d) troubleshoot and solve simple problems with the system in lieu of calling the vendor's maintenance staff, (e) load software enhancements received from the vendor, (f) load records from magnetic tape and handle associated problems, (g) run file backup operations, (h) operate printers and handle print jobs generated by the system, and (i) handle the vendor's supplied software utilities.

7.2.2 The vendor shall provide periodic review sessions and training when system enhancements are installed at sites and times that are agreeable to both the vendor and the Libraries.

7.3 Supervisor Training

7.3.1 The vendor shall train supervisory-level personnel to manage their respective functional systems on a day-to-day basis, with expected competencies to include the ability to: (a) use each functional component of their respective systems; (b) start up, shut down, monitor, and operate the equipment supporting their respective systems; (c) train other staff members in daily operation and use of their systems; (d) handle emergencies with their respective components which might arise before computer room personnel or vendor maintenance staff can arrive; and (e) troubleshoot and solve simple problems with their respective systems in lieu of calling computer room or vendor maintenance staff.

7.3.2 The vendor shall provide periodic review sessions and training, when system enhancements are installed, at sites and times that are agreeable to both vendor and the Libraries.

7.4 Data Entry Operator Training

7.4.1 The vendor shall train basic-level operators to use specific components of the system, with expected competencies to include the ability to: (a) use the equipment supporting their components and (b) use the software supporting the components.

7.4.2 The vendor shall provide periodic review sessions and training, when system enhancements are installed, at sites and times that are agreeable to both the vendor and the Libraries.

8. Hardware and Software Maintenance

8.1 Hardware Maintenance

8.1.1 All-expense, flat-rate remedial hardware maintenance for the equipment shall be provided at the equipment site Monday through Friday, 8:30 a.m. through 4:30 p.m. (all CDT/CST).

8.1.2 Normal remedial maintenance contact by vendor maintenance personnel shall be guaranteed to be within two hours after notification of need, with remedial work begun within four hours after vendor contact, except in rare and unusual circumstances, through mutually agreed upon contacting procedures.

8.1.3 All-expense, flat-rate preventive hardware maintenance for the equipment shall be provided at the equipment site at times mutually agreed upon by the Libraries and the vendor (it is desired that preventive maintenance be performed outside the normal operating hours of the Libraries).

8.1.4 An adequate supply of repair parts shall be maintained locally to repair a minimum of 85 percent of all hardware failures during a calendar year.

8.1.5 Repair parts to meet the remaining 15 percent of hardware failures shall be made available within 24 hours (continuous time), except under rare and unusual circumstances.

8.1.6 Records and reports of each remedial or preventive maintenance activity performed shall be maintained at the user site.

8.1.7 The vendor shall have a cost-free telephone number for hardware maintenance calls.

8.2 Software Maintenance

8.2.1 All-expense, flat-rate maintenance of all system and application software shall be provided Monday through Friday, 7:00 a.m. through midnight; Saturday, 9:00 a.m. through 6:00 p.m.; and Sunday, 12:00 noon through 12:00 midnight (all times CDT/CST).

8.2.2 The vendor shall have the capability to perform software maintenance by a dial-in arrangement.

8.2.3 The vendor shall provide a cost-free telephone number for software maintenance calls.

8.2.4 The vendor shall systematically inform the Libraries of ongoing system software enhancements as they are developed, shall solicit library input when critical system changes are being contemplated, and shall stipulate the cost to the Libraries, if any, for software enhancements.

8.2.5 The vendor shall guarantee the right of the Libraries to upgrade to a later-developed and improved system.

APPENDIX A (OF A SAMPLE RFP)

Workload Tables

Machine-readable bibliographic records in OCLC/MARC format will be the initial load into the public online catalog. The length of these records will average approximately 600-800 characters/bytes each. The initial load will be 450,000 records. In addition to the initial load, bibliographic records will be added regularly. An estimate of the number of records to be added in the next five years is 300,000. Therefore, the system must be able to accommodate 750,000 bibliographic records as a minimum.

Each bibliographic record will have one or more copy records. The initial load of copy records will be a minimum of 800,000. Item records will also be added regularly. An estimate of the number to be added in the next five years is 450,000. The system must be able to accommodate 1,250,000 copy records as a minimum.

Once built, the number of borrower records to be maintained online should be fairly constant. The estimated number of borrower records is 30,000. Circulation activities are as follows:

Charges, discharges, renewals	700,000
Holds and recalls	4,000
Fines and billing notices	10,000
Overdue notices	50,000

An increase of 5 percent a year for the next five years should be estimated.

Once built, the number of supplier or vendor records to be maintained online should be fairly constant. The estimated number of vendor records is 1,250. The number of fund account records (2,000) should also be constant. Acquisition activities are as follows:

Open orders	15,000
Orders in process	30,000
Claims/Cancellations	7,000
Selections and titles under consideration	20,000
Completed orders	75,000

A growth rate of 5 percent for each activity should be estimated each year for the next five years.

APPENDIX B (OF A SAMPLE RFP)

Desired Equipment

The following equipment is expected to be bid by vendors.

1—Central processing unit
1—Operator console

*—Magnetic disk drives and controllers
1—Magnetic tape drive and controller
1—Line printer and controller
50—CRT terminals
15—Optical scanners and controllers
10—Screen/Video printers
3—Miniprinters (receipt printers)
1—Microcomputer backup for circulation
*—Modems, multiplexors, and other communications equipment

---

*Amount will depend upon the vendor's plan for configuring the Libraries' hardware.

System Requirement Response Forms

Vendor responses to the system requirements in this RFP are to be recorded on the following System Requirement Response Forms. The pages should be removed or duplicated as required.

The vendor should respond to each requirement by marking an *X* in the appropriate column beside each item on the response forms. The column designations are:

Y = Available as specified. The function or feature is currently available and included in the vendor's bid.

D = Under development. The function or feature will be available as specified after the date indicated.

M = Available, with minor differences. This column is to be marked in conjunction with Columns Y or D, as appropriate. The differences must be clearly described in the vendor's response and referenced in the last column on the response form.

N = Not available. The vendor does not have this feature or function and does not plan to offer it.

Date Available = When Column D has been marked, indicate the month and year when the function or feature will become available.

References = Record the page numbers where additional information can be found.

Failure to respond to all requirements, or incorrect responses, could disqualify a vendor.

Responses are to be made to the full text of each requirement presented in the System Requirements section of this RFP. Statements in the response forms have been abbreviated to conserve space. Responses will be evaluated as meeting or not meeting requirements as stated in the System Requirements.

System Requirements Response Forms

Vendor _____

	Y	D	M	N	Date Available	Reference
1. Online Public Catalog (OPC)						
1.1 General						
1.1.1 All software for an OPC shall be supplied by vendor	—	—	—	—	_____	_____
1.1.2 Future enhancements to software shall be made available to library	—	—	—	—	_____	_____
1.1.3 The OPC shall interface with circulation and acquisitions systems	—	—	—	—	_____	_____
1.1.4 Access to OPC database via direct-connect cables, modems, and dial-in ports	—	—	—	—	_____	_____
1.1.5 Public access terminals shall retrieve records only from OPC	—	—	—	—	_____	_____
1.2 Bibliographic Records						
1.2.1 System shall accommodate file sizes and workloads in Appendix A of RFP	—	—	—	—	_____	_____
1.2.2 System shall differentiate between all bibliographic formats	—	—	—	—	_____	_____
1.2.3 ALL MARC tags and subfield codes shall be accepted and stored	—	—	—	—	_____	_____

(This is only one sample page from the System Requirement Response Form)

COST RESPONSE FORMS

Forms are provided on the following pages for listing the price of hardware, software, and other items that are bid. The forms are to be removed or duplicated, completed, and included as part of the vendor's bid. Additional cost information may be submitted to support a bid. Failure to bid separately on each item on the cost forms could disqualify a bidder from consideration.

Cost Response Forms

Vendor:			
Hardware Item	*Unit Price*	*Total Price*	*Annual Maintenance*
Central Processing Unit, including Operator Console, Cabling, etc.	$_____	$_____	$_____
Magnetic Disk Storage, including Controllers, Cabling, etc.	$_____	$_____	$_____
Magnetic Disk Packs	$_____	$_____	$_____
Magnetic Tape Drive, including Controller, cabling, etc.	$_____	$_____	$_____
Line Printer, including Controller, Cabling, etc.	$_____	$_____	$_____
CRT Terminals	$_____	$_____	$_____
Optical Scanners	$_____	$_____	$_____
CRT Workstation Printers	$_____	$_____	$_____
Communications Equipment (Itemize on Separate Sheet)	$_____	$_____	$_____
Other (Itemize on Separate Sheet)	$_____	$_____	$_____
Delivery and Installation	$_____	$_____	$_____
Hardware Total	$_____	$_____	$_____
Software Items			
Operating System	$_____	$_____	$_____
Database Management System	$_____	$_____	$_____

Vendor:			
	Unit Price	*Total Price*	*Annual Maintenance*
Other System Software	$_____	$_____	$_____
Online Public Catalog Software	$_____	$_____	$_____
Circulation System Software	$_____	$_____	$_____
Acquisitions System Software	$_____	$_____	$_____
Other Application Software	$_____	$_____	$_____
Software Total	$_____	$_____	$_____
Miscellaneous Items			
Documentation	$_____	$_____	$_____
Training	$_____	$_____	$_____
Other (Itemize on Separate Sheet)	$_____	$_____	$_____
Summary			
Total Hardware Costs		$_____	$_____
Total Software Costs		$_____	$_____
Total Documentation Costs		$_____	$_____
Total Training Costs		$_____	$_____
Total Other Costs		$_____	$_____
Grand Total		$_____	$_____

LIST OF OPERATIONAL INSTALLATIONS

Remove or duplicate the list of operational installations form on the following page. List contact information for at least three users of equipment and software similar to that being bid. Additional installations may be attached if so desired. The list of operational installations form may be removed and reproduced if desired. Include complete information as requested. Include the completed form as part of your bid.

Anytown University Libraries

Information on Bidder's Operational Installations
(Duplicate This Form as Required)

Vendor _____

Each bidder must submit the following information on buyers of system similar to that being offered to the Libraries. It is requested that a minimum of three academic library customers be listed, but other major installations may be listed as well.

1. Library _____

   Address _____

   Telephone Number _____

2. Library Director _____

3. Library Automation Contact _____

4. Telephone Number of Contact _____

5. Date System Purchased by Library _____

6. Date of System Installation _____

7. Date System Operational _____

8. Brief Description of System (Major Subsystems, Hardware and Software, Number and Function of Terminals, etc.):

9. Implementation schedule for major subsystems and enhancements:

10. Number of Bibliographic Records in Database at Present _____

11. Maximum Capacity of this System _____

12. Current Library Circulation Transactions per Year _____

13. Other Brief Information:

Glossary

Acceptance Test: An evaluation by the library of an automated library system to determine if it should be accepted and, usually, if partial or full payment should be made to the vendor. The three common acceptance tests are the System Reliability, Functional, and Full-Load Response Time Tests.

Acoustic Coupler: A type of modem that converts digital signals into audible tones. The tones can be detected by an ordinary telephone handset for transmission over the public-switched telephone network.

Adapted Library System: An automated system of a library that has been duplicated and adapted for local use by another library.

American Standard Code for Information Interchange: A standard code for interchange or exchange of machine-readable information among differing computer systems. The code consists of a series of eight bits for each of a defined set of characters. Usually abbreviated as ASCII.

Amp: A unit of electric current; an abbreviation for ampere.

Annual Operating Cost: The cost necessary to maintain and operate an automated library system for a period of one year.

Application Software: One or more computer programs written for a specific library function such as circulation, acquisitions, or an online catalog. Contrast with *System Software.*

Arithmetic-Logic Unit: The part of the central processing unit of a computer in which operations such as addition, subtraction, multiplication, division, and comparison of data are performed.

ASCII: See *American Standard Code for Information Interchange.*

Authority Control: A means of maintaining consistency in the form of names, subjects, series, and uniform titles and cross-references between these terms in a bibliographic file or catalog.

Automated Library System: A library system in which some or all processing is performed by a computer.

Automation: See *Library Automation.*

Automation Consultant: An expert on automated library systems who provides advice and assistance to a library during an automation project.

Automation Plan: See *Long-Range Automation Plan.*

Automation Project: See *Library Automation Project.*

Auxiliary Equipment: See *Peripheral Equipment.*

Auxiliary Storage: Storage that supplements the main, primary, or internal storage of a computer system, usually magnetic disk. Also referred to as mass or secondary storage.

Back Up: To prepare a duplicate copy of a machine file to be used in case the original is corrupted or destroyed.

Backup File: The file which results from making a duplicate of another file for security purposes.

Barcode: A machine-readable code consisting of bars of varying widths to represent characters of information, usually numeric.

Batch Processing: A method of processing data in which a number of records are grouped or batched, then processed together at the same time.

Baud: A term used to describe the rate by which information is transmitted over a communications channel. The speed is roughly equivalent to the number of bits that can be transferred per second.

BCD Code: See *Binary Coded Decimal Code.*

Bibliographic Utility: An organization or firm that offers an online file of bibliographic and other records for use by many libraries.

Bid Evaluation Team: A team established to evaluate the proposals or quotations in response to the library's Request for Proposal or Request for Quotation.

Binary: Pertaining to the number system with a base of two. The two possibilities are expressed as either 0 (zero) or 1.

Binary Coded Decimal Code: A computer code consisting of six bits representing each character of information. Usually abbreviated as BCD Code.

Bit: An abbreviation of binary digit, referring to one of the two numbers (0 or 1) in the binary number system.

Bits per Inch: The number of bits of data that can be recorded on one inch of a recording surface. Usually abbreviated as BPI.

Bits per Second: The number of bits of data that can be transmitted over a communications channel in one second. Usually abbreviated as BPS.

BPI: See *Bits per Inch.*

BPS: See *Bits per Second.*

British Thermal Unit: A standard unit of heat measurement, equivalent to the amount of heat necessary to raise the temperature of one pound of water by one degree Fahrenheit. Usually abbreviated as BTU.

Byte: A group of adjacent bits treated as a unit. Usually, eight bits constitute a byte, which is the equivalent of one character of information.

Central Processing Unit: The part of a computer system consisting of control, arithmetic-logic, and primary storage units. Also referred to as the central processor. Usually abbreviated as CPU.

Communications Channel: An electronic or electric link or channel, such as a telephone line or a cable, over which information can be transmitted.

Communications Common Carrier: A public utility company recognized by an appropriate regulatory agency, such as the Federal Communications Commission, as having a vested interest in, and responsibility for, furnishing communications services to the general public.

Computer: A machine or device that accepts and automatically performs prescribed sequences of processing operations on information to achieve a desired result.

Computer Program: A set of instructions that a computer follows in processing information.

Computer System: A computing system consisting of a central processing unit, storage units, and input /output devices.

Computer-Based Library System: See *Automated Library System.*

Computing Center: An organization responsible for programming, operating, and maintaining one or more computer systems and peripheral equipment, usually for use by other organizations such as the library. Synonymous with data center or data processing center.

Concentrator: A communications device that allows several low-speed devices to transmit over a single high-speed communications channel.

Console: A special input-output device attached to a computer to enable an operator to control, monitor, and communicate with the system.

Control Unit: The part of the central processing unit that receives, interprets, directs, and controls the instructions given the computer to process data.

Corrective Maintenance: See *Remedial Maintenance.*

CPS: Characters per second.

CPU: See *Central Processing Unit.*

CRT Terminal: A cathode ray tube terminal. A terminal device having an electronic vacuum tube on which output from a computer can be displayed. The device usually has a keyboard on which input can be entered. Also referred to as a visual display unit or VDU or Visual Display Terminal or VDT.

Data Center or Data Processing Center: See *Computing Center.*

Data Communication: The process of transmitting and receiving information from one point or location to another over a communications channel or link.

Data Conversion: The process of converting data to a machine-readable form. Also, the process of converting data from one storage system or medium to another.

Data Element: A predefined unit of information in a record.

Database: A collection of related files of information treated as a unit.

Database Management System: A special set of application software that organizes, stores, retrieves, and maintains records in a file or files. Usually abbreviated as DBMS.

DBMS: See *Database Management System.*

Decision Flowchart: A special type of flowchart that specifies the operations performed in a system, all decisions that must be made, and alternate courses of action to be taken as a result of the decisions.

Decision Rule: A policy on which to base a judgment as to which of several choices should be selected.

Delimiter: A character reserved to separate fields of data or subfields within a field in a record.

Detail File: See *Transaction File.*

Developmental Costs: The one-time or nonrecurring costs necessary to start up an automated library system.

Dial-Up: The use of a rotary or push button telephone to establish a communications link between a terminal and a computer.

Documentation: Information describing a system, function, piece of hardware, or other aspect of an automated library system.

Downtime: The time that a computer or other device is not operational due to a malfunction or other problem. Compare with *Uptime.*

EBCDIC: Extended Binary Coded Decimal Interchange Code. An eight-bit computer code used to represent 256 different characters of information.

Feasibility Study: A study undertaken before an automated system is acquired or implemented to determine if it is practical, economical, or possible.

Field: A group of related characters within a record treated as a unit.

File: A collection of related records treated as a unit.

File Key: One or more characters of information used to store and retrieve records in a file. Contrast with *Search Key.*

Fixed-Length: Pertaining to fields or parts of records that always contain the same number of characters from record to record.

Flowchart: A graphic or diagrammed representation of a sequence of events or operations performed in a system.

Flowchart Symbol: Boxes of various standardized shapes representing operations or processes, decisions, storage, and other activities and pieces of equipment used in constructing flowcharts.

Flowline: Lines connecting symbols in a flowchart and indicating the direction of flow of work through the system being represented.

Full-Load Response Time Test: A test to determine if an automated library system can perform operations and tasks at the rates or levels specified by the library.

Function: An independent group of related routines or operations such as charging, discharging, renewals, etc.

Functional Test: An evaluation to determine if an automated library system meets all functional requirements as specified in the library's Request for Proposal and as modified by the vendor's response to the RFP.

Gantt Chart: A project management chart useful in scheduling or depicting the activities and steps of a project and their times of completion.

Goal: A desired result of work performed in a system or of a project.

Hardware: The physical, mechanical, magnetic, electronic, and electrical components of a computer system.

Hardware Maintenance: Work required to maintain a piece of hardware in good operating condition.

History File: A file containing obsolete or noncurrent records retained for historical or legal purposes. Also called an archival file.

Information: Data symbols that have been combined or arranged to represent or convey meaningful facts, ideas, conditions, or knowledge about people, physical items, or other things. Data symbols include the alphabetic letters A through Z, the numeric characters 0 through 9, and special characters such as punctuation marks and signs.

In-House Computer: A computer physically located in the library and usually dedicated solely to library use.

Input: Data or information entered into an automated library system or computer system for processing. Also, the media containing data or information.

Input Unit or Device: An electromechanical or electronic device used to enter data or information into a computer system for processing.

Integrated Library System: An automated library system containing several component functional systems, such as acquisitions, circulation, cataloging, online catalog, and serials control. The systems are interrelated and interacting within the same set or system of software.

Interactive Processing: A method of using a computer whereby an operator and the machine exchange information or messages in an ongoing, almost conversational manner. Each interacts with the other through the messages.

Internal Storage: See *Main Storage.*

Job Description: A written description of a person's job or position and its responsibilities and requirements.

K: An abbreviation referring to 1,024 bytes of storage.

Layout Flowchart: A schematic or graphic plan or diagram of the physical space, facilities, and equipment assigned to a system and the movement of information and people through the space.

Leased Line: A communications line dedicated soley to the leasee's use for the duration of the lease. Also called a private line.

Library Automation: The use of an automatic device such as a computer to perform some or all operations in a library system.

Library Automation Project: The organized process or activities of developing an automated library system.

Library System: See *System.*

Line Driver: A type of modem used for limited, short distances between a computer and a remote terminal.

Local Area Network: A data communications network for the interconnection of computers and terminals within a limited area such as in a building, on a campus, or in a city. Often abbreviated as LAN.

Locally Developed Library System: An automated library system which is designed, programmed, documented, installed, tested, and operated locally from scratch.

Long-Range Automation Plan: A master plan outlining in broad terms the purposes or reasons for automation, any constraints on the efforts, and priorities for development of automated systems in the future.

Machine-Readable: In a form that can be sensed or recognized by a computer or other electromechanical device.

Magnetic Disk: A flat, round disk whose surface is coated with a magnetic recording material on which bits of information can be recorded and thus stored and later retrieved. A number of disks rotating on a central spindle is referred to as a disk pack.

Magnetic Tape: A tape coated with a magnetic oxide on which bits of information can be recorded and thus stored and later retrieved. The tape is stored on reels or in cartridges.

Main Storage: Storage that is an integral part of the central processing unit of a computer used to hold data to be processed and instructions or programs for processing the data during execution of a computer program. Also called primary or internal storage.

Mainframe Computer: The largest of computers, characterized by its size and its capability of handling large amounts of mass storage, a wide range of peripheral equipment, and many applications and users at the same time.

Maintenance Contract: A contract between the library and a vendor to maintain its hardware or software in good operating condition.

MARC: An acronym for MAchine Readable Cataloging. An international, standardized format for recording bibliographic information in a machine-readable form for communication or exchange among libraries and institutions.

Mass Storage: See *Auxiliary Storage.*

Master File: A file containing relatively permanent, current-status records which are the major source of information for a particular application such as acquisitions or circulation.

MB: Megabyte. One million bytes of data.

Memory: Same as storage, either main or auxiliary.

Microcomputer: A small, programmable computer usually but not always designed to handle only one application at a time, or at least a restricted number of applications.

Minicomputer: A small, programmable computer, larger than the microcomputer, which can usually handle several applications and users simultaneously.

Modem: A contraction of MOdulator-DEModulator. A device that changes or modulates electronic signals to a form that can be transmitted over a communications channel, then back to the original form after transmission.

Multiplexor or Multiplexer: A communications device that accepts input from several terminal devices and combines the signals so that they can be transmitted together, simultaneously, over one communications channel. A similar device at the other end of the channel will separate the signals before they are input to the computer for processing.

Network: Two or more libraries organized to share or exchange information and other resources using established communications links.

Network Chart: A project management chart that can graphically depict the events of a project and their interrelationships.

Network Organization: The staff who manages and /or operates a network.

Offline: Equipment or a process not under direct control of the central processing unit of a computer.

Online: Equipment or a process under the direct control of the central processing unit of a computer.

Online Public Catalog: A catalog containing bibliographic records for the holdings of one or more libraries, stored on magnetic disk or other recording media, and made available online to the public. The catalog may be searched by author, title, subject, call number, and possibly other indexes.

Operating Cost: See *Annual Operating Cost.*

Operating System: A special computer program, or set of programs, that manages and controls the execution of other programs. Usually abbreviated as OS.

Operation: A predefined set of steps or tasks designed to process input into output in a system.

Operational Use Time: The time that a computer system is available for use by the library.

Operator Console: See *Console.*

Optical Character: A printed machine-readable character that can be sensed or read by an optical scanner and thus processed by a computer.

Optical Scanner: A device that can sense or read via reflected light machine-readable data and then converts them to a form that can be processed by a computer.

OS: See *Operating System.*

Output: The product or results of processing by an automated library or computer system. Also, the medium containing data or information that results from this processing.

Output Unit or Device: An electromechanical or electronic device used to present or record data resulting from processing by a data processing or computer system.

Peripheral Equipment, Devices, or Unit: All equipment of a computer system other than the central processing unit. Synonymous with *Auxiliary Equipment*.

Phase: A very broad or general part of a library automation project, consisting of a number of related steps and tasks.

Port: A channel providing an entrance or exit for the exchange of data between a central processing unit and remote, external units or devices such as CRT terminals and printers.

Power Control Unit: A piece of hardware that serves as a buffer between power entering a computer room and the computer itself. The device smooths out power surges, brownouts, and interruptions in the energy flow before the power reaches the computer.

Preventive Maintenance: Maintenance performed on hardware or software to prevent future malfunctions. Contrast with *Remedial Maintenance*.

Primary Storage: See *Main Storage*.

Printer: A device that prints output in the form of human-readable characters on paper.

Private Line: See *Leased Line*.

Problem Statement: A description or definition of one or more problems underlying or causing a need for a project to develop an automated library system.

Procedure Manual: A step-by-step manual that provides instructions showing how to use, operate, or manage a system.

Program: See *Computer Program*.

Programmer: A person who designs, codes, tests, and revises the detailed sets of computer instructions or programs.

Programming Language: The special language in which computer programs are written.

Project Constraint: A limitation, condition, or restriction placed on a library automation project.

Project Goal: A statement of the results expected of a library automation project or what is to be accomplished during the endeavor.

Project Manager: The person officially assigned the responsibility of completing a library automation project successfully.

Project Outline: A list of the phases, activities, and steps or tasks comprising a library automation project.

Project Schedule: A timetable or calendar of the events that must occur in a library automation project to ensure its successful completion.

Project Steering Committee: A special committee established to advise and assist the project manager during the development of an automated system. Sometimes called an automation committee.

Public-Switched Line: A communications line or channel that requires that a connection be made through an operator or an automatic switching center.

Record: A collection of related items or data elements treated as a unit.

Remedial Maintenance: Maintenance performed, on an unscheduled basis, to correct a specific malfunction in a piece of hardware or in software. Synonymous with corrective maintenance and unscheduled maintenance. Contrast with *Preventive Maintenance.*

Remote Processing: The use of a computer from a distance, whereby a CRT or typewriter terminal in the library is linked via communications lines to a computer located a distance away.

Request for Information (RFI): A brief document soliciting information from vendors about their automated library systems. Usually abbreviated as RFI.

Request for Proposal (RFP): A document containing requirements or specifications and other information used to solicit proposals from vendors to supply an automated library system. Usually abbreviated as RFP.

Request for Quotation (RFQ): A document containing requirements or specifications and other information used to solicit price quotations or bids from vendors for an automated library system. Usually abbreviated as RFQ.

Response Time: The elapsed time between entry or submission of a command, query, or data to a computer system and the return of results or a response.

Response Time Test: See *Full-Load Response Time Test.*

RFI: See *Request for Information.*

RFP: See *Request for Proposal.*

RFQ: See *Request for Quotation.*

Search Key: One or more characters of information to be compared with file keys for purpose of locating matches. Contrast with *File Key.*

Secondary Storage: See *Auxiliary Storage.*

Shared Library System: An automated library system that has been developed or acquired by a library, a consortium, company, or other organization, then offered for use by a few or many libraries through a data communications network.

Site Preparation: The construction or renovation of the physical space in which a computer or system will be located.

Site Visit: A visit by library staff to another library with an automated system for purposes of examining and studying the system.

Software: In contrast to hardware, the set of computer programs and related documentation for a computer system or for a specific application.

Software Maintenance: Work required to maintain software in good operating condition.

Subfield: Groups of related characters of information describing particular aspects of a field.

Subsystem: A part of a system.

System: An organized set of activities, tasks, or operations performed on information, materials, or other physical objects to achieve a specific result or purpose.

System Back Up: See *Back Up.*

System Environment: The physical space in which a system is housed and operated.

System Goal: The mission, purpose, or achievement toward which efforts in maintaining and operating a system are directed.

System Lifespan: The number of years a system is expected to last before replacement.

System Reliability Test: A reliability test of the hardware and /or software to determine if an automated library system can operate at a defined level of effectiveness for a stated period of time.

System Requirement: A specification of what a system must do or how it must be designed to satisfy the needs, wants, or desires of the library staff. A mandatory requirement must absolutely be met, while a desirable or optional requirement enhances a system but need not necessarily be met for a system to be acceptable.

System Software: The software necessary to maintain and operate a computer and facilitate the programming, testing, and revision of application software. Examples of system software include operating systems and utility programs. Contrast with *Application Software.*

Systems Analysis: The thorough examination and analysis of all aspects of a system, activities, or techniques to determine the most effective and efficient method of accomplishing what is to be done.

Systems Analyst: A person who performs the activities of systems analysis.

Systems Approach: A method by which a library is viewed as a unified whole rather than as segmented and isolated parts. The library is viewed as a number of interacting and interrelated systems or subsystems organized to accomplish a set of goals and objectives.

Systems Project: See *Library Automation Project.*

Tag: One or more characters that identify or specify a data element or field of a record.

Tape Library: A store of reels of magnetic tape not currently in use. The reels can contain backups of files and duplicates of system and application software and other information supporting an automated library system.

Task: A predefined unit of work to be performed.

Terminal: See *CRT Terminal.*

Terminal Work Station: See *Work Station.*

Timesharing: A method by which a number of people can use a computer system simultaneously.

Transaction: The record of an event in a system or subsystem.

Transaction Fee: A fee incurred or charged each time a transaction event occurs or is completed.

Transaction File: A file containing the new or recently modified records.

Turnkey Library System: A system that has been designed and tested by a manufacturer or other vendor and, when installed in the library, is ready to be operated merely by "turning the key."

Uptime: The time that a computer or other device is operational and available for use by the library. Compare with *Downtime*.

Utility Program: A special general-purpose computer program, usually supplied by the hardware manufacturer, that performs common or often-repeated tasks such as sorting, merging, and duplication of files.

Variable-Length: Data whose length varies from record to record, depending upon the particular information to be recorded.

Visual Display Terminal (VDT): See *CRT Terminal*.

Visual Display Unit (VDU): See *CRT Terminal*.

Work File: A file containing records extracted from another file to be used for special processing.

Work Flow: An organized or coordinated movement of activities or work in a desired direction to accomplish a desired goal or objective.

Work Load: The amount or volume of work to be accomplished in a system during a specified period of time.

Work Station: A table or desk, chair, and CRT terminal and other equipment used by library staff in performing operations and tasks in an automated library system.

Selected Bibliography

GENERAL SOURCES

Advances in Librarianship. New York: Academic Press, 1970–to date.

ALA Glossary of Library and Information Science. Edited by Heartsill Young. Chicago: American Library Association, 1983.

American Library Association. Library Technology Program. *Library Technology Reports.* Chicago: American Library Association, 1965–to date.

Annual Review of Information Science and Technology. Publishers vary. Vol. 1, 1966–to date. ed. White Plains, NY: Knowledge Industry Publications, 1984.

Clinic on Library Applications of Data Processing, University of Illinois. *Proceedings.* Urbana, IL: University of Illinois Graduate School of Library Science, 1963–to date.

De Gennaro, Richard. "Libraries & Networks in Transition: Problems and Prospects for the 1980's." *Library Journal* 106 (May 15, 1981): 1045–49.

Encyclopedia of Computer Science and Technology. Vols. 1–16. New York: Dekker, 1975–81.

Encyclopedia of Library and Information Science. Edited by Allen Kent and Harold Lancour. New York: Dekker, 1969–to date.

Hayes, Robert M., and Becker, Joseph. *Handbook of Data Processing for Libraries.* 2d ed. Los Angeles: Melville Publishing Company, 1974.

Library Systems Newsletter. Chicago: American Library Association, 1981–to date.

Markuson, Barbara Evans et al. *Guidelines for Library Automation: A Handbook for Federal and Other Libraries.* Santa Monica, CA: Systems Development Co., 1972.

Matthews, Joseph R. *Choosing an Automated Library System: A Planning Guide.* Chicago: American Library Association, 1980.

Maynard, H. B., ed. *Industrial Engineering Handbook.* 3d ed. New York: McGraw-Hill, 1971.

Palmer, Richard Phillips. *Case Studies in Library Computer Systems.* New York: R. R. Bowker, 1973.

A Reader on Choosing an Automated Library System. Edited by Joseph R. Matthews. Chicago: American Library Association, 1983.

Rice, James. *Introduction to Library Automation.* Littleton, CO: Libraries Unlimited, 1984.

Saffady, William. *Introduction to Automation for Librarians.* Chicago: American Library Association, 1983.

Warheit, I. A. "The Automation of Libraries: Some Economic Considerations." *Special Libraries* 63 (January 1972): 1–7.

———. "Design of Library Systems for Implementation with Interactive Computers." *Journal of Library Automation* 3 (March 1970): 65–78.

———. "When Some Library Systems Fail—Is It the System or the Librarian?" *Wilson Library Bulletin* 46 (September 1971): 52–58.

SYSTEMS, COMPUTERS, AND RELATED TECHNOLOGY

Ackoff, R. L. "Towards a System of Systems Concepts." *Management Science* 17 (July 1971): 661–71.

Arnold, Robert R.; Hill, Harold C.; and Nichols, Aylmer V. *Modern Data Processing.* 3d ed. Santa Barbara, CA: Wiley, 1978.

Bingham, J. E., and Davies, G. W. P. *A Handbook of Systems Analysis.* 2d ed. New York: Halsted Press, 1978.

Bohl, Marilyn. *Flowcharting Techniques.* Chicago: Science Research Associates, 1971.

Bonn, Jane H., and Heer, Phillip R. "Terminal Equipment for On-Line Interactive Information Retrieval Using Telecommunications." *Special Libraries* 67 (January 1976): 30–39.

Carter, Ruth C. "Systems Analysis as a Prelude to Library Automation." *Library Trends* 21 (April 1973): 505–21.

Chapin, Ned. "Flowcharting with the ANSI Standard: A Tutorial." *Computing Surveys* 2 (June 1970): 119–46.

Churchman, C. West. *The Systems Approach.* Rev. and updated ed. New York: Dell, 1983.

Dougherty, Richard M., and Heinritz, Fred J. *Scientific Management of Library Operations.* 2d ed. New York: Scarecrow Press, 1982.

FitzGerald, Jerry, and FitzGerald, Ardra F. *Fundamentals of Systems Analysis.* 2d ed. New York: Wiley, 1981.

Fosdick, Howard. *Computer Basics for Librarians and Information Scientists.* Arlington, VA: Information Resources Press, 1981.

Hartman, W.; Matthes, H.; and Proeme, A. *Management Information Systems Handbook: Analysis, Requirements Determination, Design and Development, Implementation and Evaluation.* New York: McGraw-Hill, 1968.

Heinritz, Fred J. "Analysis and Evaluation of Current Library Procedures." *Library Trends* 21 (April 1973): 522–32.

Hice, G. F.; Turner, W. S.; and Cashwell, L. F. *System Development Methodology.* Rev. ed. Amsterdam: North-Holland Publishing Company, 1978.

King, Donald W., ed. *Telecommunications and Libraries: A Primer for Librarians and Information Managers.* White Plains, NY: Knowledge Industry Publications, 1981.

"The Library and the Computer Center." *Journal of Library Automation* 12 (December 1979): 362–78.

Martin, James. *Introduction to Teleprocessing.* Englewood Cliffs, NJ: Prentice-Hall, 1972.

———. *Telecommunications in the Computer.* 2d ed. Englewood Cliffs, NJ: Prentice-Hall, 1976.

Nadler, Gerald. *The Planning and Design Approach.* New York: Wiley, 1981.

———. *Work Design: A Systems Concept.* Rev. ed. New York: Irwin, 1970.

Optner, Stanford L. *Systems Analysis for Business Management.* 3d ed. Englewood Cliffs, NJ: Prentice-Hall, 1975.

Raffel, Jeffrey A., and Shisko, Robert. *Systematic Analysis of University Libraries: An Application of Cost-Benefit Analysis of the M. I. T. Libraries.* Cambridge, MA: MIT Press, 1969.

Rosenberg, Jerry M. *Dictionary of Computers, Data Processing, and Telecommunications.* New York: Wiley, 1984.

Sanders, Donald H. *Computers in Society.* 3d ed. New York: McGraw-Hill, 1981.

Sippl, Charles J. *Data Communictions Dictionary.* New York: Van Nostrand-Reinhold, 1984.

Sippl, Charles J., and Sippl, Roger J. *Computer Dictionary and Handbook.* 3d ed. Indianapolis, IN: Sams, 1980.

Spencer, Donald D. *The Illustrated Computer Dictionary.* Rev. ed. Columbus, OH: Charles E. Merrill, 1983.

Thomas, P. A. *Task Analysis of Library Operations.* London, Aslib, 1971.

Von Bertalanffy, Ludwig. *General Systems Theory.* Rev. ed. New York: Braziller, 1969.

PROJECT MANAGEMENT

Bellomy, Fred L. "Management Planning for Library Systems Development." *Journal of Library Automation* 2 (December 1969): 187–217.

Brophy, P. "Critical Path Analysis: A Library Management Tool." *Program* 17 (October 1983): 204–16.

Cleland, David I., and King, William R. *Systems Analysis and Project Management.* 3d ed. New York: McGraw-Hill, 1983.

Crum, Norman J. "Library Goals and Objectives: Literature Review." ERIC Document ED 082 794.

De Gennaro, Richard. "The Development and Administration of Automated Systems in Academic Libraries." *Journal of Library Automation* 1 (March 1968): 75–91.

Hayes, Robert M. "Consulting in Computer Applications to Libraries." *Library Trends* 28 (Winter 1980): 381–98.

Lockwood, J. D. "Involving Consultants in Library Change." *College & Research Libraries* 38 (November 1977): 498–508.

Moder, Joseph, and Phillips, Cecil R. *Project Management with CPM and PERT.* 2d ed. New York: Van Nostrand-Reinhold, 1970.

Veaner, Allen B. "Major Decision Points in Library Automation." *College   & Research Libraries* 31 (September 1970): 299–312.

Wiest, Jerome D., and Levy, Ferdinand K. *A Management Guide to PERT/CPM, with GERT/PDM/DCPM and Other Networks.* 2d ed. Englewood Cliffs, NJ: Prentice-Hall, 1977.

Young, Arthur P. "Generating Library Goals and Objectives." *Illinois Libraries* 56 (November 1974): 862–66.

SYSTEM COSTS AND PROCUREMENT

Auerbach Data World. 4 looseleaf volumes. Pennsauken, NJ: Auerbach Publishers, 1978–to date.

Brandon, Dick H., and Segelstein, Sidney. *Data Processing Contracts: Structure, Contents and Negotiation.* 2d ed. New York: Van Nostrand-Reinhold, 1984.

Brownrigg, Edward B., and Bruer, J. Michael. "Automated Turn-Key Systems in the Library: Prospects and Perils." *Library Trends* 24 (April 1976): 727–36.

Burgess, Thomas K., "A Cost Effectiveness Model for Comparing Various Circulation Systems." *Journal of Library Automation* 6 (June 1973): 75–86.

Computer Equipment Review. Westport, CT: Meckler Publishing Co., 1979–to date.

Corey, James F., and Bellomy, Fred L. "Determining Requirements for a New System." *Library Trends* 21 (April 1973): 533–52.

Cortez, Edwin. *Contracts, RFP's and Other Procurement Documents for Library Automation.* Lexington, MA.: Lexington Books, 1983.

Datapro Directory of Small Computers. Looseleaf service. Delran, NJ: Datapro Research Corporation, n.d.

Datapro Reports on Minicomputers. Looseleaf service. Delran, NJ: Datapro Research Corporation, 1973–to date.

Datapro 70: The EDP Buyer's Bible. Looseleaf service. Delran, NJ: Datapro Research Corporation, 1973–to date.

Duchesne, Roderick M. "Analysis of Costs and Performance." *Library Trends* 21 (April 1973): 587–604.

Epstein, Susan B. "Procurement without Problems: Preparing the RFP." *Library Journal* 108 (June 1, 1983): 1109–10.

Fient, Hans G. "Management of the Acquisition Process for Software Products." *Management Information* 2 (1973): 153–64.

Freedman, Maurice J. *Library Automation: Five Case Studies.* (LJ Special Report No. 22). New York: Library Journal, 1982.

Hegarty, Kevin. *The Joy of Contracts: An Epicurean Approach to Negotiation.* Tacoma, WA: Tacoma Public Library, 1979.

———. *More Joy of Contracts: An Epicurean Approach to Negotiation.* Tacoma, WA: Tacoma Public Library, 1981.

Jacob, Mary Ellen L. "Standardized Costs for Automated Library Systems." *Journal of Library Automation* 3 (September 1970): 207–17.

Martin, Susan K. "Turnkey Systems: How to Avoid Locking Yourself In." *American Libraries* 10 (February 1979): 89–91.

Mason, Robert M. "Ergonomics: The Human and the Machine." *Library Journal* 109 (February 15, 1984): 331–32.

Merilees, B. "RFPs and On-Line System Selection." *Canadian Library Journal* 40 (February 1983): 15–19.

Mitchell, Betty Jo; Tanis, Norman E.; and Jaffe, Jack. *Cost Analysis of Library Functions: A Total Systems Approach.* Greenwich, CT: JAI Press, 1978.

Parkhurst, Carol A. "Negotiation of Maintenance Contracts." *Technicalities* 1 (April 1981): 14–15.

Price, Douglas S. "Rational Cost Information: Necessary and Obtainable." *Special Libraries* 65 (February 1974): 49–57.

Ross, J., and Brooks, J. "Costing Manual and Computerized Library Circulation Systems." *Program* 6 (1972): 217–27.

Uluakar, Tamer; Pierce, Anton R.; and Chachra, Vinod. "Design Principles for a Comprehensive Library System." *Journal of Library Automation* 14 (June 1981): 78–89.

Woods, R. D. "Compatibility of Library Systems." *Journal of Library Automation* 13 (December 1980): 244–50.

MACHINE-READABLE DATA AND DATA CONVERSION

Attig, John C. "The Concept of a MARC Format." *Information Technology and Libraries* 2 (March 1983): 7–17.

———. "US/MARC Formats: Underlying Principles." *Library of Congress Information Bulletin* 41 (April 23, 1982): 120–24.

Avram, Henriette D. *MARC: Its History and Implications.* Washington, DC: Library of Congress, 1975.

Avram, Henriette D.; Knapp, John F.; and Rather, Lucia J. *The MARC II Format: A Communications Format for Bibliographic Data.* Washington, DC: Library of Congress, 1968.

Barkalow, Pat. "Conversion of Files for Circulation Control." *Journal of Library Automation* 12 (September 1979): 209–13.

Butler, Brett; Aveney, Brian; and Scholz, William. "The Conversion of Manual Catalogs to Collection Data Bases." *Library Technology Reports* 14 (March-April 1978): 109–206.

Carter, Ruth, and Bruntjen, Scott. *Data Conversion.* White Plains, NJ: Knowledge Industry Publications, 1983.

Epstein, Susan B. "Converting Bibliographic Records for Automation: Some Options." *Library Journal* 108 (March 1, 1983): 474–76.

———. "Converting Records for Automation at the Copy Level." *Library Journal* 108 (April 1, 1983): 642–43.

John, Nancy. "Preparing for On-Line Access: Retrospective Conversion." *Illinois Libraries* 62 (September 1980): 618–22.

Johnson, Carolyn A. "Retrospective Conversion of Three Library Collections." *Information Technology and Libraries* 1 (June 1982): 133–37.

MARC Development Office. *Information on the MARC System.* Washington, DC: Library of Congress, 1974.

Peters, S. H., and Buter, D. J. "Cost Model for Retrospective Conversion Alternatives." *Library Resources and Technical Services* 28 (April 1984): 149–51.

SYSTEM INSTALLATION AND OPERATION

Bruer, J. Michael. "The Public Relations Component of Circulation System Implementation." *Journal of Library Automation* 12 (September 1979): 214–18.

Epstein, Susan B. "Implementation of an Automated System." *Library Journal* 108 (September 15, 1983): 1771–72.

———. "Implementation: Preparing the Site." *Library Journal* 108 (November 15, 1983): 2142–43.

Griffin, Hillis L. "Implementing the New System: Conversion, Training, and Scheduling." *Library Trends* 21 (April 1973): 565–74.

Illuminating Engineering Society of North America. *IES Lighting Handbook.* Edited by John E. Kaufman. 2 vols. New York, 1981.

Juergens, Bonnie. "Staff Training Aspects of Circulation System Implementation." *Journal of Library Automation* 12 (September 1979): 203–08.

Knox, F. M. *The Knox Standard Guide to the Design and Control of Business Forms.* New York: McGraw-Hill, 1965.

Martin, Susan K. "Training for the Whole On-Line Revolution." In *The On-Line Revolution in Libraries; Proceedings of the 1977 Conference in Pittsburgh, Pennsylvania.* Edited by Allen Kent and Thomas J. Galvin. New York: Dekker, 1978.

Rooks, Dana. "Staffing the Library Automation Project." *Texas Libraries* 44 (January 1983): 8–12.

Training Users of Online Public Access Catalogs; Report of a Conference Sponsored by Trinity University and the Council on Library Resources, San Antonio, Texas, January 12-14, 1983. Compiled and edited by Marsha Hamilton McClintock. Washington, DC: Council on Library Resources, 1983.

Vardaman, Patricia B. *Forms for Better Communication.* New York: Van Nostrand-Reinhold, 1971.

Weber, David C. "Personnel Aspects of Library Automation." *Journal of Library Automation* 4 (March 1971): 27–37.

Yearsley, R. B., and Graham, G. M. R. *Handbook of Computer Management.* New York: Halsted Press, 1973.

Index

Compiled by Linda Webster